Jim

from
David

Xmas 1982

Heaven and Hell in the NHL

Heaven and Hell in the NHL

Punch Imlach's Own Story

with Scott Young

McClelland and Stewart

McClelland and Stewart Limited
The Canadian Publishers
25 Hollinger Road
Toronto, Ontario
M4B 3G2

_____

Canadian Cataloguing in Publication Data
Imlach, Punch, 1918-
    Heaven and hell in the NHL

Includes index.
ISBN 0-7710-9083-8

1. Imlach, Punch, 1918-   2. Hockey coaches-
Canada – Biography.   I. Young, Scott, 1918-
II. Title.

GV848.5.I44A3   796.96'2'0770924   C82-094772-5

_____

Photo credits: page 1, top and bottom, Imlach Collection; page 2, top, Robert B. Shaver; page 2, bottom, Robert S. Bukaty; page 3, top and bottom, Robert B. Shaver; page 4, top and bottom, Imlach Collection; page 5, top left, Imlach Collection; page 5, top right, *The St. Catharines Standard*; page 5, bottom left, Willie Dagenais; page 5, bottom right, Ronald M. Moscati; page 6, all photos, Robert B. Shaver; page 7, top and bottom, Photo-Canada Wide; page 8, top, Eric Demme; page 8, bottom, Photo-Canada Wide.

Printed and bound in Canada by
T. H. Best Printing Company Limited

Contents

CHAPTER ONE

How the worst three years began

The worst three years of my long and generally happy life in hockey began on Friday, June 8, 1979. About mid-morning the phone rang at our home in Scarborough, the easternmost borough of Metropolitan Toronto. My wife Dorothy – everybody calls her Dodo – answered. Hearing her kidding around I realized the caller must be King Clancy, one of the best friends I had when I coached and managed the Toronto Maple Leafs from 1958 to 1969. While I was fired and later moved on to Buffalo to help get the NHL franchise underway there, King had stayed with the Leafs as vice-president and constant companion to Harold Ballard, principal owner of Maple Leaf Gardens Limited and the hockey team.

I was getting dressed to go downtown. Dodo called me. I picked up the phone and said, "What's on your mind, Mr. Clancy?"

He has a gravelly Irish voice. "Punch, Harold wants to know if you're interested in the Leaf job. If you are, he'd like you to come to the office and have a talk."

I can't say I was exactly surprised. Ever since April, when the Leafs were knocked out of the Stanley Cup quarter-finals in four straight games by the Montreal Canadiens, Harold had been showing signs of doing a shake-up. He was letting Roger Neilson go after two years as coach. Jim Gregory, who had worked for me with the Leafs before, was still general manager but rumours had him going, too.

For months, I'd been part of the rumour mill simply because I was available, having been fired by the Buffalo Sabres the previous December. Harold had never called me, but also I noticed he'd never ruled me out. When my name was brought up by reporters, he'd always say something like, "Punch? Well, he's not that far away, you know." In publicity, Harold is like the fisherman whose motto is, "I don't throw nothing back." Any time he talks to reporters he gives them something to quote him on. Still, most of the early stories had been that he was after Don Cherry or Scotty Bowman, both good coaches with excellent records. Late in May, Cherry, after five years with the Boston Bruins, had signed with Colorado. Bowman had the best coaching record in hockey from his years with the Montreal Canadiens. But he was deep in discussions with the Buffalo owners. I knew he was close to an agreement. Ballard apparently had got the message about the same time I did that for the Leafs, Bowman was a lost cause. Hence Clancy's call.

"If he wants to talk to me, I'll meet him for lunch at the Westbury," I told Clancy. A lunch at a hotel was one thing. A trip to his office, much more official, was sure to hit the papers.

Anyway, I called him and said sure, I was interested, at least in talking. We met for lunch at the Westbury Hotel on June 18.

We'd known one another for 40 years, in good times and bad. Ballard always maintained that he knew nothing about the night in 1969 when Stafford Smythe bounced me from the Leafs, but as far as I could make out maybe that was just one of those things he said often enough that he believed it. My understanding was that Harold left the Gardens that night before I was fired simply because he didn't want to be part of it. That's what I was told by one of his constant companions of the time, Joey Faraco, maître d' of the Hot Stove Lounge in the Gardens. In the ensuing years, sometimes Harold and Clancy would come to Buffalo to see a game and we'd sit together. He had let the Leafs run down in the 1970s, but that was mainly because nobody in the organization would stand up to him. He was far from being the world's greatest at picking hockey players himself, or keeping good ones he had, yet he always had the final say.

At lunch, he didn't take long to get to the point. He wanted me to come to work for him and get the Leafs moving again.

First thing I asked was, "What about Gregory?"

He shrugged and said he'd look after that.

"Well," I said, "I'd like you to decide definitely about him before we really talk business." I didn't want to be part of any unpleasant axing job. In the 1960s, I had protected Gregory's job twice. Once, when he was coaching in Vancouver under a player agreement we had with the minor-league club there, I had a call from its top man, Coleman Hall, wanting Gregory replaced. I convinced Coley to back off. Another time when the Leafs were thinking of getting rid of him, I'd intervened. He'd been loyal to me.

Harold agreed immediately that Gregory would be offered another job in the organization if he wanted it, or if he wanted to go elsewhere it would be with Harold's support.

With that assurance, we did go on to talk terms. My diary around that time notes: "What Bowman was offered, plus $5,000. Control of club." Meaning, that's what I was asking, in a nutshell. He agreed. I'd get credit cards, use of a car, the usual NHL pension and insurance, a bonus for every playoff series we won, a larger bonus for the Stanley Cup, and the equivalent of whatever playoff bonuses the players got. The contract would be for three years. I would be paid if I got sick. All was agreed, all verbal. Alan Eagleson, the executive director of the NHL Players Association, once said that the best kind of verbal contract to have with Harold was in writing. I don't agree. Where money is concerned, promises, even some promises he should not have made, Harold does what he says he'll do.

Looking back, the only thing I neglected was get him to agree that if I did get sick, my job would be held open for me until I was pronounced medically fit, or unfit. That was my big oversight. Even at sixty-one, as I was at the time, a guy is always learning.

When we had laid it all out and agreed on terms and conditions, I said, "I think it's okay, but first I'd better talk to my family and the doctors, see how it looks from there."

I'd had a heart attack in Buffalo in 1972, more than seven years earlier. Nothing since then. Three days after the lunch with Harold, the doctors who knew me best checked me over and said there was no health reason to hold me back. I think Dodo was all for it because she thought it was a waste for me to be sitting out. Maybe she got those ideas from listening to me all these years. Anyway, our home and a lot of friends were in Toronto; we'd both been born there. Heck, this was where we belonged. Even when I was in Buffalo I'd worked from the Statler Hilton Hotel or an apartment and we had kept the house in Toronto so that home never changed for our son and daughter, Brent and Marlene.

It all just added up, or seemed to.

Yet, if I had had even the remotest idea of what I was getting into, I never would have taken the job. At any price. I am not that stupid.

All my life I've jotted down things I have read or heard that seemed to have special meaning for me. Re-reading my diary for that year I come across an entry made just four days before Clancy's first phone call. On June 4, 1979, I had picked up from somewhere: "A ship in harbour is safe, but that is not what ships are built for."

CHAPTER TWO

What the Gardens means to me

If anyone asked me what building had more influence on my life than any other, my reply would be easy – Maple Leaf Gardens. I was thirteen years old when it opened in the fall of 1931. My heroes then were Busher Jackson and Charlie Conacher, Clancy, Red Horner, Joe Primeau, Ace Bailey, Baldy Cotton and the rest of that crew. I listened every Saturday to Foster Hewitt call the games on radio. Conn Smythe was only in his middle thirties then. His wheeling and dealing also told me something about what was possible if a guy was very sharp at the business side of the game. I played minor hockey, and by 1935 was with a midget team and going to school at Riverdale Collegiate. I also played soccer and lacrosse, but when I dreamed of glory, it was on skates.

One February supper time in 1935, a month before my seventeenth birthday, a man we knew called Red Hughes, who was involved in minor hockey, came to the door of our house on Coxwell Avenue in Toronto's east end. I'd come home from school and was there when the doorbell rang. As I recall, the conversation went something like this:

"I've been watching you play, kid, and I think you've got a chance if you want to play junior."

"Gee, do you think so?"

"I've mentioned you to Ed Wildey of the Young Rangers and he'll give you a tryout. They practise at the Gardens tomorrow morning. If you're interested, be there not later than 5.30."

Was I interested! I remember the feeling yet. Red Hughes – I've never forgotten him, a big guy, smiling – could have phoned but he had dropped around, instead. I think it was because he wanted to see my face when he told me.

I hardly slept a wink that night. My mother and dad, both Scottish, tried to keep me calm but finally gave up. Mother, a tiny woman alongside my 200-pound dad, George Alexander Imlach, got up with me at 4 a.m. to make sure I had a good big breakfast. Then, before 5 a.m., I slung my brown duffel bag over my shoulder and tramped in the dark up Coxwell Avenue to Danforth to catch the next westbound streetcar. They ran every half hour all night then on the main routes, but when I transferred at Church to an old wooden car southbound, it was icy cold and I stood by the stove in the middle of the car until we got to the Gardens.

When I hurried in through the main door, the first thing I did was look at the big clock. 5.25 a.m. I was on time. I didn't even know where the Young Rangers' dressing room was, but another kid came in and I followed him, wishing I weighed more than my 120 pounds.

The Young Rangers were sort of the Brand X junior team of the time, the big teams being St. Michael's College and West Toronto. But I wouldn't ever have wanted to miss my next few years with Ed Wildey. He was famous around Toronto then, a former boxer, big, muscular, honest, and very tough. He didn't say more than two or three words to me that first morning, just pointed to a place on the bench where I could change. I heard later that when Ed Wildey watched me that morning, a small centre trying too hard, he figured I'd never make it. I remember one of my best bursts of speed was to get to the boards about halfway through the practice and throw up my breakfast, partly from exertion and partly from excitement. From that day on I was at the Gardens every morning, without breakfast. I'd be in there at 5.25, on the ice at 5.35, and sometimes we'd skate until 8 and I'd go straight to school. My mother, after giving up on breakfasts, made me a double-size lunch and I'd eat part of it on the streetcar on the way to school. I never played a game with the Young Rangers that spring, passed my seventeenth birthday in March wondering if I'd ever make it, but working.

Then, after about two months of practice, suddenly the other guys couldn't get to me. Ed Wildey saw it too. A little later, in the summer, he came out to our house and gave me a set of dumb-bells and told me to twirl them around every day, build up my strength. "It'll make you a little handier," he said, an expression he often used. Everything, the two punching bags in the dressing room, the two- or three-round fights we'd have in there with him as referee, the summer workouts shooting a puck off the wooden floor, was said by Ed to "make you a little handier." I gained weight and strength. But also from Ed Wildey I learned a lot of principles that have stayed with me. One is that most people have to work hard for everything they get, and that sometimes very talented people who don't work hard can be beaten by others who do.

I was not one of your great stars, even as a junior, but one Saturday afternoon in the Gardens when I was eighteen, playing opposite Billy Taylor, I scored four goals, including the winner with thirty seconds to go, against the Oshawa Generals in one game of a junior playoff. We didn't win that series, but we won that game. Oshawa went on to the Canadian junior championship, the Memorial Cup. And I'd had a taste of what my life was going to be like.

When I finished school I worked as a bank clerk at Queen and Broadview. I was still living at home, where my father, after his initial disappointment that I had chosen hockey over his favourite sport, soccer, was always ready to help out when I had decisions to make. When I was too old for junior I tried out for the senior Toronto Goodyears and made the team. One night when I was knocked silly in a game in Windsor, and got up wanting to fight everybody on the ice, including my own team-mates, I picked up the name Punchy, which later became Punch.

The last time I ever played hockey in the Gardens was with the Marlboro seniors in the spring of 1941. Then I moved to Cornwall to play hockey and the following spring joined the Army, as a lot of other Canadians were doing. There were some very strong hockey teams in the services about that time, seen as a way to keep men busy and interested while they were training. I wound up playing for Cornwall Army. I was commissioned a lieutenant in 1942 and spent the rest of the war as an instructor. Tommy Ivan, later coach and general manager at Detroit and Chicago, was a ser- geant in the camp. When the war was over he wanted me to turn pro and go with him to Omaha in the Detroit Red Wings' chain, the same team that Gordie Howe broke in with. But at twenty- seven or twenty-eight, I didn't like my chances of making the NHL. There were other hockey jobs open. I took what I thought, and still think, was the best available. The Anglo-Canadian Pulp and Paper company in Quebec City liked my hockey, plus my bank experience. They'd pay me $135 a month to work in their office, plus something on the side for playing hockey with the company-supported Quebec Aces (the name ACE coming from Anglo-Canadian Employees' Association).

It was going to be another thirteen years before I put on skates again at Maple Leaf Gardens. But the Quebec experience was one I've always treasured. I played, coached, managed, and eventually became part-owner of the team. I coached some good ones, including Jean Beliveau. In 1957, when we won the Edinburgh Cup for the minor pro championship of Canada, Lynn Patrick offered me a job in the Boston Bruins organization. That year they had a deal with Eddie Shore, owner of the Springfield Indians, and part of the deal was me as manager. I coached too. By mid-season Eddie and I weren't on speaking terms anymore. He got mad at me because once I had insisted on playing my best goalie, Al Millar, whom I'd brought with me from Quebec, instead of one named Claude Evans, whom Eddie owned. Eddie wasn't any easier to beat in the office than he had been on the rink when he was an all-star with Boston. He traded Millar. I *had* to play Evans. But in the spring of 1958 we did manage to get to the American Hockey League finals, which nobody had expected us to do.

The night we got knocked out, season over, I was walking along a hallway in the rink. Eddie was coming the other way. We hadn't spoken for months. He stopped. A big hard man, whose respect is worth having.

"I guess you had yourself a pretty good year, son," he said.

"I guess so," I said.

And, as it turned out, others had noticed. It's that way in hockey. The rewards can be immediate. In Conn Smythe's memoirs, published in 1981, he wrote about troubles the Leafs were having in 1958. They'd finished last. Stafford (his elder son and hockey heir) had been checking the major and minor leagues for someone to help fill the management gap left a year earlier when Hap Day left the Leafs. "In late May, Stafford came in to see me about somebody called Punch Imlach . . . He'd been sent to Springfield as general manager but had wound up coaching as well. Under him, Springfield had done well. . . ."

At the NHL meetings in Montreal that June, Stafford talked to me. Later I went to Toronto to continue the talks. I wanted the job as general manager. They wouldn't give it to me. When we couldn't agree, Conn said, "What's the matter, are you afraid to take a chance?" He knew how to challenge a guy. I said I wasn't afraid of anything. I took the job with the title of assistant manager, after I'd been told I'd have control.

If anybody was impressed when I walked into the Gardens that September before training camp in 1958, they didn't show it. The first day I turned up for work I went in to the hockey office where I'd work, on the second floor, and asked where Billy Reay's office was; he was the Leafs' coach.

The receptionist said, "Mr. Reay is not in. Would you like to take a seat?"

I realized right then how far I had to go to make a mark when even my own receptionist didn't know me.

By next spring, things were different. We were last most of the year. I fired Billy Reay in November and took over as coach. We beat Detroit on the last night of the season to make fourth place, the last playoff spot in the old six-team league. We beat Boston and got to the finals before losing to Montreal. And we kept getting better. Lost in the final again in 1960. Battled Canadiens all year for first place in 1961, and won the Stanley Cup in 1962, 1963, 1964, and 1967.

I am going through this rapidly because it is ancient history, but the great Leaf teams of the 1960s did not come about by accident. I had my battles with Frank Mahovlich, who sometimes couldn't stand what I asked of everybody on the Leafs then; and with Carl Brewer, who quit the Leafs after our first three Stanley Cups; and to a lesser extent with Bob Pulford. But sometimes I think those cases are allowed to obscure the fact that with players like Johnny Bower, Terry Sawchuk, George Armstrong, Allan Stanley, Tim Horton, Davey Keon, and many others I had a good rapport that lasted well beyond my time with the Leafs.

The one war that I could not win was with Stafford Smythe. I could win battles, but not the war. Early on, during the honeymoon years when Imlach of the Leafs and the Leafs of Imlach were the world's best-known, and best, hockey team, I had total control. But Stafford and I did not get along. He found it galling that it was my team, not his.

When I was winning Stanley Cups, when we were giving the fans great hockey most nights of every season, when I'd stand down there behind the bench and hear the roars of Go-Leafs-Go loud enough to be heard a mile away, he couldn't do much except harass me from time to time. But all hockey eras come to an end. The Leafs were getting long in the tooth by the spring of 1967, but were just so good, so professional, so dedicated, that they had one more great playoff series in them – and if they hadn't won the Stanley Cup again that year it would have been easier for me to start bringing in young players. The following season they finished out of the playoffs and Stafford had something to hammer me with.

The final season was one of ultimatums, insults, bickering, and infighting between Stafford and me. In the end, we made the play-offs with a young team that would have got a lot better if I'd been given more time to spend with them. But we met Boston in the first round. They were just about as strong then as they were a year later when they won the Stanley Cup. When they blew us out four straight in the playoffs, Stafford fired me.

"The Imlach era is over," he told me in a little room off a corridor near the dressing room, minutes after the game ended.

I stayed alone a few minutes. The crowd was still filing out when I went into the dressing room, as I do at the end of every season, to shake hands and thank every player for what he has done.

When I had gone around the room and came to Davey Keon there must have been something in the way I said, "Thank you for the way you played for me," that made him guess something.

He followed me out and asked what I meant.

I told him I'd been fired. He stared at me. "What do you have to do, win the Stanley Cup every year?" he asked.

I found Dodo and our daughter Marlene and got them out of there before they could hear the news.

And there I was, walking out of Maple Leaf Gardens after eleven seasons and four Stanley cups, fired the way a foreman cuts a casual labourer who's been leaning too much on his shovel. I don't know yet why Stafford did it that way, except that was the only way he knew how to treat me. Almost any other man in hockey in his position would have done it differently. If I was going to be fired, so be it. But why at the instant when we had just lost a very tight one-goal game, in it to the end, our goalie out?

We drove home, Marlene and I in one car, Dodo in another (because I always drove down early on a game night, and they had come later). There was some comedy when we pulled up alongside at a stop light and I rolled down the window and yelled to Dodo that I had been fired.

"Fire?" she called back, looking around. "Where?"

But a few minutes later the news got to New York, where Montreal and the Rangers were still playing. Dodo was listening to that game on her car radio when the announcer broke in with the Toronto score, and the news that I had been fired. When we pulled up alongside one another in our driveway, Dodo was hopping mad but everything else seemed quite serene. Our old Collie, who always stayed outside, got up and stretched and wagged his tail, the way he always did.

Then, a few minutes later, friends started to arrive. King Clancy was first. His Irish eyes were sad. "Well, Punch! Son of a bitch!" He was followed by sportswriter George Gross and my longtime friend, the lawyer and piano player, Thomas B. (Windy) O'Neill, who had played for the Leafs when they won the Stanley Cup in 1945 and also with me in Quebec. In each of my four Stanley Cups in the 1960s, champagne had flowed – and each time I had put one bottle aside, taken it home, and saved it. It seemed a good time to open the four bottles of champagne and toast not only what had been good about the last ten-and-a-half years, but what was going to happen next, whatever it was.

The next morning I started a custom that I've followed ever since, when fired: I kept quiet. I didn't answer the phone, didn't bitch to anybody. Of course, the papers were doing that for me, blasting Stafford for the way he had fired me. But soon two things happened that took the sting off, or part of it.

One of my dodges with the Leafs had been that all the little fines I levied for various things during the season went into a pot that paid for a players' party when it was all over. When they couldn't get me on the phone, Davey Keon came to my house and said that the players wanted me at their party. When I was still their coach, I'd never gone. It wouldn't have been right. But that time I did.

I also felt deeply honoured when the mayor of Toronto, Bill Dennison, arranged what must have been a first anywhere – a civic luncheon for a fired coach. A lot of my players, the guys who had been with me all the way, were there. And that day, when the city where I'd been born and raised told me I mattered, I began to recover.

CHAPTER THREE

"I'm going to stuff those words down your goddamn throat, Stafford."

I don't remember many details of the next few months, except that I did have a sort of time-table worked out. I knew I wasn't going to be out of work any longer than I wanted to be, and I was in no rush. I would be paid for another year on my contract. Someone wrote at the time that every coach and manager in the league whose position was shaky, felt a little shakier because I was on the loose. Being fired by Toronto carried no stigma as far as other clubs were concerned. Everyone in hockey knew that for years Stafford and I had been feuding. He wanted to be boss. He couldn't be as long as I was there, and that was it. I played a little golf, relaxed, and listened to the offers.

The first was from the Minnesota North Stars, where general manager Wren Blair was travelling at a coach-a-year-clip. Another, later in the year, came from Jack Kent Cooke at Los Angeles. He said he was planning to relieve Hal Laycoe of the coach's job and made me a good offer. I nearly took that one. When I told him no and hung up, my family jumped all over me. They were all in favour of Los Angeles! If Cooke had called me back the next day and said, "I haven't made the move yet . . . is there any chance you'll change your mind?" he would have had me.

Another offer of a more complicated nature came from Vancouver. I say complicated because some years earlier I had bought shares in the Vancouver Canucks of the Western Hockey League. They weren't in my own name, although they could have been without a conflict of interest – the Leafs weren't playing in the same league with the Canucks, I had no part in the management, it

18

was just an investment. In the first NHL expansion in 1967, Vancouver had been turned down but was certain to get in the next time, probably soon. Whoever got the franchise would have to buy the Canucks. At the same time, anyone with ownership in the Canucks might have a chance to parlay that into the NHL franchise. Foster Hewitt, Joe Crozier (my old partner from the Quebec Aces) and I, between us, owned one third of the shares – and if the new expansion price, when named, had not been what seemed an exorbitant $6,000,000, we would have been contenders. But our understanding was that the $6,000,000 had to be paid all in one lump. That would mean too much debt. The NHL knew we were interested, but for its own reasons (no doubt partly influenced by Stafford) actually went hunting elsewhere, and decided on a Minneapolis-based company called Medicor which didn't know a hockey puck from a road apple. I was burned up about that for years. I still am. Especially when I found out that both of the clubs given franchises in December 1969, Vancouver and Buffalo, were given terms: $1,750,000 down, and the balance at $850,000 a year for 5 years. That we could have handled. I remember one time in the Hot Stove Lounge in Maple Leaf Gardens, having dinner with NHL president Clarence Campbell, and remonstrating with him for discriminating against a group of Canadians in favour of a U.S. company.

"Why don't you buy the Oakland team?" Campbell asked (Oakland being a disaster area in the NHL at the time).

"What the hell would I want to buy the Oakland team for?" I asked. It was like being offered the *Titanic*.

Anyway the Rochester team in the American Hockey League was also owned by the Vancouver Hockey Club in the NHL. Part of the deal for Vancouver's NHL franchise was that Medicor had to buy us out. I objected to some of the terms because some shareholders had been offered $200 a share and some $250. On legal advice, we felt the transaction would be open to a lawsuit if different prices were paid for the shares. Also, there had been rumours that Medicor would not honour the Vancouver club's contracts, including that of Joe Crozier as coach. I phoned Medicor and set up a meeting in Vancouver late in November to discuss these matters, the upshot being that the total price of $2,820,000 was okay, but the distribution would be made at an equal-share price of $235. Among other things, this cost Joe Crozier $15 a share for what he owned. But in that meeting, Medicor's vice-president, Lyman Walters, told me they would like me to be general manager.

"All right," I said. "But Joe Crozier is coming with me."

I thought that was reasonable – Joe is a very knowledgeable hockey man, had had enough faith in the game to put his own money in it, and had been a very successful coach and manager in Rochester and Vancouver for years.

"We don't want Joe," Walters said.

"That's the only way you get me," I said. I wasn't going to turn my back on my friend. I never bothered with that offer anymore.

On December 2, 1969, Vancouver and Buffalo were officially admitted to the NHL lodge. A couple of days later I received a telegram from Seymour Knox, head of the Buffalo group, asking me to phone him. I did, and he told me that the principals of the Buffalo ownership would like to meet with me. We decided that for the moment, this should be kept quiet. I have always preferred that negotiations be kept secret until they are completed. The idea was that I would drive to Mr. Knox's home in Buffalo on Sunday, December 7. That day, there was a bad snowstorm. Mr. Knox told a dinner audience later that his first sight of me was trudging knee-deep in snow to his front door and then taking my boots off and stepping into his house for the first time in my socks.

The Buffalo people have said since that one thing they liked about me from that first day was that when they asked a question, I didn't hurry to answer, but then told them what I thought whether they liked it or not. I told them from the start that $6,000,000 was far too much for getting the leavings of the other clubs in the league. But there was no reason for my not being frank. I was not applying for a job; they had asked me, and they had a right to my best advice, whether it sat well with them or not.

I think I was in Buffalo five times in the next few weeks, in a snowstorm every time. One of the most important meetings was on December 23. At that one, they made me an offer to manage and coach the new Buffalo team. I told them I had decided not to make any commitment until I had settled finally with the Leafs. I had been negotiating a settlement of the year remaining on my contract with Toronto, the deal to take effect January 2, 1970. This was done by lawyers, and involved no meetings with Stafford or anyone else at the Gardens. The Buffalo people understood and suggested January 6 as the date for my answer. On January 5, a

Monday, I returned my Toronto Maple Leafs' car and picked up the cheque settling my contract. On the 6th, Seymour Knox and I talked again on the phone. I was just about ready to say yes, but there were some details of the contract to be worked out. He said maybe I should come over and see him again two days later.

That day, a funny thing happened. Having given back my Leafs' car, I had to rent one for the drive to Buffalo. I had been up and down that road for years, our top farm team being in Rochester, and there was one place where I always stopped for gas. The Leaf cars had been big ones, usually Oldsmobiles. When I pulled up at the pumps in the little rented car, the guy came out and looked it over, shaking his head. "I guess things aren't quite the same, now that you're not with the Leafs," he said sympathetically.

I didn't say anything, but it hit me. When I got to Buffalo that day and we worked out the contract, I added one request. I wanted as a company car, I said, the biggest and brightest Cadillac Eldorado in town. They agreed. When I picked it up a few days later, I went in to that same gas station. Didn't say a word except, "Fill 'er up." The guy took a good look at the car, and at me, opened his mouth a couple of times, but didn't say anything.

We had decided not to make the Buffalo announcement until a few days after the Super Bowl when there would be less competition for sports page space in Buffalo, but I got a laugh when Tom Scallen of Medicor, interviewed on Toronto television, said that I was still in the running to take over the Vancouver club.

Apparently Medicor still didn't believe that I would turn down what they were offering, just because I objected to the fact that for me to take the job would mean Joe Crozier was fired. When reporters phoned me about Scallen saying I was still in the running for the Vancouver job, I replied, "I'm glad to hear that."

Our Buffalo security obviously had been very good, and we kept it that way. On the 15th, I went to Buffalo to sign my contract and have dinner with the Buffalo directors at Seymour Knox's house. Even some of the directors didn't know who they were going to meet there. I stayed overnight at Seymour's home. We kept the secret to the end. On the 16th we held the press conference. Then I got right out of there to hold another press conference in St. Catharines. I had to be in Toronto by late afternoon because I had a dinner date with Dodo to celebrate our twenty-seventh wedding anniversary. The next day, reporting my Buffalo deal, some of the Toronto papers ran photos of Dodo and me combining our anniversary night out with closing of the Buffalo deal.

And then something happened that was to loom quite large in the months to come. My first official appearance as Buffalo's new general manager and coach was at the league's all-star game in St. Louis on the Tuesday after I signed. Before the game there was a big cocktail party and reception for all the hockey people there. I went in with Charley Barton, a good hockey writer for the *Buffalo Courier-Express* who also became a good friend. As we entered, I noticed Stafford Smythe just a few feet ahead of me. When he turned and saw me – well, I wasn't going to walk around him. And Stafford wasn't going to let me. We hadn't talked since the night he fired me. He got abusive, jabbed me in the chest with his finger, and said, "I'll take care of you. Right now I have other problems, but I'll take care of you on the ice."

The other problems he referred to were with the income tax department, but that was no concern of mine. He kept at me and at me.

"You know the reason you were fired in Toronto?" he said. "It was because you are too old." I was 51 at the time, a year or two older than he was.

"I'm going to stuff those words down your goddamn throat, Stafford," I said, and then offered to buy drinks for all present, including Smythe, shook hands all around, and moved on to have a few with some of my *friends* in hockey. Then the work began.

CHAPTER FOUR

Everything makeshift, including the team

I don't want anyone to think that from the day I walked in to my makeshift office in a trust company building in downtown Buffalo, I was obsessed with anything as far in the future as playing the Toronto Maple Leafs. That was ten months away. I had too much else to do. In many ways, the future of the Buffalo franchise was going to be built in this first year – and not only on the ice, but in selling tickets, becoming accepted by the public as a good organization. I never worked so hard in my life.

The first goal was the expansion draft, in June in Montreal. The six old NHL clubs, and the newer six admitted in 1967, had everything rigged against the two new teams of 1970. I was in a good position to harp about that. The previous autumn my first book, *Hockey is a Battle*, had come out. It was a best-seller in Canada and sold a few copies in the United States as well, eventually more than 100,000 copies in hard cover and paperback. The *Toronto Telegram* and *Weekend Magazine* had bought excerpts from it and syndicated them across the country. The response had prompted the *Telegram* to offer me a syndicated weekly hockey column. It was all my own work except the typing. Because of my contacts, I probably could dig up more inside stuff to write about than most people. Anyway, I'd spent a lot of time that winter in press boxes and the first approach I made to anyone else to work in Buffalo came in the Toronto press box – before I'd even accepted my job. On New Year's Eve, the Oakland Seals were playing the Leafs. John Andersen was Oakland's director of scouting. He'd left the Leafs at the same time I had, but in the years before that had worked his way up through the Leaf organization, first in the publicity department, then as my assistant. He knew hockey management inside out.

That night in the Toronto press box I stopped behind John's seat.

"Would you be interested in coming to work for me?" I said. I couldn't tell him where, when, or under what conditions, and he didn't ask.

"Yes," he said.

I guess others knew how well we'd worked together. When my Buffalo deal was announced, Bill Torrey, who now runs the New York Islanders but then was Oakland's executive vice-president, dropped into John's office in Oakland and said, "I suppose you'll be wanting to leave to work for Punch." I called Bill Torrey and got permission to talk to John, went to Oakland, made a deal.

Right at that time Oakland was going through some ownership changes and the new group told Bob Swados, vice-president of the Buffalo club, that it did not want us offering Andersen a job. They wanted him. I got that in a memo from Bob Swados. I just picked up the phone and told him, "Too late. I've already made a deal with him."

It was a good move for Buffalo. We had to put a first-rate scouting organization together in a great hurry, to help us get ready for the June draft. I knew John could run it.

My lifetime in hockey was a help there, too. I didn't have to interview people for scouting jobs – I *knew* them. I'd just phone and say, "I need a scout in your area. Will you work for me?" John made some of the calls, same way. We had to bloody hurry. In the junior leagues, we had only five or six weeks at the most to cover teams that wouldn't make the playoffs. So we had to saturate, hire more people than we would normally need.

Doug Minor was the first. He would cover the West. For the Boston area we hired John (Bucky) Kane; I'd known Bucky when I worked for Boston in the late 1950s. Jim Cherry had coached junior in Ontario and we got him, along with Roy Cast, to cover Ontario. I needed someone for the Montreal area and Quebec junior league. Roland Mercier, a great friend of mine and Jean Beliveau's from back when Beliveau had played for me in Quebec, phoned me to recommend Mike Racicot for Quebec. Mike is still with Buffalo, a good man. In Montreal we also hired Al Millar, my old goalie in Quebec and Springfield. He'd been a pro twenty years and knew the players. Len Poore covered the Maritimes, Paul Roach the Windsor area.

All these people were directed by John Andersen, fanning them out with no overlaps, correlating what he got from them with his own knowledge from the Oakland job and mine from ice level with the Leafs. It gets down to organization, using everybody to the best advantage. And then we were very lucky that Fred Hunt, general manager of the Buffalo Bisons in the American Hockey League, agreed to help me as assistant general manager. That was one of the best moves we made. Freddy was a quiet, low-key guy, a nice change you might say from me, and he'd played and coached in Buffalo for many years. More important, he *knew* everybody in Buffalo, unions, ticket people, everybody. No one – and I include myself in that – could have done the job Freddy did. I don't think he ever got the acclaim he deserved. He is dead now. They have a hockey Hall of Fame in Buffalo. If any guy should be in it, he should be – and in March of 1982, he did receive that recognition. Maybe he would have liked to be Buffalo's general manager himself, and in a way he had earned it. But he never showed anything but loyalty. I hope I thanked him enough. My real troubles in Buffalo years later all started after Freddy died, and I think that was more than a coincidence.

Of course, the situation was ideal for me – acquiring my own staff instead of inheriting it and having to sort out the good ones from the mistakes. On the ownership side I was just about as lucky, it seemed at the time. As I told John Andersen, "They don't know anything about hockey, which is great. When they find out a little, that's when we have to look out."

The ones I worked with most closely were the Knox brothers, Seymour and Northrup, Dave Forman, administrative vice-president, and Bob Swados, vice-president and legal counsel. The Knoxes were an interesting combination, Norty a fighter, a world champion at his game, court tennis. So you know he's competitive. Of the two, he'd throw the stones. Seymour had the competitiveness, too, but also knew when to compromise. I use that in the best sense of the word, because usually the two balanced each other. Dave Forman really ran the business end, television, deals with the city on rents, everything but the hockey. He is an exceptional man and was a good friend to me.

Bob Swados was a little different, in some ways passive, not a fighter, and in other ways very stubborn. If something comes up and a decision has to be made, my way is to decide now and fight about it later, if necessary. When I'd do that, he'd be upset. As a lawyer, his attitude would be, "We can't do that on our own. We have to reach an agreement (maybe with the league, or with other clubs) before we do it." I found out long ago that in hockey you lose a hell of a lot more than you win, by doing it that way. So naturally Swados wasn't the kind of person I cottoned to.

Anyway, I got to know them all fairly well in the first few months before we went to Montreal for the league meetings, including the expansion draft that would give us our basic team, and the amateur draft in which we hoped to pick up some junior stars that could help us. It wasn't a very enticing prospect, that expansion draft. I'd been sounding off for months about the way the cards were stacked against Vancouver and Buffalo. The only chance either of us had to get even one really topline player would be in the amateur draft, where we'd have the pick of the top juniors and college players, one pick each. It wasn't really a good crop that year apart from the top few – Gilbert Perreault, Dale Tallon, Reg Leach, Rick MacLeish and Darryl Sittler, to name the ones most prominent later in the NHL. In the regular expansion draft, a day before the amateur draft, each of the twelve existing clubs could protect fifteen players plus two goalies. So the best you could possibly get was the sixteenth best player of any team. After you picked, that team could fill with its seventeenth best player, giving you a chance at the eighteenth best. And then, through the process again, there you were staring at the twentieth best. Wow! None of the established clubs could lose more than three players, plus goalies. Even worse, first-year players were exempt. That meant Montreal, for instance, after protecting fifteen, had twelve more pretty good players who couldn't be touched, and Boston eight. So the eighteen players to each of Vancouver and Buffalo would be entirely the sixteenth, eighteenth, and twentieth best of the existing clubs, plus one good junior each.

I spent much of the spring looking for an edge, and didn't find much. I did ask Seymour Knox to try to arrange that the contest between Buffalo and Vancouver for the right to go first in the two drafts should be settled on June 9. The expansion draft was June 10, amateur draft June 11. If I knew on June 9, for instance, whether I would have first or second choice, it would enable me to make judgments we couldn't make otherwise. I wore out my knees praying that I would win first choice in the amateur draft. I wanted Gilbert Perreault as I had never wanted a hockey player before. I'd seen him play in St. Catharines that spring and the hair just stood up on my neck at what he could do. He was a superstar in the making, the man the Buffalo franchise could be built around, and no mistake.

Usually, first or second pick would be decided by a coin toss. For some reason, perhaps because it made better television, the NHL substituted a big jeezly wheel, the kind you see on the midway. It was numbered from one to twelve. I won a toss to see who picked what numbers for the main spin. I chose the top ones. There was a hell of a crowd in the ballroom at the Queen Elizabeth Hotel, everybody in hockey there. When the first spin of the wheel stopped at eight, I had won first choice in the expansion draft. Everybody at our table cheered. But now came the big one.

Clarence Campbell spun the wheel. When it stopped, he looked at the winning number, and announced "Number one! Vancouver wins first choice in the amateur draft!"

But I was on my feet and so was everybody at our table, pointing and yelling, "Eleven! Eleven!"

Clarence took another look. The digits in the double figures were one above the other.

It's always amused me that Clarence didn't say, "I've made a mistake." He said, "There has been a mistake. The winning number is eleven. . . ." The rest was drowned out in the wild uproar, not only at our table but through the room, with only Vancouver and its supporters remaining quiet. Even glum.

It was a funny time, for me. I always stayed in the Mount Royal Hotel in those days. In the past, when I got in for league meetings, my phone would be ringing off the hook, people offering players or trying to deal for mine. Now I had nothing to deal with. We'd inherited a couple of players when the Sabres (the name decided on by a contest) bought the old Buffalo minor-league franchise. I had picked up four more minor-leaguers when I asked for, and got, permission to take part in the minor-league draft on the grounds that Vancouver already had about forty minor-league players from the purchase of the Rochester and Vancouver minor-league clubs. But I had nobody that anyone wanted.

Getting first choice in both the other two drafts changed that, a little. And I don't want anyone to think I was lonely. Far from it. Newspaper friends dropped in, out-of-work hockey guys. The two Buffalo hockey writers who were going to be very important to the franchise, by their understanding and good writing, were Dick Johnston of the *Buffalo Evening News* and Charley Barton of the *Courier-Express*. They usually wrote their stories in my suite. There were coaches, scouts, old players, hangers-on. Somebody called it Imlach's Army as we walked back and forth between the meetings at the Queen E. and the Mount Royal.

One of my best breaks came one night as I was waiting for an elevator with three or four other guys. Sid Abel, once a great player for Detroit and then coach and general manager, came along. We'd been rivals, not always friendly. Sid was mad as hell at me a couple of years before when I was quoted as saying that Detroit wasn't going anywhere in the playoffs because he was always giving them days off to go to the races. But this night when he saw me, it was only a few hours after I'd won first choice in the expansion draft. He hooked his arm through mine and said so the guys with me could hear, "Come with me, Punch. I want to *give* you something."

"I'll bet you do!" I said.

We walked to a quiet corner.

"Look, you know Tom Webster?"

"Yeah." Boston had him, a right wing, only twenty-one. He'd been a big scorer in the minors, but not good enough yet to break into the powerful Boston club. The protected lists were out and Webster was not protected. Detroit wanted him, badly. Obviously.

"If you'll pick Webster first, we'll trade you Roger Crozier for him," Abel said.

Music! Whatever else we got in the draft, we just had to come up with an NHL goalkeeper. But Crozier was beyond my wildest dreams. He had won the rookie award in his first full year, the Conn Smythe trophy as the most valuable player in the playoffs a year later, and had a low 2.65 goals-against average in the season just ended. But he wasn't happy in Detroit and they thought he was sick too much. That's when you can get a guy.

"You got a deal!" I told Abel.

Later Milt Schmidt, another former star player and then coach and general manager with Boston, came to me and asked me to lay off Webster. In return, I was promised someone else. To Milt I was non-committal. I didn't want to say a flat no, for fear he would protect Webster and screw up my deal for Crozier! He claimed the next day that I double-crossed him when I took Webster, and immediately traded him for Crozier. But I had never told him I would lay off Webster. He just *thought* I was going to go along. He had taken a gamble by leaving both Webster and Gary Doak off his protected list (a strong team has to take those chances) and he lost both of them in the first two picks. Incidentally, also before that draft, Chicago asked me not to take Jerry Korab, a minor leaguer then. They'd give me goalie Dave Dryden for that favour. I told Tommy Ivan okay.

As the draft went on, anybody looking closely could have seen my pattern. With the goal position nailed down, I did the best I could to build up the defence. Four out of my next five picks were the best defencemen available. Then I took Don Marshall from New York and Phil Goyette from St. Louis, both old Canadiens. It was among the forwards, starting with Marshall and Goyette, that my main idea surfaced. I wanted offence. I was sure of Perreault, who would be great. I wanted the best skaters and scorers I could find. When I had the Leafs after the 1967 first expansion, I would see those new clubs come in and play kitty-bar-the-door hockey, dull as ditchwater, just up and down, up and down, check, check, check and hope the other team would make a mistake. Sometimes they would win that way, in fact, they won a lot more than some people expected. But it was dull, dull hockey. I was not going to try to sell the Buffalo public dull hockey, even though I was getting eighteen hockey players that nobody else wanted. We would have to improve on them as quickly as we could, by trades.

One thing I liked was that in the new divisional alignment we were in the strongest section, against all the old NHL teams exept Chicago. When you play the best, you can see exactly how much better you have to get. Not everybody looked at it that way, but it made sense to me.

So okay, we drafted our eighteen, and the next day when the time came I stood up first. I felt *so* lucky that moment when I said, "Buffalo picks Gilbert Perreault from the Montreal Junior Canadiens." Even so, I didn't know how lucky I was going to be.

There were a couple of other small items I should mention.

One was that in the Mount Royal Hotel, the Toronto suite presided over by Stafford Smythe was right below the Buffalo suite. Ballard and Clancy were there, with Jim Gregory as general manager and John McLellan as coach. (John would have been my choice, too.) On our last night in town, my joint was jumping when the room-service waiter came in with another load of ice and mixes.

I said, "You working the Toronto suite, too? How are things down there?"

"I was down there earlier, Mr. Imlach," he said. "Things were very quiet."

"Very quiet, eh?" I said. "Haw, haw, haw."

And Stafford didn't let the occasion go by without another put-down. A reporter interviewed him about the rivalry that would build between Buffalo and Toronto, each of us within range of the other's television, drawing on the same fans in the Niagara peninsula.

"How do you think Buffalo will do against your Leafs this first year, Mr. Smythe?"

"They won't win a game," Stafford said.

The reporter then asked what I thought. I had just looked over my list of players. *Jeez!* But what I said was, "When the NHL schedule comes out, just circle the date for the first time Buffalo plays in Toronto. That'll be the night."

When I got back to Buffalo the first thing I did was have a big sign made and pasted on the wall behind my desk in our makeshift office in the trust company building. Everybody who walked in, or even walked by, could see it.

Two words. BEAT TORONTO.

CHAPTER FIVE

A night to remember

When I'm talking about that first season in Buffalo, I hardly know where to start. I'm walking back and forth underneath the stands. We hadn't been able to get the balcony built for that season. We didn't even have our own dressing room . . . and the hockey team was unbelievable! If I said it to myself once I must have said it a hundred times – what the hell am I doing here with these yo-yos after having the best? For eight or nine years in the 1960s I'd had the best, the champions, best teams, best players, dedicated players, the whole bit. Now I had these guys! They'd practise and then go over to Fort Erie and get loaded on beer every afternoon. I knew about it. But I used to say, "Well, what am I going to do about it?" Sometimes I'd be upset, and I certainly didn't like the idea of turning a blind eye to what I'd massacre a *good* hockey team for, but I knew I had to put it in the right perspective – even if they didn't drink, they weren't going to play any better. That was the key. So why go crazy over it? Trade, get rid of them, get better hockey players. That was the answer. And once in a while I'd think, well, Imlach, it could be worse; you could have a team of *good* hockey players who were blowing their brains out by boozing it up.

I remember one time early in the season. I'm living in the Statler-Hilton Hotel. I'm in bed about four in the morning, when the bars close across the street, and I hear this big commotion outside. I get up and look out and here's practically my whole hockey team falling out of the bar! The next morning at practice – actually just a few hours later – they all wondered how I knew what had happened to them.

There were exceptions, of course. One was Gil Perreault. People

31

sometimes tell me I'm a hard taskmaster about how the game should be played. But I know when to get tough and when not, most of the time. With Perreault I just told him, "Look, kid, take the puck and go with it. I mean, you're going to make all kinds of mistakes but eventually, by making the mistakes, if you're smart you're not going to make them again. You're going to develop, and build your game up." It worked for Perreault that year and for Ricky Martin the next, when I told him exactly the same thing. Even Perreault made me shudder a few times. . . . He'd go in front of his net, somebody would take the puck off him and put it in. What the hell, everybody does it at one time or another but he seemed to do it more than was necessary, at first. Yet I had the privilege, I repeat, the privilege, to watch him play every game from the beginning. In other cities people would see him play a few times a year. I watched him every night and saw him do things nobody else can. If he had the desire of Rocket Richard, or the concentration of somebody else, say Wayne Gretzky, he's got the talent to be the greatest of them all. But those other intangibles are missing. He just wants to play. Sometimes he *would* do it all, get motivated by something, and I'd see him come up with such great, great hockey.

Yet, to get back to those first days, I was supposed to build a hockey club in Buffalo, eh? I had the authority to do it. I was going to do it. And apart from some down times, I enjoyed doing it. We used to get beat. They'd make the dumbest mistakes when they first started, and I'd be walking up and down behind the bench saying my favourite Buffalo word, "Unbelievable!" Sometimes I used to put another stronger word between "un" and "believable." But they got better, or they'd have good nights. Sometimes I really did enjoy watching those buggers, but all the time I'm thinking of how to make the team better.

One thing, I did have them ready to start that season. We had training camp in Peterborough. I hired a couple of real tough apples from the Royal Military College at Kingston to get them in shape, off the ice. It was a tough training camp. We'd asked more than seventy players to camp. The physical training instructors from R.M.C. were there for one reason, to get these guys into the best condition they'd ever been in. Right beside the rink is a track for harness racing. The R.M.C. guys would get them running around that track. Some of them used to die out there. They weren't ready for it. Goyette and Marshall were the two stars, you might say. They'd been on top before. They would rebel and go home to Montreal. Then they'd come back. Then they would go home again! The last time they went home I left them there, because of another idea I had.

I laughed at some things that happened. One of our real characters was Reggie Fleming, a good street fighter, you know, and not a bad hockey player. One day when the R.M.C. guys were teaching unarmed combat, Reggie decided he'd give them a little lesson on how it's done in the NHL. The next second he's flat on his back! That was the end of that.

There was one player in that camp I felt sorry for, big Moose Vasko. When he played defence for Chicago in the 1960s he used to come in at about 220 pounds. He reported to our camp at about 270. He tried to get it off, and it just about killed the guy. For two weeks he gave everything that was in him, worked and worked and worked. He would go in in the morning and never leave the rink. Others would go for lunch, but he was trying to get the weight off and hardly ate at all. He kept driving but was just too far out of shape to make it. I really felt for the guy, he tried so hard, but it just wasn't there any more.

Our first exhibition game was against the New York Rangers. We didn't belong on the same ice with them, but got them down 4-0 before they got mad. From then on we never had the puck. Even so, it took a shot from behind the net that bounced in off one of our defencemen for them to get a 4-4 tie. Incidentally, in that first game Buffalo ever played, the first goal was scored by Billy Inglis, who went on to coach the hockey team years later, after I was fired.

One of the good things about those weeks before the season began was that the Buffalo owners didn't know the first thing about hockey, so they took my word for what to do. For instance, we needed a play-by-play broadcaster. The applicants sent in tapes and some were pretty good. I took the better ones to a CBC man I knew in Toronto and we listened to them together; we got the list down to three, and then picked Ted Darling, who is still the voice of the Sabres. I had a little trouble with our first publicity man, Chuck Burr. He put out an excellent training camp guide but then complained about my announcing things in Peterborough instead of releasing everything through him, in Buffalo. I phoned

Knox and said, "Let's get something straight. The publicity should come from here, because the team is here. Secondly, the hockey club is not being run for the benefit of the publicity department. It's the other way around." So we got that straightened out, although Burr later left to handle publicity for the Buffalo Raceway.

To sell tickets, we put ads in Toronto papers, just a picture of me with the line, "Remember me? I'm in Buffalo now. Come over and see me!" One of the first to subscribe was Stafford Smythe. He bought four season tickets because, as he told *Sports Illustrated*, "I never want anybody in the Leafs' organization to be in a position where he would have to ask Imlach for tickets."

Anyway, we got ready for our first league game in Pittsburgh October 10, and won it 2-1. That was a nice way to start, being able to go out and win our first league game, with *that* team. A few days later we were in New York. I remember standing behind the bench and looking at the Rangers. There wasn't one guy on our team who could have made the Rangers! They beat us 3-0. The next night we were in Buffalo for our home opener against Montreal and it was murder. They played that funny game where they don't let you have the puck. I remember before the game, at the reception the Knoxes threw for opening night, somebody said that everybody there would do anything they could for the Knoxes, except play goal. The game that night showed how true that was. Roger Crozier was just magnificent in our goal, but they outshot us 44-14 and beat us 3-0.

We did our best with what we had during October, but still ended the month last in the league. That was okay with me. In fact, I'd deliberately left Goyette and Marshall at home in Montreal. I knew how much those two could help us, but there was another factor. I didn't exactly want to be leading the league in the first month. Or even out of last place. My thinking was this: when players were put on waivers *before* the end of October, the club that had finished last in the spring got first shot at them. But as of November 1, the club that was in last place *then*, had first chance. I wanted that club to be Buffalo. Not that I went out and tried to lose games to achieve last place. I didn't have to try! Barring a miracle, that's where we would be. Then maybe we could pick up some players on waivers who would help us.

And that's precisely what happened. Late in October I had a chance to get Paul Andrea from Oakland. He was available, but if he'd been put on waivers other teams would have had a chance at him before us. I asked Oakland to wait until November 1. That day, in last place, I started making moves. First thing I heard was that Bobby Baun, who'd been with me in Toronto in the 1960s and helped win four Stanley Cups, was going to be put on waivers by Detroit. St. Louis wanted him. We made a deal. I claimed him on November 3, and the next day traded him to St. Louis for Larry Keenan and Jean-Guy Talbot, another former Montreal Canadien. Both could skate and score. Andrea was put on waivers by Oakland and I took him. And now that the crucial date was past, I was anxious to get in the best possible shape for the game in Toronto on November 18. I sent John Andersen to Montreal to talk to Goyette and Marshall. Okay, now that training camp was over, they were willing to come back. They only had three or four practices before we were due in Toronto. But they were big leaguers for sure and with the other players we'd picked up, I figured that would make a difference. At the practice Tuesday, the day before the Toronto game, I asked them whether they felt they could play in Toronto the next night. I said I would probably give them only spot duty, such as on the power play. They nodded that they were ready.

After that Tuesday practice, I went back to the office for a while. When John Andersen and I were leaving I glanced at my watch and said, "It's six o'clock, John. Exactly twenty-four hours till we walk into the dressing room at the Gardens." We went and ate and when we were having a beer I happened to glance at my watch again. Eight o'clock. "Exactly twenty-four hours before they'll be dropping the puck," I said.

I had my own car there, so the next day I drove back alone, a little ahead of the bus carrying the team. On the Queen Elizabeth Way cars would go by me and maybe the driver would glance over and recognize me and then slow down and give me a thumbs-up sign. One fished in his pocket and waved his game tickets. A lot of thoughts were going through my head. I figured that Stafford would have the Leafs up for this game like there was no tomorrow. Some of the players would feel a special motivation, too. I'd feuded with Mike Walton of the Leafs when I was there, and when he wanted to play, he could play. Also, the previous weekend Bobby Baun had been traded by St. Louis to the Leafs, his fourth club in ten days (I'd claimed him from Detroit, traded him to St.

Louis, and they'd sent him to Toronto for Brit Selby). Baun had resented that I'd had him riding the bench most of the time in the 1967 Stanley Cup Final. The rest were mainly players I'd brought into the Toronto club myself, some of them my friends. But that wouldn't stop them from shoving it to me if they could.

But we were feeling pretty good, too, with our additions since November 1. We'd beaten Oakland and tied Montreal in our last two games. If Roger Crozier played his game, that would be worth a few goals to us, for sure. I wished Jean-Guy Talbot wasn't injured, but. . . .

In the Gardens I walked along the corridors that had been my mother-house, sort of, since that day long ago when I first walked in, sixteen years old, at 5.25 a.m., carrying my gear. A lot of the photos blown up on the walls were of Stanley Cups I'd won with the Leafs, along with the big men from those teams – Johnny Bower, Terry Sawchuk, Allan Stanley and the rest.

I had a cup of tea and kept as much to myself as I could. Some friends, including Foster Hewitt, my old travelling companion, came in to say hello. Foster asked for a prediction. I think I said we'd win 4-1. But to tell the truth I wasn't as confident as I let on. How could I be?

Just before the game I went into the dressing room. I didn't really have to tell the players how much this game meant to me, and basically that is all I said.

A lot of people have said since that the minute or so before the puck was dropped had a lot to do with the game. I don't know. I never used to go to the bench until after the national anthem had been played. When the players went out, I sat down in the dressing room and one of our trainers stood behind me and kneaded some of the tension out of my neck muscles. With the last bars of the anthem, I stood up and walked along the corridor.

I don't know what I was expecting, probably the usual, just as sometimes when I was still coaching there, a mixture of boos and cheers. But what I got was something else. When the lights went up and people in the crowd saw me behind the bench, they started to applaud. Then some stood up and cheered, and more followed. It was a standing ovation. Even John Ashley, the referee, stood at centre ice, holding the puck uncertainly. Then he dropped it, and the game was on.

The Leafs poured it on early. Roger Crozier made a series of saves that had the Leafs shaking their heads, especially during an early power play. Then Garry Monohan slid into the net with the puck in a play that Crozier couldn't have stopped. Baun got a tripping penalty and I put out Goyette at centre on our power play, with Marshall on one wing and Perreault on the other. We took the puck into their end and never let it out. For a minute Bruce Gamble in the Toronto goal held the fort, then Donnie Marshall flipped in the rebound of Cliff Schmautz's shot and tied it. In the second period Gerry Meehan put us ahead for the first time, but Mike Walton, the most fired-up Leaf, playing the game of his life, tied it. A minute later Larry Keenan got his first goal, and put us ahead for good. He got another one a few minutes later, both on passes from Floyd Smith and Al Hamilton. Toronto had outshot us 15-11 in each of the first two periods, but we were ahead 4-2. That tells you something about the way Roger was playing goal. And it kept on in the third. Leafs outshot us 16-10 in that one, but Crozier didn't let one of those 16 shots past him, and we scored three – Meehan his second of the game, Steve Atkinson one, Paul Andrea one. After we got ahead, the Toronto crowd cheered and laughed with every goal. I almost felt sorry for Johnny McLellan behind the Leaf bench. I'd seen Stafford in his box across the ice behind the penalty box during the first two periods, but he didn't show there in the third.

Near the end of the game, when the Toronto crowd gave us another ovation, Reggie Fleming put my hat on his hockey stick and waved it at the crowd. They yelled, "We want Punch!" Some Buffalo fans who had come over for the game yelled back, "You can't have him." I felt humble, for once. I didn't stay out for the ovation at the end. I followed my team into the dressing room, and all I could do was hammer my fists on an equipment trunk and yell, "Way to go!" When the three stars of the game came in, Crozier, Meehan, and Keenan, the team cheered them. I went around and thanked every one. When the reporters came in, I tried to put the compliments where they belonged – on the players. A lot of them were not going to be with me forever, I knew that, but they had made this night one of the most memorable in my life. I tried not to gloat but I guess I did, a little, because one of the papers the next day quoted me as saying, "Did I shove it down far enough? Did I?"

After a while I went out and sat with Dodo in the seats. There were still people around wanting pictures, autographs, and just to talk. We were sitting there when the Leaf players filed out. Johnny Bower, my great goalie through the best of my Leaf years, working as a scout that year, was one of the few who spoke. Shaking his head, he said, "I don't even want to talk to you."

The papers the next day played it with big photos on the front pages. One headline read: "Punch's Sabres prove his point." A day or two later I put in an ad that just said, "Thanks." It was the only way I knew to reach the people who had helped make that night the way it was.

When Dodo and I walked out of the rink and drove home, I knew that as important as the night had been to me, it was even more important to her. She had hated to see me humbled, to see me fired. If we had lost that night, she would still have had that bugging her. But for both of us, in a sense, it was gone. I knew the Leafs would beat us from time to time, maybe even in our next game in Buffalo, but this was the night we would remember.

Before I went to sleep I was thinking of something else – another move to improve the team. I thought I had a chance of trading for Eddie Shack and Dick Duff from Los Angeles. Eddie the Entertainer was one of my favourite people. Even when he made me maddest, I couldn't help laughing at him. Duff had been a great player for me with the Leafs, and later with Montreal. He was getting near the end of the trail, but I thought, if so, I'd like him to end it with me. It was another week before I could make the deal, but it was a great one for Buffalo in more ways than one. Shackie gave the team colour. He put the show on the road, and the people into the seats. In that first year, Roger Crozier, Gil Perreault, Reggie Fleming, and Eddie Shack made our team exciting; in effect, I have always thought, they made the franchise.

CHAPTER SIX

Nothing the matter with my head, just my heart

In a way, I hate to get into this subject, but I can't avoid it. Heart attacks have been one of the few things in my life in hockey that I would like to have missed. I have tried to figure it out. Maybe the stress of running hockey clubs is part of it. Or maybe I am so intense that whatever I did in life that fully involved me, as hockey does, would have brought the same result. I don't know. I can get knocked down and get up again, as I did when I was fired by Toronto and came back to build the Buffalo club into one of the best in the league. But I have often gone back over my first heart attack, and the months that led up to it, and I can never think of anything I would have done differently even if I'd been aware that an attack threatened.

The first one was a total surprise. The night before, the phone rang a lot. I didn't sleep well. Dodo remembers that in the morning when I was putting on my tie I said I was tired, and, "I don't know, this is rough, maybe I should give up the coaching job."

She replied, surprised, "I never heard you say *that* before."

That was January 7, 1972, halfway through our second season, with nothing very pressing up for decision, as I recall. A little later I was in my office when Floyd Smith came in. He'd played six games for us at the start of the season and obviously was near the end of his playing days. There was no way I would just drop him, after he'd played so honestly for me in Toronto and again in Buffalo in our first season. So I'd asked him, "How about hanging up the skates as a player, and staying with me as assistant coach?" As captain of the team, a veteran, and much respected by the players, I knew he could help – and I felt he had a good coaching career ahead of him, which proved to be correct. He was thirty-six at the time. With Freddy Hunt as assistant general manager and Smitty now in his third month as assistant coach, I had two good men to help me carry the load. So it wasn't that I was overworked, any more than I wanted to be.

"Geez, Smitty," I said to him that day. "I'm really feeling lousy. Tightness in my chest. Don't know what the hell. . . ." Then the pain went away. A little later the phone rang. It was Joe Crozier calling from Cincinnati.

I think I've made it plain that some people in my life are friends forever, no matter what. Joe is one of them. In our first season, during our first trip to Vancouver, he had been fired by the Vancouver club and his contract hadn't been paid off. Local newspapermen were surprised when our club came in and I refused to talk to them because I didn't think they were fighting hard enough for Joe's contract to be honoured.

That got them on my back. When Vancouver beat us, the major sports-page headline was, *Take That, Punch Imlach!* (Although a few weeks later when we walloped them and I needled the Vancouver newspapermen about giving me equal time, they did, with a big headline saying, *Take That, Tom Scallen!*)

After that, Joe's claim had dragged on. Dodo and I were in Nassau on a holiday after our first season when I got a call. Joe's case was coming to court and he said he needed me to testify. "Can't win without you," is the way he put it. The last thing I wanted right then was to fly all the way from Nassau to Vancouver to appear in court, but I made the preparations – and just before I left got a call saying the case had been settled out of court.

But that's the kind of thing Joe and I would do for one another. He'd been at the expansion draft meetings in 1970, out of work, and got off a good line about how far back he and I went. He was just dropping in to see me, he said. "Last year Punch was out of work and I bought the lunch. This year I'm out of work and it's his turn. The way it works is, the guy who has a job, buys the lunch."

Now he worked for me. After our first year, when we sent our surplus players to Salt Lake City in the Western League, we'd got enough players to start our own farm team in Cincinnati. I had hired Joe as general manager and coach. He was doing a good job there, bringing along players who would do well with the Sabres later on.

Anyway, when I answered Joe's phone call that day in January, 1972, suddenly the chest pain came again, worse than ever.

He started to talk. I interrupted, gasping out the words, "Joe, I feel lousy, talk to Smitty."

Joe, to Smitty: "What the hell's wrong with Punch?"

Smitty, watching me: "I don't know. He looks white as a sheet, says he has chest pains."

Joe: "Hang up and get the bloody doctor. Right away!"

Smitty hung up and was trying to get the doctor when I thought I was going to fall down. I stumbled out into the reception area outside my office. There was a chesterfield there so I lay down. But I couldn't stay down, had to get up again, the pain was so bad. Somebody yelled, "Get oxygen from the dressing room! The doctor's on his way!"

So someone runs to the dressing room to get the oxygen. They get the tank up to where I am and it's empty! I'm lying there groaning and one thing I groaned was, "Those goddamn trainers are supposed to keep that tank up! If I ever get out of this mess alive I'm going to fire both of those bastards!" Of course, I didn't, but I have to laugh about it now – I'm dying, or could have been, in one of the few places where oxygen is always available, and the tank is empty! I don't think it ever was again.

So then there were sirens, the fire department with oxygen, an ambulance, and people calling Dodo and the Knoxes. They get me into intensive care at the Deaconess hospital but as soon as the pains start to fade back a little I'm telling the doctors. "You can't keep me in here! I've got to get out! Toronto is coming on Sunday. . . ."

Well, a lot of teams came and went before I got out. That time I was in hospital twenty-five days, twelve in intensive care. I spent a lot of time trying to figure out what the hell had brought it on. I went back in my memory month by month. I was getting better, and knew that probably the season was over, for me, but still. . . . What had happened in those last few months, which I had enjoyed so much, that had been so tough? Nothing much, really. . . .

I guess we could start with the draft meetings, the previous June. The top junior in the country then was Guy Lafleur. He would be drafted first, for sure. I remember one time a few months earlier in our first season when the Sabres were in New York. Gil Perreault was starting to show why he was going to be a superstar on his way to winning the rookie award with a record thirty-eight goals and thirty-four assists. Seymour and Norty Knox took me to dinner at a club where Norty was playing court tennis. At dinner one wine on the list was a Chateau Lafleur.

"I'll take that Lafleur," I said, laughing. "Might be the only chance I'll get."

I said that, because the last-place team always got first choice in the next amateur draft, and I was damn sure Buffalo wasn't going to be last. At least, pretty sure. But the idea sort of captured the Knoxes.

"Can you imagine us with both Perreault and Lafleur?" one said. "How can we get him?"

"Well," I said, "maybe if we lose every game we play between now and the end of the season, we might nose out California for last place and get first pick. But there's no way we're going to do that."

Which was right. We actually finished tenth overall in the league that first year, beating out Vancouver, Detroit, Pittsburgh, and California and tying Los Angeles. California's first draft choice had been traded earlier to Montreal Canadiens, so they got Lafleur. Detroit, with second choice, took Marcel Dionne. Richard Martin should have been third. I couldn't believe my luck! Vancouver picked Jocelyn Guevremont as third, and St. Louis took Gene Carr fourth. I felt very good standing up and saying, "Buffalo drafts Richard Martin from Montreal Junior Canadiens."

Then we had a little argument around the Buffalo table. I'd gone out west during the season to look at players, and I'd seen Billy Hajt of Saskatoon looking very good. When it came time to make our second choice, I said I wanted to take Hajt. John Andersen and the scouts put up an argument. John said, "Craig Ramsay is the best hockey player still available."

I said, "He's a forward, and Hajt's a defenceman, and for gosh sake we need defencemen."

John: "Ramsay is better."

I'm not a totally stubborn guy all the time. Besides, you have to listen to the scouts, otherwise there's no use having them. So I looked at them and said, "All right, Ramsay had better be as good as you say, because I'm going to take him. If he isn't, you're all on the hook." So I drafted Ramsay, and wouldn't you know, Billy

Hajt was still there fourteen choices later when we got our third pick, so I got them both. We wound up that draft with Richard Martin, Craig Ramsay, and Billy Hajt – all guys who could play on our hockey team. If anybody else ever got three players of that quality in three picks, I haven't heard of it. Of course, you can't do everything right. Ramsay turned out to be a good hockey player for Buffalo, but one other guy available at the time we picked him was Larry Robinson, who went on the next pick after Ramsay, to Montreal.

Maybe I should get into the signings, here. First Martin. One of the things I wouldn't do at that time was deal with lawyers; I dealt directly with players. My theory was, they should look me in the eye and tell me, "I want to play for you." After we'd drafted Martin, I wanted to talk to him. He was in Montreal. I said, "Meet me in the hotel and we'll have lunch." So in he comes the next day and says, "I got my lawyer, Larry Sazant, with me."

"I'm not talking to your lawyer," I said. "If you have lunch with me, we'll talk contract and then you go out and talk to him. He's not having lunch with me."

So he talked to me and then went out to talk to Sazant. You never settle anything the first time. You're lucky if you get a deal settled after ten meetings. Ten guys, a hundred meetings. It consumed a lot of time. Eventually, though, we get things straight with Martin and he's coming to Buffalo early in September.

"I'm going to bring my lawyer," he said.

I said, "I don't give a damn if you come with your lawyer, but he's not going to get in. You can talk to him as much as you like, but I'm not talking to him." At that time we still had the makeshift office in the trust building in Buffalo, no reception room, no nothing, just a hallway. I won't let Sazant into the office, so I had to take a steel office chair out for him to sit in the hall. I was embarrassed, but I had to do it. That's the way I felt.

I discussed the contract with Martin and got the whole thing straightened out and said, "All right, you take that out and show it to him. You discuss what the heck you want and then come back. If you don't want it, we'll try again. If you want it, come back in and we'll sign it."

And that's what happened. But that's the last lawyer or agent I treated that way. I don't know that Sazant ever held it against me. I did have dealings with him later on, and in better surroundings.

Martin, of course, was great right from the start. We played him with Perreault for a while, then moved him around a bit. He got his first hat-trick (three-goal game) three weeks into the season. The French Connection wouldn't come into being for another few months, when I traded Eddie Shack to Pittsburgh for Rene Robert. I'd actually had Robert briefly during the 1971 draft meetings when I'd been pulling a fast one in the intra-league draft to get enough players to stock the Cincinnati team. Each time I drafted, I had to drop a player to make room on my roster for the new one. If the team I'd drafted from picked up the player I'd dropped we were square. If they didn't want the one I'd dropped, I owed them $20,000. Well my system was to drop a player I didn't think anybody would want to pick up. Not hard with that club. Then he'd become mine again when I paid the $20,000. I spent $80,000 that day, using Reggie Fleming four times without having anyone take him. But the whole exercise was valuable. I got six players with NHL experience to stock Cincinnati. The other general managers didn't like what I was doing. They appealed to Clarence Campbell to stop me. He couldn't find a rule against it, which I'd checked out before I started. The only time I lost somebody I wanted that day was when after claiming Rene Robert from Toronto, I dropped him to protect Dick Duff – and Pittsburgh took Robert. Sometimes, finding a little crack in the rules gets a guy some good hockey players.

Sometimes staying on the job helps, too. At the trading deadline the previous spring, John Andersen and I had decided to stay in the office right to the midnight deadline, even though nobody was calling us and we figured we didn't have much anybody wanted. At 11.30, as we sat twiddling our thumbs, the phone rang. It was Ned Harkness in Detroit. He badly needed a goalie and wanted Joe Daley, who had played good goal for us when Crozier was ill, or being rested.

"Okay," I said. "But I want Don Luce and Mike Robitaille."

"I'll call you back," he said. We crossed our fingers. At 11.55 he called back: "It's a deal!" Both played for the Sabres and Luce was one of the backbones of the Buffalo club all the time I was there. If John and I had gone home that night, Buffalo would not have had that Don Luce backbone.

A few things happened that fall that you might consider stressful, but none that I can recall bothered me much. We went back to

Toronto for our first game of the second season and beat them 7-2 again. One columnist wrote, "Buffalo and Toronto played their annual 7-2 hockey game here last night in what is speedily becoming an NHL tradition."

All this time I had continued writing the column for the *Toronto Telegram* newspaper syndicate. That got me into trouble eventually. First the Professional Hockey Writers' Association rejected my membership renewal because I was a general manager. Then the NHL took action against me because I was a writer! Some of the hockey people were getting a little hostile at my reviewing their mistakes and so on across the country, but nothing really happened until an owners' meeting in Florida that October. I attended with the Knoxes. One night I was sitting with Wren Blair from Minnesota, having a drink before dinner, and he started in on me.

"When are you going to stop writing that column?" he asked. "It's not right that you're writing about us all the time." He was talking loudly.

I said, "Oh, I don't know, I'm enjoying it. As long as I keep on enjoying it I'll keep on doing it. . . ." Then Charlie Finley, the California owner, walked over.

"I agree with him," he said to me, jerking his thumb at Blair. "I'll tell you, if you ever write anything about me I'll have you in court! I'll have lawyers on top of you like there's no tomorrow!"

"Is that right?" I said. "Well, you'd better get them geared up, and buy a *Toronto Telegram* tomorrow, because you're in it, front and centre!"

"What?" Finley said.

"You heard me! Front and centre!"

I never heard anything more from him, but I couldn't believe the coincidence. Right when he's threatening me, that column was already in print. It was about one of the great NHL players, Bernie (Boom Boom) Geoffrion. He'd started a previous season as coach in New York, but had to step down because of an ulcer operation. Then, at the draft meetings in June, some Toronto director had asked him if he would consider returning to the NHL as a player. He was told they'd give him a two-year contract and use him mainly on the power play, where his shot from the point should be worth a lot of goals. So Boom Boom worked all summer, skating, getting in shape. But he never heard from the Leafs. When he called they wouldn't even talk to him.

So okay, Toronto had treated him badly. Then, at the league's annual meeting in Montreal the following summer, he was approached by Garry Young from California about a coaching job there. Boom Boom said yes. He and Charlie Finley thrashed out terms, shook hands on it. Boom Boom, who technically still belonged to New York, then let Emile Francis of the Rangers know about the California deal and resigned from the Rangers. He packed his bags and waited for California's training camp to open. Again, he never heard. He made some calls and eventually was told, "Mr. Finley has changed his mind." So both Toronto and California had, you might say, screwed him. Good thing Emile Francis was a different type. Emile had him reinstated as a New York scout. And then, would you believe it, a few weeks later when California fired Fred Glover as coach, they approached Boom Boom again about the job. He told them what they could do with it.

So that was the story involving Charlie Finley that was in the paper the day after he threatened me. But I knew the facts, had checked them out everywhere, including reading the story to Geoffrion before it was printed. Net result, if any, was that I was excluded from the owners' meetings.

One other little jab I managed in November 1971 was to fly Joe Crozier from Cincinnati to Vancouver to coach the Sabres for one game. Soon after, we retired Dick Duff from Buffalo, giving him a private luncheon to tell him how much we valued his eighteen-year career in the NHL. That would be his first Christmas at home since he started to play pro hockey. When we retired Duff, we brought Craig Ramsay up from Cincinnati. In his first game, only twenty years old, he scored all three Buffalo goals in a 3-1 win over Minnesota, who had been unbeaten in nine games up until then. Ramsay had arrived to stay, and the scouts who had persuaded me to draft him were off the hook. Ramsay and I had plenty of differences later, but I have never had any doubts about his hockey ability.

One more thing I should mention here: the drinking. Problems with alcohol in pro sports have been there for a long time but have only recently gone public with players, like Darrell Porter of Kansas City in baseball, realizing they were in trouble. Don Newcombe, one of baseball's great pitchers until alcoholism got him, visits baseball training camps giving talks now, and players who know they're in deep with booze or drugs may come to him after. Some are helped. But it's an old, old story in sports – a tough game, you have a beer or two to replenish body fluids, more with dinner, more later. It adds up.

You have a lot of older players, or at least some types of older players, who start out as rookies with a beer or two after a practice and before long are up to three or four, and then up to ten, or twelve or more. Once Eddie Shack's car was found out in a field near Fort Erie, just sitting there. He'd at least had the sense to get out and go home, but it didn't prevent a charge being brought against him. The judge fined him $23, that being his sweater number. But the worry I had was that not all judges would have a sense of humour, and not all incidents would be trivial – trivial in that nobody was hurt. It's always been my fear that players who have a few too many, for instance, on a chartered plane home after a game, get to their cars at two or three in the morning, want to get home fast, and get involved in something serious. Then the law might come down on the player, of course, but it also would come down on the hockey club that provided, or allowed, booze for him on the plane; and give a black eye to pro hockey in general.

I remember one afternoon game in Vancouver, Oct. 30. The night before when the rooms were checked most of the beds were empty – right up to 3.30 a.m., when I left notes on pillows, with the time, to let them know I'd been around. Some of that was comical, like a six-foot-two defenceman, Jumbo Watson, trying to flatten himself against a wall so I couldn't see him coming in. But some wasn't so comical. If the game had been at night they might have recovered from a night like that, but in the afternoon there was no way. They flew in the first period, and died in the third to blow a two-goal lead and scrape out a tie, 4-4. I must have been raving on the plane to Oakland a few hours later because I really alarmed Don Uren, our assistant trainer. Everybody called him Sockeye. "Listen, Punch," Sockeye warned me, "you keep that up and you'll get a heart attack."

I knew I couldn't stop it entirely, but I had a set of rules that put some control on things. One was that no player was allowed to drink in the hotel where we were staying. That meant that if I wanted to go into the hotel bar for a drink, it wouldn't be a situation of both management and players conspicuously drinking in the same bar. Another was that if I happened to go into a bar where some of the players were drinking, if I bought them a drink they could stay and I'd leave. If I didn't buy, they would finish whatever they were doing, drinking or eating, and then they would go, but without ordering any more booze.

I didn't want to be embarrassed, and I never went looking for them. I told them, "If I know you're there, chances are I won't go in unless I'm awful upset about something." Those rules worked in Toronto for me for eleven years, and I didn't see why they shouldn't work in Buffalo. I still think it is a reasonable approach.

Of course, the writers who travelled with the team knew these rules and were able to watch from the sidelines, sometimes knowing more than I did. This brought about one memorable night on the road early in our second season. Charley Barton and I had been out to dinner with Floyd Smith and were going back to our hotel in a cab when we happened to pass a bar. Charley must have known something. He had a definite twinkle in his eye, when he said, "I dare you to go in and see who's there." Well, daring me is like putting the red flag in front of the bull.

I said, "Okay!" In I went. And sure enough at least two-thirds of the team was there. Good thing in a way – at least they were all together! They were sitting along a great big table loaded with booze like you wouldn't believe! They had a curfew at twelve o'clock. I guess this was around 10.30.

I just looked at them and said, "You know the rules. Out!" But nobody moved.

So I went up to the bartender and said, "Don't serve those people any more booze!" Here I am telling him what to do in his own bar.

"Who are you?" he asked.

"That's my hockey team," I said. "I happen to be the boss. I don't want them to have any more."

So I looked at them and they looked at me. I walked up to the bar and sat down and told them again, "Get going!" For a long time they stayed put. Then one did get up, realizing, I guess, that this was the way it was; first that one, then another, and then they all left.

Later, when I got back to the hotel, Barton was there, chuckling away. "I guess I put you right in the middle," he said.

Still later, about midnight, curfew time, I told Smitty to go and check the rooms. When he came back he said they were all in, "But one or two want to have a meeting with you."

"What the hell are you talking about?" I asked. "Are you out of your mind? They've had a few drinks – it's a waste of time having a meeting. You tell them we're having a meeting at 11 a.m. The usual team meeting. If they've got anything to say, that's the time to say it. If they want a meeting right now, you have the meeting and explain the facts of life to them."

The next day we had the meeting. Nobody said a word. I mean, what the hell, I can understand players going out to have a get-together, a few drinks. Nothing's wrong with that. What's really wrong is if they don't get to bed until two or three in the morning, which they'll do sometimes if you're not around to force the issue. I mean, they're human. We all go through that kind of stuff.

So at that time I wasn't exactly taking it seriously enough to cause a heart attack, if you know what I mean. But a little later I did get real serious. A flight out was delayed one night around the middle of December. We phoned to the players, most of them living in Fort Erie, "Don't come to the airport until we call you." Turns out they then all gathered in one house and had a few drinks. Then we called and said, "Come." Everybody got there fast except for three or four. This was a regular flight, not a charter, so we couldn't hold it long. Eventually the plane had to move off.

We were out on the runway when the gate called, "They're here!" The pilot turned the plane around. The other passengers couldn't have been too pleased about that. I also learned that these guys hadn't hurried through the terminal, just strolled along saying, "Ah, they'll wait for us!" Big shots, you know. When they did get on, a couple of them were reeling. But that wasn't the worst of it. Some guys get a few drinks in them and then want to argue. Doug Barrie and Al Hamilton, both defencemen, came along the aisle and said to me, "We want to talk to you!"

"Go away!" I said.

Our defence was no hell in those days. Maybe drinking was part of the trouble. I think it was Chicago we were flying to that night. I know that right away I dealt Barrie to Los Angeles and I did it on the phone from Philadelphia a day or two later. Larry Regan was L.A. general manager. They were in worse shape than we were. That's the time when you can make deals; a guy may be causing trouble to one club, but the jolt of trading him sometimes straightens him out. They're just kids, a lot of them, away from home, on their own, entitled to make mistakes, but young enough to change.

Anyway, for Doug Barrie and Mike Keeler, a minor-leaguer, I got Mike Byers and Larry Hillman, who was a lot older, an experienced defenceman, and a tee-totaller! Good deal. I also thought trading Barrie that fast might tell some of the high livers in our club what could happen if they stepped too far over the line. I don't know if it did the team much good (it wasn't playing as well as the previous season), but it did *me* some good. I was really getting tired of some of the yo-yos that the good young players were carrying on their backs.

One thing strikes me now, thinking about it – the tremendous way I was treated by the Buffalo Sabres when I had my first heart attack.

There was nothing the matter with my head, just my heart. Because Smitty had been my assistant, he handled the Sunday night 2-1 loss to the Leafs. There wasn't really enough time to do anything else. But even before that game, I think during the previous afternoon, I had laid out what I wanted done. "Putting Smitty in as coach isn't right," I told the Sabre owners, in a message through Dodo, who was the only person allowed to see me. "Bring up Joe Crozier from Cincinnati, send Smitty to run things there, and make Freddy Hunt acting general manager."

It was done exactly that way. Seymour Knox said in an announcement, "Crozier will act as coach and Hunt as general manager until Punch is able to resume those duties." Seymour and Norty Knox came to the hospital every day even though they knew they wouldn't be allowed to see me. They talked to Dodo, and their daily concern and kindness helped her a lot.

A few days after the attack, John Andersen sent another message through Dodo: We have a chance to get Jim Lorentz from the Rangers. Should we make the deal? John thought the Rangers would take in exchange our second-round draft choice later that year. We had another second-round choice through an earlier deal, so I didn't mind giving one up for a player who could step right in and help us. "Tell him to make the deal," I told Dodo from my bed in intensive care.

Also, when Joe was called up, he knew the call came from me. Once, when I was sick in Toronto in February of 1967, Stafford Smythe called Joe Crozier in Rochester to come up and take over the coaching. Joe told Stafford, "I'll come when Punch asks me to come, not before." He knew as well as I did that Stafford would have loved to replace me then. We'd been losing. That was the year Clancy filled in for me, won a lot of games, and we won the Stanley Cup after I came back.

"This time," said Joe when he arrived in Buffalo, "I got the message that Punch wants me to come in, so I will, but only until he's ready and able to take over as coach again." Which, as it turned out, was never, but he had laid out the conditions – that he had come only because the message came from me.

So maybe you get the picture, or part of it. In the first few days after my heart attack, I got a lot of messages. Three telegrams from Harold Ballard. A call from Tiny Tim, one of the entertainment stars of the time, who was also a Toronto Maple Leaf nut although he lived in New York. Nice notes from Johnny Wayne and dozens of others whose names aren't as well known, but whose sentiments I valued as much.

One kind letter was from Dan Meyer, owner of the Salt Lake Golden Eagles of the Western Hockey League, our first farm team connection. A couple of weeks after writing that letter he was in Bloomington, Minnesota, for the NHL all-star game, when he left a meeting in the hotel where all the all-stars were staying. He said he had to make a phone call. A few minutes later he was seen by some of the all-star players in rooms a few floors below his as he climbed out of a window above them and plunged nineteen storeys to his death. Bobby Hull ran upstairs in bare feet and was first into Dan's room. Apparently it was suicide. Dodo was delegated to tell me the shocking news before I could hear it elsewhere.

When I was told on February 1 that I could go home to Toronto the next day to convalesce, the Knoxes made sure the trip was made in style. While the Cadillac Eldorado they'd given me two years before was still in good shape, they bought me a new one and sent it around, with John Andersen driving, to take Dodo and me home. The Knoxes also sent a message that I wasn't to worry, everything was okay, and they just hoped I'd be back in fighting form for the draft meetings in June. On that trip, incidentally, Dodo was in her usual good form, protecting me. John had arranged that we be taken out of the Buffalo hospital's ambulance entrance, to avoid news media people, but when we got to Toronto reporters and photographers were waiting at our home.

Dodo stormed at them, "Get lost!" The only photos of me then were with long-range cameras. People don't fool with Dodo when she's on the warpath.

But the good part of convalescing then was the feeling that I never stopped being part of the team. Joe, Freddy Hunt, and John Andersen phoned me about anything that needed my decision because it had a long-range aspect that I would have to live with. It was that way early in March when we got a chance to get Rene Robert from Pittsburgh. I'd always liked him; he was a shooter, at twenty-three a really well-rounded hockey player. We got him for Eddie Shack and some cash. My old friend Eddie has been pretty good for me over the years, despite the battles we had. In Toronto I traded him once to Boston for Murray Oliver and $100,000 (in U.S. funds!). But no one could ever put a price on the laughs he gave us when he was in Buffalo. Not that we needed much more to make us laugh in those early years when Reg Fleming was taking on the phys ed instructors, and Shackie and his snowmobile, which he drove the same way he skates, were terrorizing friend and foe alike on the streets of Fort Erie. For one brief stretch Eddie had played on a line with Gil Perreault. Eddie was impressed. "Trying to follow his moves," he said once, "I even deked myself. Trying to play with him, I was like a calf slipping in its own manure." Sitting at home remembering these things after I had okayed the trade, I was sorry to see him go. It turned out, though, that deal, with Shackie the key man from our side, soon put together the best line in hockey in the 1970s – Perreault, Martin, and Robert, the French Connection. Also, for a guy who was down a little, it was great therapy picking up the Buffalo papers and finding lines like the one in a Charley Barton story, quoting Dave Forman, Buffalo's administrative vice-president, saying, "Punch is the club's Number One asset."

In those circumstances, it wasn't hard for me to make the decisions I had to make; one being to tell Charley Barton, who phoned me every few days, that I wouldn't be coaching any more that season, and perhaps not ever again. There were daily phone calls to Joe, Fred, and John Andersen. I watched TV and read the papers. In mid-February I got back to writing my weekly column. It had been switched to the *Toronto Sun* when the *Telegram* folded and the *Sun* started up. In one column I did some reflecting about why I had had a heart attack. I thought of the Leafs' Johnny

McLellan and hoped he could weather the trouble that club was in. It made me think of something I once told a player, "Too bad we can't put you behind the bench where you would have the pleasure of watching yourself go through the motions." Any coach who finds that he has a lot more interest in winning than his players seem to, had better have a strong heart.

When I felt well enough, Dodo and I went to Florida, and then I came back for the last Buffalo game of the season. We hadn't done as well as the first year, scoring twelve fewer points, and finishing twelfth instead of tying for tenth. Actually, we only beat two teams, Vancouver and Los Angeles. Yet I had a feeling that the kids we had coming along might just be on the threshold of forming a good team, if we could draft well in June, and pick up another player or two with the leadership qualities to mould the whole thing together. During that stay in Buffalo I made it official: I was through as coach, Joe had the job if he wanted it.

There was one other sad duty to perform. The previous summer in Montreal, Charley Barton had taken ill. It was cancer of the kidneys. He'd come out of hospital again and in our second season covered the team almost to the end, then had to go back in. I went to see him. He said, "Can you imagine? All my life I wanted to be covering the National Hockey League. Now I am. And I'm going." It was so sorrowful. What he wanted in life he wasn't going to get. He died a few weeks later on May 20, 1972.

CHAPTER SEVEN

Tim Horton

I have always had a special feeling for Tim Horton, and always will. When I took over in Toronto in 1958 he had already been a pro hockey player for nine years and although he was known as the strongest man in the NHL, he didn't have a mean bone in his body. He always called me George. "Aw, George," he'd say with that shy grin of his, on top of a neck that looked like part of a fire hydrant, "don't worry, we'll win it for you." I'd tell him that if he could only get a little mean, like Gordie Howe, he'd be an all-star every year. "Aw-w-w-w, George, you don't really think that." One of his particular favourites on the old Leafs was Davey Keon. Tim didn't like to go to bed without saying good night to Davey. One night in a hotel on the road when he went to say good night, Keon's door was locked, Keon asleep, and when Tim knocked all he got was a sleepy voice telling him to go away. He broke down the door, overturned Keon's bed, dumped him out on the floor, said, "Good night, Davey," and left. Grinning. When a few of the Leafs made it known to newspapermen that they didn't exactly see eye to eye with some of my coaching habits, the two-a-day work-outs, the way I drove them, a reporter went to Timmy and asked him earnestly what he thought about playing for me. "Well," Tim said, grinning, "George preaches a strange gospel, sometimes, but it seems to work." When I was fired minutes after our last playoff game in 1969, reporters flooded the Leaf room looking for comments. "If this team doesn't want George, I guess it doesn't want me," Tim said. Can you imagine a first-team all-star today deciding to retire because his coach had been fired? I never ran into any. And at the time he'd been a first-team all-star twice in a row, both times with Bobby Orr; the second time Tim was thirty-nine, Orr twenty-one. He got more involved with his growing business, a chain of doughnut shops. A few months later Harold Ballard met him on the street. "How much would it take to get you back?" Ballard asked.

Tim later said he intended his answer as a joke. "If somebody said they'd double my salary, I might consider it," he said.

The Leaf people howled and pleaded and told reporters, "No way," but Tim stuck to it. Salaries in those days were no hell. He'd been getting $45,000 a year, and when the Leafs finally got it up to $90,000, Tim spun it out until after training camp was over and then accepted. Later, he retired regularly every year; from New York, then from Pittsburgh. According to him, he was never paid a decent salary until he started retiring every year. Also, by unretiring at the right moment he managed to avoid training camp. He hated training camp and practices in general. "What I get paid for is the practices," he said more than once. "I would play the games for nothing."

In 1972, when I went to Montreal for my third draft on Buffalo's behalf, Tim had announced his retirement from Pittsburgh. He was forty-two, and he and Orr still were the only defencemen in the league who had been on six all-star teams, Orr with five first teams and a second, Tim with three and three. And I had something in mind. I knew Tim could help our team if I could talk him into going back to work. I was going to draft the best young defencemen available and they would need an anchor. I drafted him in the intra-league draft, and picked as my first two amateur choices two defencemen, Jim Schoenfeld, nineteen, and Larry Carriere, twenty. Tim had been playing pro hockey before either was born, was an NHL all-star before Schoenfeld was two years old.

I talked him into signing for a year. The pay was good, better than $100,000. Tim told a reporter, "I'd be a hypocrite if I said the money didn't matter, but it wasn't the only thing. George was very persuasive." More amazingly, he signed in the summer, before training camp.

It was another good draft for us, and Tim helped make it so, because I hadn't really expected that both Schoenfeld and Carriere would play with the Sabres, but playing with Timmy they played very well. Our sixth pick that year was Peter McNab, so once again we drafted three amateurs who would play in the NHL.

But I'm getting ahead of myself. That was a tough summer for me. For instance, I have here a letter dated July 10, 1972. It was from George Imlach, general manager, to Seymour Knox III, president, and read, in full: "This is to advise you that I am resigning my position as general manager of the Buffalo Sabres due to illness."

I never handed in that letter, but had it typed up for a meeting on that date. In other words, the World Hockey Association damn near made me quit hockey. That was their first year and they were signing Bobby Hull, Gerry Cheevers, Derek Sanderson, Bernie Parent, and other NHL stars for staggering sums, some in the millions, and giving rookies and fringe players double what they were worth, just to lure them away. The way they went about it was something entirely new to me, and to every other general manager. Everything went berserk. A lawyer would come in with a contract demand for a player. I'd look at it and say, "He's not worth that, here's his record . . ." and the damn lawyer would interrupt and say, "Look, we don't care about his record, that doesn't mean a thing. He's got an offer from the WHA for so many dollars and you've got to pay that, or goodbye." Like $90,000 for some fringe player who'd ordinarily be lucky to get $35,000 and might not even have much chance of making our team. And we had the team in Cincinnati to stock, too. We wound up stocking Cincinnati with players on big salaries, all because of the WHA. Like everybody else, we were being raided but my argument was, okay, the guys we have to get, we'll get. Still, I was keeping private what I was doing, not giving it out to the press or anybody, just pecking away, getting things done.

Of course, what was worrying the Knoxes was that now they were assured of selling out for almost every home game, but might not have a hockey team. As a result, they started pressuring me. Maybe because of my heart attack six months earlier I was a little testier than usual, but why not? Every contract negotiation was tougher than ever. I was doing the right things but when the Knoxes and others kept asking questions I felt, jeez, who needs more aggravation? I wanted to be able to lay it all out for them, the job completed. They set up a meeting, wanted me upstairs. Okay. I dictated my resignation for health reasons, in case I needed it, and went upstairs.

It started right away, "We have to get this done, we have to get that done." Clearly, they were worried about the sort of team we'd have. Instead of blowing up, I said to John Andersen, "Go downstairs and get that list of players we've signed." Gil Perreault had signed originally for two years; I already had him on a new one. I'd signed everybody else including the draft choices we needed most. When John came back, I handed the list to the Knoxes.

Norty Knox read it, looked up and said, "You son of a bitch, you had this done all the time."

I said, "I do things my own way."

He said, "I'll say you do things your own way. Okay, I've got nothing more to say." The things that had to be done were done. I know my business, and they had temporarily forgotten that.

Anyway, by late in August I was ready for a little break. I didn't know exactly what it would be, but that was the year of the first NHL-Soviet series. Although I had just about decided to drop the column I was writing, the *Toronto Sun* persuaded me, like I had persuaded Horton. "Just go to these Russia games and write about them for us," said George Gross, the sports editor. It looked as if it fitted as a break after the heavy summer. The series would open in Montreal, go across the country, and then to Moscow. I could get clean away from the Buffalo Sabres and let Joe Crozier run his own show as coach, and be back in time for the final cutdown decisions and the start of the season.

"Okay," I said.

I don't think I would have agreed to the Moscow portion of the trip except that George Gross, who had covered the Leafs all through the 1960s and was a good friend of mine, told me he'd meet me in Copenhagen and go to Moscow with me. He didn't, and I don't really blame him, because he came out of Czechoslovakia as a refugee in the early 1950s and had a thing about never going behind the Iron Curtain again. But when he cancelled I was already on my way, so I was upset. Also, I wasn't feeling well. Didn't know what the hell was the matter. I would feel fine, eat and drink a lot, and then go to my room and throw up. For the Moscow end of the trip Dodo came with me, and she was worried, too, but we kept on going and I'm always glad we did, even with the troubles we had.

The first of these was that when we got to Moscow, we were put in the Minsk Hotel. We'd understood we were going to the new Intourist Hotel, but *nyet*. Our room was quite a shock. It was like one in a Kirkland Lake hotel forty years ago. There wasn't a spring in the bed and the mattress consisted of one-quarter inch of foam rubber doubled over and sewn between two white sheets.

I can remember the days when trainers would carry boards on the train to put between the mattresses so players with bad backs could rest comfortably on overnight train trips. They would never have had to worry about this in our hotel. We didn't blame the Russians. They were doing the best they could, but their tourist facilities were not capable of handling 2,500 affluent Canadians who, compared to Russians, were downright spoiled.

We were well-off, though, compared to Rocket Richard, who stayed in the Bucharest Hotel which had no showers or hot water in the rooms. The showers were in the basement. Can you imagine some 200 Canadians lining up at the same time to use showers?

Our first reaction was: "What are we doing here?" But the second day was not so bad, and by the third day we were used to it and starting to enjoy the experience. Certainly the people were pleasant and polite, going out of their way to be friendly.

I have read where other Canadians felt they were being harassed or followed, but as far as I was concerned there were no curbs. I could leave the hotel, hire a taxi, and go anywhere in Moscow, or use their beautiful subway in the same manner and shop in any store as long as I had the rubles. A Russian once even stopped to give me a lift when I couldn't get a taxi.

Sometimes we would go on guided tours, but I also walked around Moscow as much as I could. And I had the usual troubles of a first-timer. For instance, I tried to cross Gorki Street, not realizing you had to go underneath it. I was starting across and a soldier grabbed me and in sign language told me where to go. Another day my wife and I ended up in a military museum. I'm interested in that to some extent, and what do you know, there was Gary Powers' U-2 spy plane in a corner. "We got it!" the Russians seemed to be saying. I enjoyed that. One other time we were supposed to go to an author's home, with a busload of Canadians. When everybody else went in I decided not to, and roamed around the neighbourhood instead. I was surprised at the quietness. There were no cars, no kids. I went down a street off the main drag and all the houses were made of logs. I couldn't believe it. They were nice, very nice, all bungalows except instead of being brick, they were of logs. I never saw a soul and I walked for maybe half an hour down and around and then thought I'd better get back in case the group came out and said, "Where the hell is he?"

Incidentally, the two players Buffalo had with the team, Gil Perreault and Rick Martin, had already gone home before I got to Moscow. Later I was criticized for giving them bad advice, suggesting they go home, but they hadn't been playing and they made that decision on their own. I don't blame them. If they weren't going to play, why the hell waste their time? These were two kids trying to get their bearings in the National Hockey League, Perreault with two years in the league and Martin with one. Why would they want to be spectators? They wanted to get back to our own team, so they went. Jocelyn Guevremont went home with them, too. They must have decided, you know, three French kids, to hell with this. Especially Perreault, he had enough trouble speaking English. He certainly couldn't speak Russian. There they were in an alien situation, so they got depressed and thought, let's get back to the environment we know and love.

One thing I didn't enjoy at the hockey games were the antics and tantrums of some players and coaches, and of Alan Eagleson. One incident that's been written up a lot was when Eagleson got into a fracas with cops during a game. I was up in the stands in a perfect position to see. For a few seconds while the cops were holding Eagleson I saw someone in plain clothes, must have been a senior man, leaning in an exit watching. The cops holding Eagleson looked over to this other guy as if to say, "Do we take him or let him go?" I saw the man nod, and the cops let Eagleson go. I know that isn't the official version printed later, but it was what I saw, and I think Eagleson was *that* close to landing in the clink. Eagleson said later he'd rather be a bum in Canada than a major-general in Russia. Well, his qualifications to be a major-general in Russia can certainly be challenged.

I really enjoyed the time we spent in Moscow, but especially being part of the tourist crowd, rather than the hockey and press crowd. I saw and heard a lot of things the reporters and hockey players didn't. On the last night, after Paul Henderson scored the winning goal with thirty-four seconds to go, all of us came out of the rink and it was snowing. Then this whole group of 2,500 Canadians spontaneously started singing *Jingle Bells*. Some things stay in the mind. Every time I've heard *Jingle Bells* since I associate the song not only with Santa Claus, but with Moscow.

But the trip wasn't over for me, yet. On the way home we stopped in Copenhagen. A few of us went downstairs into our hotel's restaurant. I should have known better because of the way I'd been feeling, but I tucked into the drinks and some fancy herring dishes, as starters. About seven o'clock that night I had the worst attack I'd ever had. My wife, very worried, went downstairs to get help. By luck a doctor from Ottawa was on the trip with us. He had been John Diefenbaker's doctor, J. C. Samis. A tremendous guy. It didn't take him five minutes to figure what was wrong with me. He gave me some pills, and told me to get a thorough checkout back in Toronto. Which I did. After tests by Dr. Bruce Tovee I had a gall bladder operation and felt a lot better. My old travelling companion, sports-writer, Rex MacLeod, put a memorable phrase on that operation. He wrote that rumour had it they'd removed my bladder, but left the gall.

There are times in hockey when a team of good young players suddenly comes of age. With Tim on our blue-line we developed a steadiness to go with the hotshots up front. We didn't lose one game in October. Rick Martin's forty-four goals the previous season had broken the rookie scoring record of thirty-eight set by Perreault the year before. Now he started out with nine in our first seven games! This included a four-goal game on October 22 against Atlanta. But we were in tough. The NHL's East division, where we played, had five of the original six pre-expansion teams, including the powerhouses in Montreal, Boston, and New York. By early January, when we swept weekend games with the Rangers and Philadelphia, we were tied with the Rangers for third place, with Detroit close behind and Toronto, Vancouver, and the Islanders trailing. We were dynamite at home, unbeaten twenty-one games in a row before sellout crowds. By the end of January the French Connection line had seventy-seven goals. But when February came we faded a little and from then on we were sometimes in fourth place, the last playoff spot, and sometimes Detroit had it. On the final night of the season we led Detroit by one point, with Detroit playing in New York and us at home against St. Louis.

I changed the starting time of our game that night from 7.30 to 8.30, so that during the game our players could keep track of what was happening in New York – what they had to do to make the playoffs. Detroit tied Rangers 3-3, meaning that a tie or a win for us against St. Louis would do it. Our defence was great that night, limiting St. Louis to twenty shots on Roger Crozier. When we won 3-1 we were not only in, but had finished fifth overall in the league, up from twelfth the year before! Only Montreal, the New York Rangers, Philadelphia Flyers, and Chicago Black Hawks were ahead of us in points. Sure, our kids of previous years were developing quickly, but adding Tim was the principal factor in giving us the mix we needed. At the end of the season the players themselves voted him the team's most valuable player – not bad for a man of forty-three!

Oddly enough, however, one consequence of that win over St. Louis caused a little rift between me and Joe Crozier. A picture in the paper the next day showed champagne being waved around in our dressing room. I got mad at Joe, demanding, "Why booze in the dressing room? You know I don't want booze in the dressing room!"

"Well," he said, "I never made the NHL playoffs before and neither have these guys!" Somebody had presented him with the bottle. I'd been in the playoffs, won the Stanley Cup and everything else, so making the playoffs wasn't such a big thing to me but it was to them. I realized I was being too strict; but that's the way I am. So, between Joe and me, both being high-strung, there was a little bit of tension over that incident.

Then in the playoffs, we go in against the league's top team, the Canadiens. The first two games are in Montreal. We lose both, 2-1 and 7-3. The third and fourth games are in Buffalo. In the third game, Joe got kind of boxed in. He was matching lines, trying to keep the French Connection playing against a line it could handle. But that made him look out-coached, because what happened was that he didn't get Perreault, Martin, and Robert on the ice enough – just four minutes in the first period and five in the second, in the game he's got to win, right? I brought it to his attention and he did better in the third period, but still we lost, 5-2.

The next game was one of the great thrills. We were down 1-0 when Schoenfeld tied it. Then Gil Perreault put us ahead. We went into the third with that one-goal lead, not much against Montreal. But Rene Robert made it 3-1, Don Luce got another on a breakaway, and Perreault sewed it up with his second of the night. Stanley Cup fever hit Buffalo that night, and it kept right on growing when we went back to Montreal for the fifth game, down 3-1 on the series.

Now, very rarely, in my experience, does a hockey club's public relations director provide part of the reason for winning a hockey game. But our man, Paul Wieland, was something special. Paul had been in the job since the first year after Chuck Burr left. One day he told me he played goal for a local amateur team. I kidded that he should come out and practise with the Sabres, if he had the nerve. And he did. When Roger Crozier saw him come on the ice the next day he asked, "Are you crazy. Do you want to get killed?" One time we had a practice game with Paul in one net, and his whole team kneeled down at centre ice and pleaded with me not to make them play with him in goal. But Paul's team won that game!

The point I'm making is that he was not only a good writer and quick-witted, but was extra interested in goalies. In a game with Montreal in mid-March his ears had pricked up a bit when the Canadiens protested that Dave Dryden's goal stick was longer than the rules allowed. That got us a minor penalty at the time and caused Paul to look up the rules about goalie equipment. When Montreal came in for the third game of our playoff weeks later, Paul had a plan.

When nobody was around he went into the Montreal room, strapped on the pads of Dave Dryden's brother Ken, the Montreal goalie, and measured them. Then he wrote me a note saying that Ken Dryden's pads measured a fraction more than ten inches across, making them illegal. The rule read that while you could lodge a protest during play, the actual measure would not take place until the next intermission. Joe and I talked it over. I asked when he intended to use it. He first said, "At the start of the game." That would give them a penalty, to start the second period. My idea was different – that the ideal moment would be right at the end of regulation time with the score tied. That would give us a man advantage to start overtime when one goal would automatically win the game. This we agreed on.

We hadn't needed that edge in the fourth game, but the fifth, in Montreal, was as close as a game can be. Frank Mahovlich scored in the first period. Rick Martin tied it in the second from Perreault and Robert. Then Robert, from Perreault, put us ahead. We held that until late in the third period when Guy Lapointe scored – 2-2.

As the game wore on toward the end, I was sitting with John Andersen in the crowd. "Do you think Joe will remember?" I asked him. "Just in case he doesn't, go down and jog him."

With twenty-nine seconds left to play, Joe called Referee Bruce Hood over and protested Dryden's pads. There was a holdup of several minutes. Hood was really upset. At one point a few minutes later he even threatened to give us a penalty of some kind, to even things up. As if we were trying to cause trouble for him, or something. Then Hood had the final twenty-nine seconds played before the hunt was on for a tape measure which in time would give us a power play situation to start overtime, as we had planned.

Something I'll always remember happened before that overtime. The intermission dragged on longer than usual because of the pads argument, with referee Hood and NHL referee-in-chief Scotty Morrison and NHL president Clarence Campbell all in the act, plus Scotty Bowman, the Montreal coach, demanding a measurement of Roger Crozier's pads (which might have been a shade illegal, too)! But Clarence Campbell ruled that as Montreal had not made the measurement request during the regulation time, Roger's couldn't be measured before the end of the first overtime period, so we would start overtime with a power play.

I don't know where Joe was at the end of this confusion. When it was over I went into the dressing room for a minute and called out, "Look, they've got a penalty, this is a big chance, take advantage of it, do your best!"

I was going out when Horton grabbed my arm. "Where are you going?"

"Out."

"Stay in here," he said. "I've been here before and so have you, but most of these people have never been in the playoffs in sudden death overtime. Tell them what it's like."

I looked at him. "Aah, that's up to Joe."

But Tim wouldn't let go of my arm. "You tell them! You can help, too, you know!"

I said okay and turned back to the players. "Look," I said, "it's really not different. The most important thing I can tell you is to get the puck out of your own end of the rink, and then don't wait to admire it – follow it out! Go out after it just as hard as you can! Canadiens are the top team, they're going to come after you. They're going to come in, they're going to commit themselves deep. If you get it out and follow fast you'll be able to capitalize. Good luck!"

I don't know if it did any good or not, but maybe the reason I remember those moments, is Horton's faith that I had something to offer a hockey team in that situation.

Another important thing was that the time used up in Joe's original protest, plus the extra time needed to measure and re-measure Dryden's pads, had given extra minutes of rest to our big line. This showed in the overtime. We didn't score during the Dryden penalty, but might have; Jim Lorentz beat Dryden and hit the post. From then on we seemed to have the momentum, maybe because the Montreal team was naturally upset over us pulling a fast one like that. After about nine minutes of overtime, it happened just like I said. The Canadiens were in deep. We got control of the puck. Schoenfeld passed from behind the Buffalo goal to Rick Martin, who fed it up to Perreault. Perreault saw Rene Robert breaking into the clear. His pass was perfect. Robert cruised in, waited for Dryden to make the first move, and scored the winner.

Then, of course, we really had Cup fever in Buffalo. But it wasn't to be. Montreal beat us 4-2 and went on to eliminate Philadelphia and then Chicago, to win the Stanley Cup. We'd made it tough for the best team in hockey because Horton had done a tremendous job in helping those kids and Joe had done a hell of a job bringing them on by driving hell out of them, because he's a tough-minded, hard-nosed coach and at that particular time that's exactly what they needed.

CHAPTER EIGHT

Bad night in February

Yet, I can never think about that season, really, without thinking of events that seemed to me to be linked to it. As if there's a kind of pendulum that swings all the way up and all the way down.

When the playoffs were over, first thing I had to do was decide whether to stay on in Buffalo. My original contract was up, and I was wondering about my health. Some people were telling me that maybe I couldn't stand the strain. It's true that nothing in hockey ever runs smoothly. You're dealing with a lot of hyper people all the time, so it's a stressful life, no question. I was thinking seriously about retiring. Then I would think, what the heck am I going to do if I retire? This is what I love. I might be cutting my life short, but do I live by doing things that I don't want to do or do I live by doing things that I want to do? So I went for medical checkups. The doctor told me, as I was to hear often in later years, "You're at risk, naturally, but if it's what you want to do, I can't tell you not to do it and I can't tell you to do it. We can't see any difference in the cardiograms and stuff like that. You have to make your own decision." So I decided, what the hell, I'd go back again.

We called a press conference in Buffalo on May 10 and I got a fairly good press on it. The writers all said I looked better than I had for years. Maybe we were serving good brands that day. "I have decided to un-retire, before I retire," I said. "It's too easy to lose a job in this league. It doesn't make much sense to quit while they still want you."

The announcement said I'd signed a two-year contract as vice-president/hockey and general manager. I must say I didn't take the vice-presidency thing as seriously as I might have. A reporter asked what the title meant and I said that the title, and thirty cents, would get me a ride on the Toronto subway. I think maybe I was a little too casual about that, because titles do mean a lot in business and the Knoxes thought I'd be pleased. To me, it was still just as easy to get fired as a vice-president as it was as anything else. But Seymour Knox said, "It's just our way of recognizing Punch's stature in the world of hockey." I might have been a little more polite about it.

One other question that day was about Joe Crozier. There'd been talk about us having squabbles in the playoffs, but to me the talk meant nothing right then. I said I wanted Joe back, if he wanted to come. With that in mind, I went to the annual draft, which was not a vintage year, and wouldn't you know, right after the draft I came back to Buffalo feeling lousy with stomach pains and general aches, and had to go to hospital. But a thorough examination didn't reveal, the doctors said, any recurrence of cardiac complications – exactly what I'd been told before I signed my new contract.

So I went back at it.

Signed our first draft choice in a blaze of publicity (Morris Titanic, my first strike-out; an injury ended his career before it really began).

Congratulated Perreault on winning the Byng Memorial trophy, awarded annually to the player "exhibiting the best type of sportsmanship and gentlemanly conduct combined with a high standard of playing ability." Added to his rookie award two years earlier, that gave him two league awards in three years, somewhat higher than the national average.

The WHA was giving us hell worse than ever. I was writing letters and having meetings and making phone calls trying to get our most important people signed, all the other things that keep a hockey man busy in the summer when everybody thinks he's playing golf.

Over a period of many weeks, and four or five meetings, I worked on Horton. Training camp started, exhibition games were played. Still no Horton. Of course, I knew one of two things was happening. Either he was engaged again in his lifelong battle to avoid training camps, or he really was serious about quitting. I was pretty sure it was the first. But how could I tell? About three or four days before the *end* of training camp, I set a public deadline. I had to. "If Horton doesn't show up at camp that day," I told reporters, "I'll have to assume that he's giving all his time to the Tim Horton doughnut business." On the appointed day the press and other news media were on hand, cameras and pencils ready. No Horton.

The very next day, I had a phone call. "George," he said. "I think I'm ready to conduct our final negotiations." He was in Oakville at the time, at his office.

"Okay," I said. "I'll meet you halfway, in St. Catharines."

We set a time to meet at Archie Katzman's Parkway Hotel. Of course, he was late. He tried to make up the time and got a ticket for speeding.

"You're going to pay for the speeding ticket," he said.

"Like hell – that's your problem."

As usual, when Tim decided it was time to move, things moved fast. We pretty well agreed on the amount of money. I can't remember the amount, but it was closer to $150,000 than he'd ever been in his life. That was a lot of money in 1973. We lined up all the playoff and other bonuses fine.

Then he said, "There's just one more thing."

"What's that?"

"You're going to have to give me a Pantera."

"What the hell's a Pantera?"

"A Ford car," he said.

Well, I thought to myself, what the hell, here am I talking to a player in terms of $150,000 or whatever it is, what's a $5,000-car? Little did I know. "All right," I said. "But where do I get one?"

"Oh, they're around. You'll be able to find one in Buffalo."

"So everything else is okay?"

"Everything's fine, George." Big smile. "And I haven't wasted all my time in training camp."

"If I get you the car we got a deal?"

"Yeah."

Back in Buffalo I called our administrative vice-president, Dave Forman. "Look," I said, "would you find out for me, you know the people, is there a Ford Pantera in Buffalo and can we buy it?"

He got back to me. There were two in Buffalo, only one for sale. It was then that I realized Tim wasn't hitting me for any $5,000-car. When I heard the price, $17,000, I knew pretty well what to expect. I had a look and didn't like it, one of those hopped-up sports jobs that went like a bat out of hell. But Tim was a car enthusiast and had been ever since his first pay cheque with the old minor-league Pittsburgh Hornets in 1949, when he was only nineteen.

We got the contract written up and I called him. "When you come to Buffalo the car will be here for you," I said. "Let's meet in St. Catharines and you can sign." So we met at Archie Katzman's hotel.

I'll always remember that when I signed him I said, "You know something? I'm dead against giving you this car. You're liable to kill yourself with the damn thing."

He grinned at me. "Aw-w-w-w, George, you're crazy. I know how to drive those things."

It was just a strong feeling I had. I kept on about it. I told him I didn't know why I was giving it to him.

But I did know. I wanted him to play, and that car was the condition he had set and I had agreed to, without even knowing what kind of a car it was.

So he signed and got the car and one night he just about scared me to death on a ride to the airport in it. We started to play, not badly, but struggling a little. Gil Perreault broke his ankle on October 28 and missed twenty-three games. Enter Paul Wieland again, for one of the few pieces of levity we had that season. When Perreault was recovering he would work out with Paul in goal for an hour or so every day. Once Perreault cut too close to the net on a fast rush. Paul swept his feet from under him. Perreault crashed into the boards shoulder first and lay still. Paul stood there white as a sheet, imagining a headline: "Perreault out for season, tripped by PR man at practice." Then Perreault got up, laughing, and put about ten past him. I think it's about then Paul quit working out with the Sabres.

But as a result of the breakup of the French Connection during that Perreault injury, Rene Robert seemed to suffer more than anyone. He was running at a pace of only about half his forty goals of the previous season. Perreault didn't come back until January, a little while after Joe Crozier and I got at loggerheads again over a trade I'll get to later.

And then the season's biggest disaster happened. At practice on Monday, February 18, Tim hurt his jaw badly. I'm not sure how it happened, but a stick or puck or pads or the boards hit him. The jaw swelled up tremendously. He told Joe he couldn't practise, the pain was too bad, and asked if he could drive home and at least do a little business in his Oakville office before our next game in Toronto Wednesday night.

By Wednesday the swelling had gone down a little but not the pain. Still, we were fighting Toronto then for a playoff spot. It wasn't the kind of game Tim would miss. When the team drove over by bus Wednesday he met them at the Gardens and then asked the Leaf doctors to examine his jaw. They did and told him they thought it was cracked. He asked if they would inject it to freeze that side. They refused on the grounds that it was too risky. Remember, he was just past forty-four then.

Tim went out and played anyway. That's the kind of person he was. He hardly played at all in the third period, the pain got so bad, but had played so well in the first two that he was named one of the three stars of the game.

I was staying home in Toronto that night, so my car was parked in a lot off Church Street. When I came to the Gardens' Church Street exit, Tim was talking to Dodo. He'd told her that the reason he finally had to stay off the ice in the third period was that every time anybody hit him it was just like a shot going through the top of his head. Normally, Tim never talked about it when he was hurt. The three of us walked up Church Street together. At the parking lot, along came Tim's old friend Davey Keon.

I laughed, "There's your pal – the one you used to break down doors to say goodnight to." So Tim went over, and when Dodo and I drove away they were still standing there talking.

That was the last time I saw Tim alive.

The next morning about 7.30, my phone rang. Dodo answered. It was Dave Forman on the phone from Buffalo. Dodo told me what Dave had said. About 4.30 that morning Tim's car had rolled on the highway just outside St. Catharines, he had been killed, and was in the morgue there. I don't know what I said. I can only remember the way I felt.

"Somebody has to tell Lori Horton," Dave said. "The provincial police are going to release news of the accident at 8 a.m., so somebody should get to her first."

The police had found Joe Crozier's phone number in Tim's wallet so had phoned him first to come over and identify the body. Joe had gone with one of our doctors, John Butsch. They had made the identification but then, for God's sake, they had gone back to Buffalo without phoning Lori Horton! They'd phoned Dave Forman and asked him to call her. Now he was asking us.

I got off the phone, shocked. I sat down and thought, "Isn't there somebody better than me to tell her?" I wanted to break it the easiest way I could. There's no easy way to do it, but I was burning because nobody had called her before. Whoever had been there, the doctor or Joe or the police, should have called her. I didn't know Lori that well. I was Tim's friend, but hardly knew the family. Then I thought of his business partner, Ron Joyce. I knew he was a close friend of the whole family. I phoned him and told him. He sounded befuddled with the shock of it, hardly believed me at first. I convinced him. "Okay," he said.

But I guess he couldn't face doing it on the phone either. He jumped in his car and started over to Horton's. But it was morning rush hour, and a fair distance. I heard it on the radio at eight o'clock, so the news was out. At 8.15 when I was just about to leave for Buffalo I said to Dodo, "Let's call Mrs. Horton and see if there's anything we can do."

Dodo called and asked for Lori. She came on the phone. Dodo asked if there was anything we could do – and then suddenly held her hand over the phone and whispered to me, "She doesn't know!"

I said, "Oh, my God!"

Dodo had a lot of presence of mind. With Lori guessing right away that something had happened to Tim, Dodo asked first for the Hortons' oldest daughter, but she had left for work. Lori had a friend there with her. Dodo asked to speak to the friend, and told her. She then told Lori. And I guess right after that, Tim's partner, Ron Joyce, did arrive.

Normally they would have had the radio on, but that day they didn't. So that was a blessing, anyway. But the daughter got all the way downtown without knowing until she walked into work and somebody told her.

In a little while I drove to St. Catharines and stopped to get Archie Katzman at his Parkway Hotel. He knew his way around town. He took me to the police garage to see the car. It was a mess. Tim must have been going very fast. I knew he had been taking pain-killing pills because of his jaw. Right where the accident happened there is the slightest little bend in the road. Tim had driven by it a thousand times. The way the police figured it, one wheel just got off the road a few inches. When he tried to get it back, with all that power and the car's quick responses, it rolled out of control through the median and into the lanes on the other side.

I stood there looking at the wreck of that damn car that I had handed to him less than five months before. While badly smashed, there was hardly any damage on the driver's side. If Tim had been wearing his seat belt, he might have come through all right. The police guessed that when the car first rolled, the door flew open and Tim went out, and then the car rolled on him, breaking his neck. I stood there remembering the very first time I saw Tim in a game, saw how strong he was, and thought that he could never be hurt. Why did it have to happen to him? I guess everybody thinks that, when they suddenly lose someone who means a lot to them. Just four days earlier, on Sunday night, I'd had him on my television show and we'd been kidding about whether he would play another season after this one.

The Sabres had to play at home that night. They wore black armbands and at first seemed numb, preoccupied, absent-minded. They were losing 4-1 before they came back and tied it 4-4. Paul Terbenche, who was Horton's closest friend on the team, his roomie on the road, said later, "It just seemed as though I wasn't there at the start of the game, just not there at all. But the more I worked the more I forgot and just played hockey. But then it all came back after the game." There was a lot of anguish in that dressing room.

The eulogies have never really stopped. In 1977, when Tim was inducted into the Hockey Hall of Fame, I had the privilege of giving the citation, telling of him as he was to me, fun and strength and a great man. And still, when hockey players and fans of his years get together and talk of the great ones, you hear that respect for Tim. Pallbearers at his funeral were old Leafs Allan Stanley, George Armstrong, Dave Keon, Dick Duff, Billy Harris, and Bob Baun. The people at the funeral read like a roll call of hockey's great, and some maybe not so great, but who had found a kind of greatness in knowing Tim.

CHAPTER NINE

The occasionally interrupted friendship

A lot of people have been puzzled from time to time about what goes between me and Joe Crozier. It's no real puzzle. Joe is a strong-willed person and so am I. It is inevitable that we will disagree sometimes. But business is business. As far as I'm concerned you can fight with a guy, but it shouldn't affect your relations with him once it's over. Maybe that is asking for utopia, yet to me that's the way it should be. To a certain extent, I think Joe thinks that way, too. But in Buffalo there turned out to be one big difference between us that we hadn't run into before. In Buffalo when we got into an argument, I followed my usual procedure of keeping it private. Joe took it to the papers. As simple as that. No one can find a newspaper story or broadcast tape where I blasted Joe Crozier. I don't cut up people I'm working with, unless it's private, face to face. He talked to the papers about me; I replied in private. I remember when I took the Buffalo job, sportswriter and broadcaster Dick Beddoes said he was glad to see me back in hockey because I'm such an easy target. I'm beginning to think he's right.

I know exactly when the big problem with Joe started. At our contract talks in the summer, at first he wanted a four-year deal. A little later in the negotiations he asked if he had a chance to be general manager in Buffalo eventually, if I got sick or quit. I told him that job was not one I could hand out (obviously, or I wouldn't have been fired myself, years later). He told me in that case, "Forget the four-year deal. Just make it for one." He was keeping his options open.

At the time, Jim Pattison was running the Vancouver Blazers in the World Hockey Association. Of course, Joe was big in Vancouver, colourful, a draw. It's hard to know which came first, the chicken or the egg, but Joe's story was that about the time our 1973-74 season started, Pattison got his home phone number and started calling.

In November, on our first trip to the coast, I found out later, Joe had lunch with Pattison. That's only one month into the season. Pattison made an offer about 30 per cent higher than Joe was getting in Buffalo. Joe sent his brother-in-law, a Quebec lawyer named Mike Sheehan, to see me a few days later in Los Angeles and tell me about the Vancouver offer. Well, I wasn't going to be whipsawed like that, especially during the season. I resented it. Joe had asked (through Sheehan) that I speak to him about it. So I did. I told him he should accept the Vancouver offer, if that was what he wanted. That was the point, I believe, at which Joe decided that he was leaning toward Vancouver. Maybe I would have, too, with more money on the line plus a chance to run my own show as general manager. Coaching is a precarious profession. There is no doubt that Joe wanted to be general manager *somewhere*.

I'm just giving that as background to our first really serious public rift. All that to me was minor stuff, not necessarily unfixable. Maybe this would have been fixable, too, if it hadn't escalated.

On December 12, I went to Finland and Sweden to look at hockey players. When I got back a week before Christmas I had a chance to add speed and muscle to our defence by getting Jerry Korab from the Vancouver Canucks. I had talked three or four times with Hal Laycoe in Vancouver and had told Joe that there was a chance I was going to make the deal, with Tracy Pratt one of the names being mentioned. Joe apparently mentioned this to Pratt, asking if he wanted to go to Vancouver. Tracy didn't. Joe told me that, but it was all none of his business. Korab was twenty-five. Pratt was thirty, an honest player who at the time had the club's best plus-minus record (goals scored while he was on the ice, versus goals against). He had been one of our originals in 1970, one of the few left around. But I knew it would be a good deal for the club if I could swing it.

Nobody can run a hockey club making trades, or not making them, based on liking or disliking people. You've got to ask, is this guy a better hockey player? Can he do more for the club than the other fellow? A lot of people you like you have to get rid of, that's the business, and you hope each one realizes that it *is* business and that your friendship persists. If you did it another way, only keeping the people you like, eventually you'd all be doddering around together. Not winning many hockey games.

Anyway, Laycoe and I agreed on the deal, Pratt and John Gould for Korab, at just about the time Joe was going to Quebec for a couple of days at Christmas. I said to Laycoe, there was no way we were going to announce this until after Christmas – and as it shows in the NHL Guide, the trade was officially made on December 27. But it leaked to the press on Christmas Eve. Immediately I'm an ogre for interfering with everybody's Christmas. When we found the news was out, I got Fred Hunt to call Pratt and tell him. He already knew. I tried to call Joe but couldn't get him. Neither could any of the newspapermen right then, so he wasn't reachable by phone.

But when the press did get to him, he did what I considered a bad thing. He said he didn't think the deal would help the hockey club. In effect, he criticized the management, which I didn't think he would like himself if he became a general manager. He made it obvious then and later that he resented Korab, which sure as hell isn't the right way to get a guy playing good hockey for you. In fact, it was stupid.

So that started the whole damn thing on the wrong road. By letting the media in on our fight, he poisoned the atmosphere. And that was the year so many other things were going bad, Perreault's broken ankle, Larry Mickey's two broken legs (one in training camp and one later), a back operation on Jim Schoenfeld, Roger Crozier sick a lot (although Dave Dryden played well), and the death of Tim Horton. Joe even defied the *reason* I got Korab – which was to play him on defence. He'd been playing some left wing for Vancouver but I wanted him only as a defenceman. I told Joe, "Put him in there with Schoenfeld and we'll have a defence pair that'll make people think when they're going in on them." Which was true. They were both tough, they'd take on anybody when they first got together.

The disagreement between Joe and me really heated up then. I thought his criticism should have been voiced in private, where it wouldn't hurt the hockey club. As it was, I started getting shafted in the *Courier-Express* for making the deal at Christmas, not listening to good old Joe's wise counsel, and a lot of other crap. I think

Joe was being used by the *Courier-Express*. Since Charley Barton died, that paper seemed out to get me. A nice controversy between a coach and his manager, of course, is meat and drink for a paper with that in mind, and Joe was co-operating to the hilt. He was talking. I wasn't.

After Tim Horton's funeral I got back from Toronto to my desk one morning to find the paper again full of the so-called troubles in the Buffalo Sabres' executive suite. Joe was being quoted in some places. Other things they printed they could only have gotten from him. Maybe his words were being twisted, but it all made me red hot.

I picked up the phone and called Joe. "Have you seen the morning paper?"

"I never read the paper."

Of course, that was pure bull. "Well," I said, "there's plenty in there that I don't think much of. As a matter of fact, I don't know what to do about it."

"Well, I can't help it," he said.

"Okay," I said and hung up. I thought about it for a little while, and knew what I should do. I called one of the club doctors and said, "I want you here at four o'clock to examine me and tell me whether I'm capable of coaching the hockey club – tonight."

"Okay," he said, sounding a little surprised, "I'll be there." I called the heart specialist to be there as well. I should have asked them for three o'clock. They were a little late. By the time they got through looking at me, bringing in the cardiogram machine, and so on, at five minutes to seven they said, "Okay, you're capable of coaching the hockey club as far as we're concerned."

Five minutes to seven! The game was at 7.05. I couldn't go down and take over the hockey club five minutes before it went on the ice. I'd been hoping the whole examination would be over by six at the latest. Then I would have gone down, fired Joe, done what I thought I had to do. But at seven o'clock I wouldn't do it.

Then I started thinking – ah-h-h, that would be the way it would happen in Toronto, it's not the right thing to do. I cooled out. During the game I decided I'd let it ride until the end of the season. If I'd been able to get the examination done in time, I sure as hell wouldn't have changed my mind. But everything happens for the best. You get mad in the hockey business and you can get over it. Sometimes you look at a problem and it's a mountain. Two weeks later it's a hill. In another few weeks it's just a grade, means nothing. That's one of the things I've learned. If I have time I'll take lots of time to make a decision. If I don't have time, I'll make it right away – like you do behind the bench when everything that comes up has to be handled instantly.

But I don't put things off forever. I was sore at Joe because he was ignoring my wishes to have Korab play only on defence. Late in the season, young Rick Dudley, who'd scored forty goals for us in Cincinnati the year before, was playing pretty well on the wing. He deserved to be there. But Joe benched him and put Korab up front. If I'd been interfering as much as the papers said I was, I wouldn't have stood for that. But it was my job to supply the players, and the coach's job to decide how to use them. As a result of being benched, Dudley was so mad that he privately began talks with the World Hockey Association's Cincinnati club that eventually led to him leaving Buffalo a year later.

When it came up to contract time, there were not only those things, the steady infighting, bothering me about Joe. There were persistent reports in the Vancouver papers that he had already agreed to be general manager of the Vancouver Blazers the following season. Sources I had inside the WHA assured me he had signed the contract. One time Al Eagleson called Jim Pattison about a player's contract and Pattison said, "You'll have to discuss it with Crozier." When challenged, Joe said sure he had a contract, but it wasn't signed. After we missed the playoffs that year, with no last-minute heroics to confuse the issue, I decided I wouldn't offer Joe a new contract. According to his account to newspapers later, he made the decision – sat down and listed the advantages and drawbacks of both Vancouver and Buffalo. He put the rift with me at the top of the Buffalo drawbacks, and decided on Vancouver. I think maybe he knew that I wasn't going to make him an offer anyway.

It was interesting to read in the *Courier-Express* the whole list of his grievances, some new to me. He said I got sore at him because he wouldn't let me in the dressing room before that all-important St. Louis game the year before, the one that got us into the playoffs. He said I never talked to him during those playoffs, which wasn't true. He said I locked the dressing room door on him in Montreal during the pad-measuring incident and was in there talking to the players. That was the time Tim Horton had begged me to come in; I didn't lock the door and also, I can't imagine Joe Crozier not kicking it down, if he had objected at the time. He said he didn't like me forbidding a couple of players to take a television engagement in which they might have been injured and thus lost to the fans who paid their salaries. He said the Knoxes had urged me to hire him for another year; they had not. And he got in a cheap shot about me looking *relieved* – as if relieved at not having the competition any more – when he told me he'd taken the Vancouver job. That's Joe.

I was relieved because it was good for him, good for both of us, and might allow our friendship to be resumed, proving that we could fight and still remain friends. Which turned out to be the case.

The *Courier-Express* writer got in his final jab in the last few lines: "Now the word from the club is that, with Joe Crozier gone, the operation of the Buffalo Sabres will be 'more tranquil.' Maybe so, but not from a player's standpoint, if a 'yes man' replaces him."

I won't dwell on it, but the paper was saying, in effect, that without Joe Crozier, or somebody like him, the Sabres would be in trouble. With Joe keeping everything in a turmoil all year, we had finished well out of the playoffs – the only real achievement being that on the last night of the season Rick Martin scored a hat trick that gave him fifty-two goals on the season. The next year, when I brought in Floyd Smith, the Mr. Nice Guy who often can function very well as a coach when following a Mr. Tough Guy, we not only made the playoffs but got right to the Stanley Cup final and would have won it if we'd had better goal-tending. If that's a disaster caused by letting a troublesome coach go, I'd like more of them.

Looking back, the only bright spot that season was Real Lemieux. Real Lemieux, you might say, who's he? Journeyman hockey player, bounced around, dead now. But in January of 1974 Joe said he needed an experienced man, a good skater, as a penalty-killer. Real was available. He'd been with the Rangers only a few weeks after being dealt from Los Angeles, but Emile Francis already knew he could spare him. I made a deal. I've always got along pretty well with French-Canadian players. Real and I talked on the phone. He had his family to move. I told him to go ahead and move them, then report. Which he did, along with an expense account that landed on my desk. I went ten feet off my chair when I saw it. Then I couldn't stop laughing. I took it in to Bob Pickel, the comptroller, and said, "Pay him." You'll find that original expense account in a frame hanging in Pickel's office today. It was all on one sheet of paper, misprints and all (as to spelling, I'm sure I wouldn't do any better in French than Real did in English):

I MOVING FAMILY N.Y. TO MONTREAL AND TO SOREL

Taxi to Kennedy airport	$ 10.00
Type porter at airport for luggage	8.00
One-way ticket for my mother to help my wife packing	34.00
One ticket for my dog	10.00
Bought cage for dog for plane	60.00
Bought boxes for packing dishes etc because air freight wouldn't accept big heavy trunks	45.00
Air freight for boxes and lite trunks	92.80
Type for porter at Montreal airport	8.00
Fair from Montreal airport to Sorel, family	20.00
Fair from Montreal airport to Sorel for dog, trunks and luggage	25.00
Helper at home, luggage and trunks, etc.	25.00
In N.Y. wife call long distance to have shipment for car to have her pick up air freight in Montreal, etc.	20.00
Lost gift certificate in N.Y.	30.00
Lost food in N.Y. because can't take across customs boarder	100.00
Drugs trow away because customs	55.00

II MOVING OF CAR N.Y. TO SOREL

Car ass to be inspected before leaving, see if it was ok, he was declared ok	$ 32.50
Auto driveaway to N.Y. to Sorel; details, N.Y. to Montreal $100, going truw customs $75, Mtl to Sorel $50 Total	225.00

III   Mr. Imlach give wife holiday, baby sitter
for three weeks   100.00

Air fair two ways from Mtl to Buffalo   89.00

Total $989.30

Thank you. (Signed) Real Lemieux

Real only played eleven games for us and a few years later I was
sorry to hear he had died, but his expense account lives on.

CHAPTER TEN

Close but no cigar

Somebody once asked me, "Would you say that the biggest aggravation in your life is the salaries you have to pay these guys?"

"Hell, no," I said.

"What, then?"

"Making them play up to their salaries."

Year in, year out – especially some time later when I got back to Toronto – that was almost always the problem, except for that 1974-75 season in Buffalo. Guys that sometimes were a pain in later years, I just couldn't fault that year. Joe Crozier told somebody in Vancouver that the Sabres weren't far from being a championship club, and he might have got them there himself if I had found him the few extra people he needed. "But he'll get them for Smitty, you wait and see." As if I'd been holding them back from him, on purpose.

The amateur draft was on May 28 in 1974, held by a telephone conference hookup instead of at the meetings later in Montreal. Partly this was to get a jump on the WHA so the whole league could work on signing the best amateurs, fast. The WHA was hurting us plenty by then. They had forced salaries up so high that we had to make a difficult decision and close down our team at Cincinnati. It was strictly a business decision: are we going to lose a million dollars a year in the minors when the money could be better used in our top club? I went to Cincinnati and talked to Floyd Smith about coming to Buffalo as coach. We'd made an arrangement with Hershey in the American Hockey League to send them our surplus players. I wanted everything ready in my organization before the draft. I remember telling Smitty, "Listen, we've got to win this year."

I loved his optimism. "Don't worry. We're going to win."

I signed him May 23 and, with John Andersen and others, we talked over our problems. We needed help on defence to fill the gap left by Horton's death. We were short in goal, too. Dave Dryden had played more than fifty games for us the previous season, Roger Crozier only twelve (because of recurrent illnesses). Dryden had played well but now had jumped to Chicago in the WHA. Rocky Farr and Gary Bromley had been up and down between Buffalo and Cincinnati playing goal and Floyd had a lot of confidence in Bromley, but I wasn't so sure. I also couldn't see any goalie in the amateur draft who could step right into the NHL, which meant keeping my eyes open to deal for a goalie.

That was the first year we were allowed to draft players under twenty. We picked a nineteen-year-old defenceman first, Lee Fogolin, eleventh overall. That was the year Washington and Kansas City came into the league, making eighteen teams, so our next choice was twenty-ninth overall – and that's when we got Danny Gare. Through Montreal's system of trading surplus players for draft choices, they had five first-round choices that year! Still, they passed by not only Gare but also Bryan Trottier, who in retrospect must both be considered high among the class of that draft. Sure, I passed on Trottier, too, but with the loss of Horton we were determined to make our first pick a defenceman, and we thought highly of Fogolin. Trottier did not go until the twenty-second pick overall. For a few years there wasn't a club in the league that didn't sometimes wonder, "Why didn't we pick Trottier or Gare? Or both?" I guess we can just be happy Montreal didn't pick them both, which they had ample opportunity to do.

But the Gare pick was one that sticks in my mind. Sitting in our Buffalo office, we had a few minutes before each pick to make our decision. And when we were considering Gare, along with some other players, we got a call from Gare's agent, Larry Sazant. How he knew exactly when to call I don't know. The whole thing was supposed to be secret. He must have had a pipeline in somewhere.

"I just wanted you to know," Sazant said, "that my player is available."

I laughed and said, "How in hell did you know it's our choice?"

"Never mind," Sazant said.

So I hung up the phone and we talked. I called Sazant back.

"Look, it's between Gare and someone else, with us. I want to know what Gare's going to cost me."

He replied that they'd be asking something like $300,000 over five years.

I said, "If I draft him, am I pretty sure of that figure?"

He said yes. So we took Gare. When the draft was over, we went to work immediately to sign our picks. Alan Eagleson represented Fogolin. It was the first time I'd ever taken a player that had Eagleson as an agent. We met in Montreal at the Ritz Hotel, had dinner together, Fogolin, Smitty, Eagleson and me, and I think John Andersen, too. We made a deal, and toasted it in champagne. Then I called Sazant again about Gare.

All of a sudden the rules had changed. Somebody in the WHA – everybody told me later it was Joe in Vancouver – had offered a lot more money for Gare than Sazant and I had agreed on.

"I had a deal with you!" I told Sazant.

"I know, but he's got this offer and he's going to take it, if you don't come up. What can I do?"

In the end, Gare cost me another $150,000, I think, to sign. That's what the WHA was doing to us – making it a question of not how much the guy was worth, but how much money he would insist on. So we paid, and I'm glad we did, because Danny turned out to be a pretty good hockey player for us. At least he played for us – I signed Claude Deziel that year for almost as much money, and he never did play for us. Again it was a situation of being whipsawed by WHA offers. It made me so mad that early in June I made a proposal to the rest of the NHL clubs that we should do to the WHA exactly what they were doing to us – go out and buy away their stars. I offered right then that if any NHL club could recapture from the WHA somebody whose NHL rights we owned, for the good of the league we would let him go. I thought we should fight back, not be such patsies. Incidentally, after Fogolin and Gare, our next three draft picks that year did not play for us, right down to Derek Smith. We picked Derek sixth. Being that low on the draft he was not hard to sign. When Derek came to camp that year he looked every bit as good as Perreault, but he got a head injury that set him back a lot.

After Derek Smith, we had just about everybody we wanted to take. But the draft was still on. Waiting for our next call with not much to do I said, "Let's have a little fun." The others looked at me. The players we were drafting from then on weren't likely to make our team – at least, we didn't think so. "Let's draft a Japanese hockey player," I said.

Chorus from around the room: "What the hell are you talking about?"

I went out of the office. Dave Forman's secretary was there. I said, "Do you know any Japanese names, common ones, like Smith in Japanese?"

"I know a Japanese florist," she said. "I'll call him."

She got the florist on the phone. He was somewhat mystified. She held her hand over the receiver and said, "He says Tsujimoto is common, and Taro for a first name is common, too."

I got her to spell it for me and then said, "Ask what is the name for sword in Japanese?"

"Katana," she relayed.

"Thanks. That's all I need to know." I went back in. When it was our turn, I said into the phone, "Buffalo drafts from the Tokyo Katanas, Taro Tsujimoto."

All along the conference line people started to laugh. Somebody asked, "How do you spell Tsujimoto?"

I spelled it. Well, nobody in the league, eighteen clubs listening, maybe a hundred people, knew who the hell Taro Tsujimoto was. Neither did I!

We talked over later about actually getting a Japanese guy and bringing him to camp. We didn't carry it that far. But when we eventually went to camp, reporters would ask, "When is this Taro going to report?"

"Any day now," I'd say.

Of course, having Paul Wieland as public relations director helps make a gag like that work. He could do a deadpan press release on anything.

When we finally confessed, it caught on as a joke with the Buffalo fans, especially the ones who make signs and hang them around the rink. They'd use the name Taro as in those old Confucius Says jokes. Over the years there must have been hundreds. "Taro says Dave Schultz is German for Game Misconduct," is one I remember. And our young defenceman, Bill Hajt (pronounced height) prompted this one: "Taro remembers Bill's allergic brother, Gesund Hajt."

During the summer I struck out in various deals I tried to make for goalies. I could have had a first-rate one – for Richard Martin, which made me laugh. Then, in October, just after the season opened, I did manage to pick up another promising defenceman, Jocelyn Guevremont, from Vancouver. We got him along with minor-leaguer Bryan McSheffrey in exchange for Gerry Meehan and Mike Robitaille. And away we went.

I had a sign put up in my office that year which read: "Love is having a hockey club like the Buffalo Sabres."

After the previous season, when there had been all the bitching in the papers about the lack of rapport between Joe and me, and complaints about me interfering, this one was like the difference between day and night. Of course, it's hard times even for the most active of rumour-mongers when a team keeps winning like the Sabres did. There were no incidents. It was just go and play hockey and enjoy it. No crabbing, no nothing. It was a wonderful year. Part of it, without a doubt, was the difference between Joe and Smitty. Joe was tough, always pushing, in his first half-year bringing out what was in the players but then not able to do it again. Then Smitty comes in, easy-going. They'd had the hardgoing type for so long, in me and then in Joe, that it was like a holiday for them. This kind of thing only works for so long, but it does work. It's a matter of being the right sort of coach in the right place at the right time, and that's how it was with Smitty that first year in Buffalo. The rink was full, 15,863 seats sold, every time we played. By mid-November Martin had ten goals, Robert nine, and we'd gone ten games unbeaten. We won by just about every kind of a situation you could imagine, including the occasional shorthanded goal. The French Connection was flying. By mid-December each of them had twenty goals. Gare was playing well on a line with Luce and Ramsay. People called our third line the Kamikaze Kids – Lorentz, Rick Dudley, and Brian Spencer – not scoring a lot but creating mayhem with their forechecking. Every defenceman was six feet and 190 pounds or more. Our average age was twenty-three, lowest in the NHL.

We were pretty good at centre, with not only Perreault, but Luce playing his finest season, Lorentz, and Peter McNab up from Cincinnati. Still, in January when we had a chance to get insurance at that position in Fred Stanfield, we traded to Minnesota for him. He'd been in the league ten years, could play the power play. By then we had a really well-balanced hockey team with only that worry about whether our goalkeeping was strong enough.

Montreal would have traded me Bunny Larocque for Jocelyn Guevremont, but that seemed to be giving up too much at one position to strengthen another – and then maybe not strengthening it enough. So I kept on trying, and waiting, as you have to do in hockey. Jim Proudfoot wrote in the *Toronto Star* that my wait for a goalie was characteristic. He said I was always driving past gas stations with the gauge showing empty, but confident I'd get where I was going. Late in February, I had my chance. Not for a Ken Dryden, or Tony Esposito, or young Johnny Bower or Terry Sawchuk. But for one I thought would do.

I'd known Gerry Desjardins for years and liked his work. He'd played junior for the Toronto Marlboros and worked in the mail room at Maple Leaf Gardens. Then he'd backed up Tony Esposito in Chicago, which is like being unemployed. The Islanders took him in the 1972 expansion draft. He played well, then jumped to the WHA. When the Michigan Stags breached contracts by not being able to pay their players, and breached them further by moving to Baltimore, I went to see Desjardins. We sat in the Baltimore stands one night and he told me he'd be overjoyed to play in Buffalo. I signed him. The NHL, pussyfooting as usual when it came to the WHA, at first refused to okay the deal on the grounds that it broke a WHA contract. I got on to Ron Roberts, his agent, and eventually to Bud Poile, who by then was president of the WHA. Poile talked to Clarence Campbell and told him that in the circumstances Desjardins was a free agent as far as the WHA was concerned. After that I had to deal with the Islanders, who still owned his NHL rights. But they had Chico Resch and Billy Smith, and agreed to let me have him for cash and future considerations.

Only then, early in March, was I able to use him. I told Smitty to play him every game. We had to see right away if he was good enough. In his first three games he only allowed eight goals, for two wins and a tie. In his nine full games before the end of the season, he allowed twenty-five goals for an average of 2.78 per game, which was better than any but a few goalies in the league. Not as good as Bernie Parent of Philadelphia, Rogie Vachon of Los Angeles, Ken Dryden of Montreal, or Roger Crozier in the twenty-three games he'd played that season for us. But good. Suddenly we looked like a solid club, ready for a run at the Stanley Cup.

By the middle of March, we had clinched our division title and for a while were alone in first place of the league's overall standings. The euphoria showed everywhere, including Paul Wieland's April 1 deadpan press release, sent on the regular hockey TWX wire to all NHL clubs, for local distribution and information. Incidentally, I had told him long before that he could quote me on anything as long as I could back it up. On April 1, 1975, now tied for first overall, our press release read:

TO: ALL P.R. DIRECTORS, NHL CLUBS

FOR RELEASE AT 5.00 P.M., APRIL 1, 1975 . . . .

THE BUFFALO SABRES TODAY ANNOUNCED THE CLUB WILL TRAIN NEXT FALL IN HONDURAS IN CONJUNCTION WITH A PAN-AMERICAN GAMES PROJECT TO FOSTER HOCKEY IN THE OTHER AMERICAS.

IN AN ANNOUNCEMENT JOINTLY RELEASED BY THE U.S. STATE DEPARTMENT SABRES' VICE PRESIDENT/HOCKEY AND GENERAL MANAGER GEORGE "PUNCH" IMLACH SAID THE DECISION TO TRAIN IN HONDURAS WAS MADE AFTER MONTHS OF MEETINGS WITH OFFICIALS OF THE PAN AMERICAN GAMES ORGANIZING COMMITTEE, THE STATE DEPARTMENT, THE NHL OFFICE IN MONTREAL, AND THE HONDURAS ICE HOCKEY FEDERATION.

"THERE'S A GENERAL AGREEMENT," SAID IMLACH, "THAT SOUTH AND CENTRAL AMERICA COULD TURN OUT GREAT HOCKEY PLAYERS IF THEY HAD A CHANCE TO PLAY THE GAME. STUDENT RIOTERS IN MANY COUNTRIES TO THE SOUTH SHOW ALL THE ATTRIBUTES OF THE BEST OF THE NHL, AND WE THINK THESE ATTRIBUTES CAN BE CHANNELED INTO HOCKEY."

IN A RELATED DEVELOPMENT TODAY, THE CAHA SAID IT WOULD NOT PLACE A CANADIAN TEAM IN ANY PAN-AM GAMES COMPETITION IN THE FUTURE UNLESS CANADA WAS ALLOWED TO USE ANY PLAYERS IT WISHED. CAHA SECRETARY GORDON JUCKES SAID HE HAS RELIABLE INFORMATION THAT A PANAMANIAM HOCKEY TEAM PLANS TO USE THAT COUNTRY'S TOP PROS UNDER THE GUISE OF AMATEUR STATUS IF AND WHEN THERE IS PAN-AM HOCKEY.

END RELEASE

Maybe we were all a little nuts that season, especially on April Fool's day. There was also the time Ted Darling, our play-by-play guy bought a live lobster in Boston to bring home. Somehow it was let out of its packing box and through most of the flight was crawling around the plane snapping at things. Darling had to hunt it down after all the rest of us got off.

But I guess one of the most amazing communications I ever got, in Buffalo, Toronto, Quebec or anywhere, was this:

The ADVOCATE
2121 South El Camino Real San Mateo California

Dear Manager:

As you probably know, the ADVOCATE is the largest gay publication in the United States. You will be interested to know that we are expanding our editorial content to include sports news and personalities.

As the major vehicle for gay peoples' self image, we are very concerned with presenting positive role models to present our people with the story of gay athletes.

Could you help us by letting us know which of your players are living a gay lifestyle? I would appreciate it if your publicity department would set up interviews with them for us.

Thank you for your cooperation.

When I read that one I was tempted to send it along deadpan to Wieland and ask him to do what the man wanted. Then I wondered whether Paul had written it himself. But the letterhead was real.

I didn't answer it. Couldn't think of a thing to say.

The euphoria that year *almost* lasted long enough. Almost.

The league that year had been split into four divisions in two conferences. We won our division by a mile, and on the second-last night of the season travelled to Toronto for one of the most important games the Sabres had ever played. A win would give us the Prince of Wales trophy, the conference championship. Montreal was close, but had fewer wins, so a win for us would be decisive. I was rather annoyed that nobody in Toronto seemed to know how important this game was to us. The papers and other media ignored that aspect, treating it as a nothing game for both us and Toronto. We won 4-2 and celebrated the Prince of Wales, the first trophy the Buffalo Sabres ever won, by taking the team across the street to the Westbury for champagne, before we hit the road back to Buffalo.

Our quarter-final against Chicago was no contest. Desjardins allowed ten goals in five games, and we won four of them. That put us against Montreal in the semi-final. There had never been such hockey excitement in Buffalo. That series also proved that my heart was standing up okay.

A good thing. When it gets down to the series like that, I live and die with every play. And when I sit with my wife, she doesn't do much to keep my excitement level down. Our daughter Marlene once said to her, "Mother, if you were a hockey player you'd always be in the penalty box." In the first game we were up 3-1 in the first period, and let Canadiens come back to go ahead 4-3 before Perreault tied it again. We had out-shot Montreal in the first two periods, but the third had to be seen to be believed. Jim Lorentz put us ahead 5-4 early in the third and we just kept pouring in on Ken Dryden. We outshot them 12-4 in that third period, but they were still in the game. In the last minute, only about thirty seconds to go, they pulled Dryden and had six skaters against our five. Then with play going mad around our goal, Jerry Korab slid into the net somehow and caught his skate in the mesh! He couldn't get loose. That meant, in effect, they had six against four. Jacques Lemaire had the puck in the corner. He shot for the front of the net and Danny Gare, who had been checking like mad, stuck his stick out to deflect it back of the net – but put it in, instead; 5-5, and overtime.

In the fifth minute of overtime, Montreal had survived a tripping penalty to Bob Gainey and was starting to come on again. There was a face-off in our end. Luce, over-eager, fouled the face-off. He was waved out of the face-off. I got ready to pull my hat over my eyes. Craig Ramsay was waved in to take the face-off against Lemaire, one of the best in the business. Ramsay figured, probably correctly, that he couldn't outdraw Lemaire, so he tried something. He let Lemaire win the draw but whipped his stick around behind Lemaire in an attempt to get it on the puck – and did. He went around Lemaire like a rocket, pushing the puck in front of him. Luce and Gare broke with him. The Montreal defence opened a little to play the wings so Ramsay headed for the space between them. Larry Robinson recovered almost in time and got a hip on Ramsay, but Ramsay held Robinson off with one hand and with the other shoved the puck to Gare. Gare pushed Henri Richard aside, took the pass and shot without breaking stride. It was in at 4.22 of the overtime. We had won, which we deserved, but still – I'd been around lots of times when people deserved to beat the Canadiens but didn't.

They weren't through yet. We took them 4-2 in the second game, and went into Montreal and got blown right out of the Forum two games in a row, 7-0 and 8-2. Back home we came from behind in the third period to tie 4-4 and then it came down again to an overtime face-off in their end. Perreault won the face-off, got the puck to Rene Robert and it was in.

So we led the series 3-2 then, but had to go back to Montreal with the memory of those two blowouts in our minds; the memory also of outshooting Canadiens 21-5 in the first period of the fifth game and still having to come from behind in the third and win it in overtime.

For the sixth game, we had two regulars injured – Rick Dudley and Don Luce. Not only their scoring ability was out (Luce thirty-three goals, Dudley thirty-one) but they were tough checkers, none better. That's when it first began to look as if our depth had some quality. Pete McNab took over at centre between Ramsay and Gare. Both McNab and Ramsay scored, along with Rick Martin, in the first period. Stanfield was hurting, too, but played anyway. It was interesting that the Canadiens, intent on tying up the French Connection because of the 131 goals the line had scored that year (Martin fifty-two, Robert forty, Perreault thirty-nine), realized too late that Buffalo wasn't a one-line team any more.

It wasn't just the Luce-less Luce line, that got them. Our third line was not exactly red hot on paper, but it had what it took – Brian Spencer and Jim Lorentz on the wings with Fred Stanfield. In the second period, that line hit everything that moved. In the first period Desjardins had made sixteen saves, but in the second they only had three shots on goal, two in the last ten seconds, while Lorentz scored our fourth, the eventual winner. In the third, the Canadiens brought the score to 4-3 with sixty-five seconds to go and Dryden out for a sixth attacker. I have to tell you, by that time I was talking to myself. But in the last minute, when Dryden was out again, the Canadiens had three face-offs in our end. Stanfield won all three, and we had put the Canadiens out.

In the dressing room Peter McNab expressed something I'd often hoped I would experience again. "The feeling is unbelievable, to be on one of the two best hockey teams in the world," he said.

A strange thing happened on the plane on the way home from Montreal that night. Maybe it was a hint of trouble in the years to come. I noticed that while everybody else was happy, singing and yelling, Craig Ramsay was just sitting there looking grim. I walked back along the aisle once and he stopped me. "I want to talk to you," he said.

"Yeah, what about?"

"I'm very disappointed in you."

"What are you talking about?"

He said, "Korab is getting a big bonus, he says, for being in the final. Told everybody in the dressing room."

"So, maybe he is, I don't know."

He said, "Well, I'm not getting one and I don't think that's right."

"Look," I said, "you made a deal and he made a deal. Whatever your contract calls for, you get. What his calls for, he gets. Maybe you're making more money than him. That's not important. Never mind what he makes, you should be happy you're going into the final."

I went back and thought about what he said. It proved something. He didn't want anybody else to get something unless he was getting it, too.

No more was said about it, though, and we got home with a week to wait, get over injuries, and bask a little, while the Islanders-Philadelphia series went to seven games before Philadelphia finally put the Islanders away.

That Stanley Cup Final with Philadelphia had its moments. During one game the weather was so hot in Buffalo that a thick fog rose from the ice. Before the next game I asked what was going to be done about the fog. "Don't worry, Punch! We've got it licked." That night I saw what they meant – a bunch of kids who really couldn't skate very well came out on the ice waving bedsheets to dispel the fog! I couldn't believe my eyes. And one night a bat got into the rink and had all the players and audience ducking, until Jim Lorentz hit it with his stick. Too bad for the bat, but it got the game started again.

In the end we lost to Philadelphia in six games. Bernie Parent's goalkeeping beat us. One of the wall signs in Philadelphia during that series read: "Jesus saves – but nobody saves more than Parent." We would keep the puck in their end for minutes at a time – and then they'd break out to our end and score. It started out as a homers series, making me wish that somewhere along the line we had got even one more point so that we would have had the extra home game. The crowds in both Buffalo and Philadelphia were huge factors. They beat us twice before their home crowd, and we beat them twice before ours.

We went to Philadelphia to play the fifth game, with the series tied. When the first puck dropped we put it in their end and they never got it out. The first time they got it out, they scored. We put the damn thing back in again and we were all over them again and they got it out and scored again. We never recovered. They beat us 5-1 and won the Stanley Cup 2-0 in the final game, before our fans in Buffalo.

I sit now and think about that series and know that if we had changed goalkeepers, it would have been no contest. I'm not taking anything away from Gerry Desjardins. He played as hard as he could but he was not Bernie Parent. Few goalies are.

As I write this, it is still the best season the Buffalo team ever had – to finish tied for first in the eighteen-team league, to win the divisional championship, then the conference championship, to have six thirty-goal scorers in the lineup (Martin fifty-two, Robert forty, Perreault thirty-nine, Luce thirty-three, Gare thirty-one in his first season, and Dudley thirty-one as well). And Luce won the Bill Masterton Memorial Trophy, the professional hockey writers award for the player "who best exemplifies the qualities of perseverance, sportsmanship and dedication to hockey."

Of course, I won an award, too – the close but no cigar award, held by many a general manager before me. Plus the right to explain why, when we came so close that year, we couldn't keep on improving over the next few years until we did win the Stanley Cup. To that one, I have a lot of clues, but no answers.

Come to think of it, the only thing that season that did bug me a bit was the problem of trying to sign Rick Dudley. I can only guess at the background. He was sore at Joe Crozier the previous spring when he was benched so that Joe could use Korab on the wing. At the same time Dudley got an offer from the Cincinnati club in the WHA which, I later was told, but can't prove, he accepted to take effect a year after, at the end of this 1975 season. I kept trying to verify this but couldn't get to first base. I think Dudley's lawyer figured that if I really did know about Dudley's WHA signing I would have taken some action, maybe not played him, or traded him, or whatever.

They went out of their way to make me think Dudley hadn't agreed with the WHA. Once a meeting was actually set up at the Bristol Hotel near the Toronto airport ostensibly to talk about a new contract. The agent specified a five-year contract which I wouldn't sign for anybody and an amount of money that he knew I'd never pay. So, whether it was a really serious negotiation or just an attempt to make me think Dudley still could be ours, I don't know, but I've got my suspicions. Then Philadelphia finally beat us on that last Sunday night. The next morning, during a team meeting, I got a phone call. It was Dudley's agent.

"You're not going to like this," he said, "but Dudley has signed with Cincinnati."

He was right. I didn't like it. I'd been conned. But I blame the lawyer, not Dudley. The reason I don't blame Dudley is simply because he played a tremendous hockey season for me. He never played as well again. Moving to the WHA was a bad move for him. He should have stayed right where he was and I'm certain he would have been a star in the National Hockey League.

Buffalo never has had as good a season as that since. We won forty-nine, lost sixteen, tied fifteen. And in the matter of plus-minus records, we did not have a minus on the team. Even in Toronto, when we were winning Stanley Cups, we had a couple of guys with a minus on our team. Don Luce was plus 60! Funny thing was that the French Connection was Perreault plus 2, Martin plus 5, Robert plus 7. They were the guns – Robert got 100 scoring points, Perreault 96, Martin 95. So they were on for a lot of goals, at both ends, but they made things happen. There are always a few good reasons for being minuses, of course. Such as a line that's playing against the best line of the opposition all the time. But that year we usually had Luce, Ramsay, and Gare playing against the best opposition in the NHL, and they had the best plus-minus record on the team. There is no way you can be a loser under those circumstances.

CHAPTER ELEVEN

I should have traded Schoenfeld

Someone asked me what is different about the players coming into the league today from, say, Tim Horton, Dave Keon, Allan Stanley, and a lot of others. There's no difference. The kids coming in today are just the same – *when they come in*. They have the same ambitions as the rookies of years ago. Then many change. They forget what it was that got them there, or they try to be something else.

I'm thinking of Jim Schoenfeld, for nearly ten years a major hero on the Sabres – the guy I gave the captaincy to when I traded Gerry Meehan. Schoenfeld had just turned twenty-two at the time. I took his C away a few years later when he stopped being the kind of player I wanted as captain. He has been traded from Buffalo since, but I should have traded him years earlier. I can remember the very day when I should have done it.

Schoenfeld was never a dirty player, but when he came into the league he was tough, would back up from nobody. He was six-feet-two, 208 pounds. He took on three people one night playing against the Boston Bruins, Wayne Cashman, Bobby Orr, and somebody else. He was a better hockey player in his first two or three years than he's ever been since, because in those days other players gave him that little extra bit of room they always give to the tough ones.

When we got Jerry Korab, and he and Schoenfeld were out on that blueline together, they'd take on *anybody*. Nobody wanted any part of them. If something started in a corner, or a fight in front of our net, they'd look at each other and then just wade in. That made a hell of a difference, lifted everybody, the knowledge that when trouble brewed these two six-foot 200-pounders were coming in like there was no tomorrow.

But over the years Schoenfeld changed. His life changed. He didn't play it tough anymore. It was as if there had been a shift in his priorities and hockey no longer was on top. Hockey players sometimes seem to feel that the game has changed, when actually it is they who have changed.

I'd had such respect for him earlier that I thought we should talk about it. I called him into the office one day in 1976 or '77. I told him that he wasn't playing as well as he could. "When you came into the league," I said, "you were very, very aggressive. Because of that, other players gave you room to manipulate." Schoenfeld couldn't skate well enough, wasn't mobile enough, to operate efficiently unless he had that extra space. "You've lost it because when a guy comes in to check you now, he knows nothing bad is going to happen to him. He knows you're not going to make him suffer."

Well, Jim said he thought that way of playing was no longer in his best interests. And then he added something that raised what little hair I had on my head. He told me the worst thing anybody can say to me about his way of playing hockey! "I'm not going to fight any more for those other people up in front. They're big enough, they can fight for themselves. I'll make sure they don't get jumped from behind, I'll look after that. As far as I'm concerned, if somebody hits me, I'll clobber them, but they'll get the first shot."

He'd make sure that nobody else would get in the act, but he wasn't going to do the fighting for them! They're going to fight for themselves! What the hell! It doesn't take long for players who aren't good fighters but do a lot of other things for the team, to catch on. Then all of a sudden everybody is looking after themselves as individuals, not as a team. If that's a team, that team goes down the drain. It just takes half a year, maybe a year, and it gets around that well, hell, nobody's going to come in to fight my battles for me; therefore, I'm going to look after myself, not take chances. The edge you get from having a guy behind you who's going to take care of you if needed, is lost. That's bad enough, coming from anybody, but from Schoenfeld it was worse. He was the *captain*. The captain is telling me he won't stand up for his teammates! I should have traded him that day. Why didn't I? I think it was the family atmosphere we had on that team. You can argue, but how do you kick your kid out of the house? So I stuck with Schoenfeld, but eventually gave the captaincy to Danny Gare. I never gave a reason for the change. I don't knock my players. But as the years went on the others – Gare and Ramsay, Lee Fogolin, and other people who did fight for their team- mates – had to take Schoenfeld's share of the load. Later I didn't always get along with Gare and Ramsay, either, but I would never take anything away from them as men who would stand up for teammates in trouble on the ice, as well as being damn good hockey players.

I don't think I was especially hard to get along with, for people who gave what I thought they should be giving. I'd do what I could for them. In the summer of 1975, after Gare's thirty-one- goal rookie season, he was given a day out in his home town of Vernon, B.C. He asked me if I'd come. I didn't feel any too well, was still on orders to avoid getting tired because of the 1972 heart attack, but because Gare had asked, I flew to Vancouver, rented a car and drove for several hours to get to Vernon. A lot of NHL players showed up. They held one of those summer exhibition games that nobody is supposed to know about (and I never told). Later I was sometimes easy on Gare because of the way he was playing for me. Once, I think in his second season, we had a couple of players who had to be watched because of their drinking habits. They were going into places I didn't want them to, so I hired a guy to keep tab. There was one tavern in Buffalo that had a real bad reputation, not only for booze. One night the guy I'd hired to keep a lookout followed our heroes in. He had a beer or two himself, watching them. At 3 a.m. he walked up like Joe Fan, and asked for their autographs. They all signed autographs on cocktail napkins bearing the name of the joint they were in!

One was Gare, another was Jacques Richard, a very talented player who had a considerable drinking problem at the time, and since has done well with the Quebec Nordiques. I can't remember who else, but there were three of them.

I didn't tell anyone in the Sabre organization about this. It was my business.

I called Gare in and said, "Look, I want to give you a little ad- vice."

He's not very big, you know, five-nine, about 170 pounds, with a boyish face. Fans and writers used to call him baby face. Women thought he was just a darling. My wife often said that she couldn't be prouder of Gare if she were his own mother. He looked at me with that baby face and said, "What's the advice?"

I tossed over his autograph from that night and said, "Never sign an autograph on a doily or anything else with a tavern's name on it. It's a dead giveaway that you were there, regardless of whether it's legitimate or not legitimate. You never know when somebody's going to get hold of that autograph and claim that it wasn't legitimate. You're not going to be legitimate every time. Everybody knows that. I know it. Don't put yourself in the jackpot."

He looked startled, then laughed. "Jeez! I never thought of that."

That was the end of it. I didn't tell him I knew what time he'd signed it. The point is that I was not an ogre when a guy played hard for me. And sometimes maybe I should have been tougher. For instance, I used to try everything I could to keep Jacques Richard from drinking. He'd had an impaired driving charge in Buffalo, and those things embarrass a hockey team at least as much as the player. Nice kid, good hockey player, really talented. But I could see him wasting his talent. I've seen so many. You lose something when you booze all the time. You don't know you're losing it, but you are. Your reflexes are going. You may get some back but you'll never get them all back. You don't get your brain back, either. With Jacques, trouble seemed to follow him around. One time in 1976 he and another young player named André Deschamps were in a tavern in Quebec City – I used to live in the district so I know the place – when a guy came in and started blazing away with a gun. One shot went right between Jacques' legs and hit Deschamps!

I tried to get Jacques straightened out in Buffalo. Of course, I couldn't keep an eye on him all the time at home, but on the road it was a little different. So I thought. We played in Minnesota one afternoon and were flying to Los Angeles later that day to play the next night. After a game players like to have something, maybe a beer or two, before they get on the airplane. I know that. But for the real drinkers this gets to be a lot more than one or two. So on that trip I played cards with Richard all the way out, to keep him occupied.

We got to L.A., checked into the hotel, and I thought everything was okay. But after the check-in, he, Al Smith, (the veteran

The best day in a hockey job is the day you sign the contract. That's the only day everybody's happy. Floyd Smith, me, Harold Ballard, 1979.

An earlier "best day": when I signed with Buffalo in January, 1970. With the Knox brothers, Norty and Seymour.

The Entertainer at work. In Buffalo after Eddie arrived we'd often lose and still send fans home laughing. Gerry Ehman provides the ride.

Gil Perreault broke the NHL's 45-year-old record for goals by a rookie. Other people saw him only once in a while. I had that great privilege every night.

Behind the bench is the best job in hockey. I wanted to coach every night.
But a few days after this photo a heart attack ended coaching for me.

The night Tim Horton died. He asked for a Pantera in his contract.
I said I didn't want to give it to him, it would kill him, and it did.

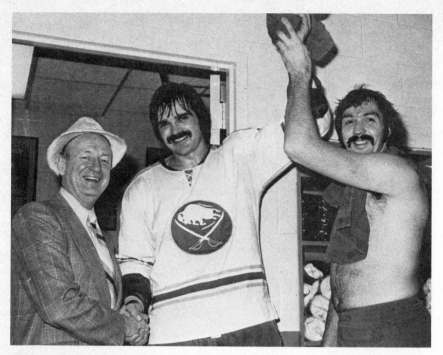

The night Sabres beat the Russians 12-6. We out-shot and outskated them, and Jerry Korab's body checks helped. Nobody has walloped them that way, since.

Frank J. Selke congratulated me after the Russian game. It bore out his idea, he said, that our best would always be a little better than anybody else's.

People a G.M. hangs out with: Tiny Tim,
with Ward Cornell and Bob Gordon of
Hockey Night in Canada.

A couple of general managers
practising how to worry. With Emile (The Cat)
Francis, a veteran like me.

Roger Doucet's singing of national
thems became famous in the NHL and around
the world. A good Canadian.

On the night of Buffalo's first home
game, Canadian Energy Minister Joe Greene
came to Buffalo to shake hands.

What's happening (top left)? It didn't turn out great (top right). In these situations I prefer the view from inside my hat (bottom left). But standing up, I've found in hockey, often is good for a pain in the rear end, however caused.

In my first year back with Leafs the team book went on sale in one store.
Buy now! They will all be traded this year! But I didn't change enough.

Dodo has seen a lot of hockey with me since I stopped coaching. She's loyal to her
favourites, but her own family comes first with her and always has.

In Buffalo's Hockey Hall of Fame I'm a charter member. In 1981
Seymour gave me a sword and the fans an ovation. Dodo and I
were very quiet on the way home.

Outside courthouse after Carl Brewer hearing, 1982. After my
coronary bypass operation I felt the best I had for years,
but that didn't get my job back.

goalie I'd brought in to be backup to Desjardins) and a couple of others went out for a few drinks. One thing led to another. Al had been around a lot and was not exactly the best housemother for a guy who shouldn't be drinking. The next thing you know they're in a fight. Richard hits somebody and sprains his wrist badly. The following night I go to the game, walk in the dressing room, and there is Richard in his street clothes.

"What the hell happened to you?" I asked.

"I fell and hurt my wrist."

I have to laugh now, but it was serious then – and of course it soon got to me about the bar and the fight. The sum of it was that a guy we really needed couldn't play. Some of the things that prevent you putting your best team on the ice! After that we gave up on Richard for a while, sent him down to Hershey, but he worked his way back up to the Sabres eventually and later went to Quebec, where he has played well.

In 1975-76, the year after we lost to Philadelphia in the Stanley Cup Final, we were not bad but not anywhere near as good as the year before. When a good team has reached its peak and is going down, you should be able to keep injecting new blood, or replacing the worn parts, or however you want to put it, so that everything continues to function as before, or even better than before. But how the hell can you make that decision about a young team that has just finished tied for first in the league? It was two or three years before I began to realize that the Sabres had reached their peak in 1975, getting there early, and just weren't going to get any better. It's the old story: talent can get you there, but it takes character to keep you there.

The maddening thing was that they had it when they wanted to. This was proved in the middle of the 1975-76 season. There have been a lot of meetings between Soviet hockey teams and the NHL since, but give me, as a memory, the Sunday afternoon and Monday night of January 4 and 5, 1976.

The two best Soviet teams, beefed up with stars from other teams in their top league, landed in North America around Christmas. On December 28, Soviet Army had the New York Rangers 7-1 before Rod Gilbert and Phil Esposito scored in the last five minutes to make it a slightly more respectable 7-3. The Soviet Wings led Pittsburgh 5-0 the next night and won 7-4. Soviet Army then went into Montreal on New Year's Eve and tied 3-3 in a game where the Canadiens were outstanding. Our brand of hockey was being trampled. The next game, against the Soviet Wings, was ours.

I was high about that one right from the moment the game date was set. Smitty made some remark about it only being an exhibition game. I said, "It's no exhibition game as far as I'm concerned. You make damn sure you put it to the players that this is the most important single game they'll play this year."

Then I did what I could to back that up. At that time I usually didn't bother watching films of teams we were going to play. That was Smitty's job. But now I ordered a set of films of the Pittsburgh game. I got them on the Thursday of that week, and looked at them closely by myself. On Friday I called the team in. We watched the film together. I ran it back and forth to show mistakes on both sides. One bit I remember in particular, a Pittsburgh player just going through the motions, as if he didn't care. I stopped the film and ran it back and said, "If any s.o.b. in this place thinks he's going to play *that* kind of a game, you're wrong!" I told them, "This is our business, our hockey, that we represent. Everybody in Canada is going to be watching this game, and you represent them. You better be ready to play on Sunday."

I went on about other things I saw in the film. I mentioned the way the Soviets made what is, in effect, a double pass, with two possible receivers. Sometimes the first guy takes it. Sometimes he lets it go to the second guy. I said, "You can step in between and pick it up."

I told them what our system would be. No different than I'd always used, if I could get people to play it. Basically, on offence, our guys would be on their own. It was up to the Soviets then to stop them. But when the Soviets had the puck, with all their criss-crossing and leaving positions and so on, we weren't to go chasing all over the rink with them – until they crossed our blueline. "When they go over our blueline, you stay with your guy until we get control of the puck. Don't ever quit on the check. That way the defence doesn't have to look at what you're doing, because you're with the guy and you're going to look after him. And if there's nobody to take, go in behind the defence and pick up whatever comes." If all that worked, nobody had to worry about one of the Soviet defencemen coming in late, because there'd be one of our guys open to take him. We had a lot of talent and a lot of power. If we used it, I thought we could beat them. The whole answer, I told them, was in tight checking. "Sure they're good, they're strong, they can skate all night, they throw passes to spots instead of to the man who is going to arrive there – but if you're on top of them and they have to pass too soon, or pass too late, it won't be on target. Or if you slow down the guy who's supposed to get the pass, the action won't happen."

I kept them there two hours after we'd seen the film. Some didn't like that, but I didn't give a damn.

I remember George Gross of the *Sun* asked me before the game if I'd promised them a special bonus for winning and I said, "What the hell are you talking about? I *pay* them to win, but I sure promised them a lot of aggravation if they lose. If they work they can win." Work and wins go together.

I also told George I thought we'd have to score five goals at least, to win.

Well, we got twelve. Nobody in the NHL before or since has beaten a top Soviet team the way we did, 12-6. I think maybe the goal I enjoyed the most was in the first period. We'd gone ahead 3-0 on goals by Guevremont, Perreault, and Martin. Then the Soviets got one on a power play. Less than a minute later Martin stepped in on one of those double-pass plays I'd warned about, intercepted the puck, and went in to score. He told me after, "Jesus, you were right."

It was some afternoon. Busloads of people came over from Toronto. The game was on the CBC national network. In three games up to then all the NHL had managed was the one tie in Montreal. The CBC had me as a colour commentator. I was jumping up there, seeing the Sabres play the finest game they ever played as a team, even though we were missing Jim Schoenfeld, down with mononucleosis. Jocelyn Guevremont had the flu, but played anyway. We had them 4-2 after the first, 9-4 after the second. We outshot them every period, 17-9, 17-7 and 12-5. Outscored them every period. We had five power plays, and scored on four of them.

More important, we proved they were human. We outplayed them so badly that late in the game they were doing what they hardly ever do, throwing the puck into our end and chasing it. We plugged up centre ice, where they liked to freewheel. Ruined their pattern style. Jerry Korab shook them with some tough checks.

Perreault and Martin simply outskated them going for loose pucks. We got rave reviews right across the country (except that Frank Orr in the *Toronto Star* somehow managed to ignore our total superiority by saying that the Soviet goalies we played weren't as good as Vladislav Tretiak of Soviet Army).

Actually, I think people in North America tend to over-stress the good points of the Soviet game. We play two different systems and it just happens that when the two systems collide the good parts of their system, being new to the fans, seem more noticeable. To me our game is the best. We fill the rinks in Buffalo, Toronto, Montreal, the good hockey cities. They don't fill their rinks for most league games, even in Moscow. Despite occasional complaints, I think the weight of public opinion is on the side of our kind of hockey. During the 1982 world championships held at the same time as our Stanley Cup, sometimes I would switch back and forth between a Quebec-Boston game and a world title game. No comparison; our games were better by a mile.

I've been disappointed that in all that is written about Canada-Soviet hockey, that game of ours in Buffalo sometimes seems forgotten. Maybe that's so because it was in Buffalo instead of Toronto. One letter I received after the game was from Frank J. Selke, who ran the Canadiens for so long. He congratulated me "on the excellence of your team," a fulfilment of his hope "that our best will always be a little better than the best of any other country."

The game also proved something I've always contended – that we should send a club team, not an all-star team, against the Soviets when we play them. Then those players have to accept the challenge, put their own pride as a team on the line, accept that if they lose they will be blamed and properly so. Not like an all-star team that scatters after a loss, so that nobody really has to shoulder the blame.

The second big thrill for me at that time came the next night. After beating the Soviets, we flew to Montreal. When we came on the ice that Monday night, the big Forum crowd stood up and just yelled. It was an amazing ovation. Red Fisher in the *Montreal Star* called it "a thunderous display of admiration for a team which had excelled. It was public, yet somehow private. It was something these 18,000 people wanted to share with the Sabres, and with them alone. It was rich and warming. It may never happen again to a team coming in to play Montreal, but those who were there to hear and to witness it, will never forget it."

I know I never will. And what made it better was that the high we had reached against the Soviets hung on there with us for one more night. Richard Martin scored three goals and we beat Canadiens 4-2.

But when you get on a high like that, you have to pay. There is a letdown. In the next two weeks, while the Soviet teams played four more games, the Wings beating Chicago 4-2 and Islanders 2-1 while the Army beat Boston 5-2 and lost 4-1 to Philadelphia, we hardly did a thing right, dragged through to finish the season fourth behind Montreal, Philadelphia, and Boston.

That meant that in the Stanley Cup we had to play in the preliminary rounds, because we hadn't even won our division. Due to a hassle with the Buffalo basketball team about playoff dates in Buffalo, I agreed to open the three-game preliminary series in St. Louis, instead of at home. The rest of it would be in Buffalo. We had finished thirty-three points ahead of St. Louis in the standings, but Ed Staniowski in goal for them stonewalled us in the first game and we lost 5-2. Then we were life and death in two overtime games in Buffalo to win, Danny Gare winning the second game at 11.23 of overtime, and Don Luce getting the third for us at 14.27 of overtime. That, from a team that never should have been close to us. Then New York Islanders put us out in the quarter-finals in six games. Season over.

Oddly enough, there was also a negative result from our great Soviet game. It seemed innocent enough at the time, but it started something. Peter McNab said on television right after we'd beaten the Soviets that he and the others were playing that game 100 per cent for Canada. Some Buffalo fans took offence. I know it wasn't meant that way. Normally, Buffalo fans are the best. Later that season McNab was booed. He was playing his option year and because of the boos over something he'd thought was completely natural, he decided he didn't want to play in Buffalo any more. That June of 1976 Boston had a player, André Savard, one of their first round draft choices, who didn't want to sign again with Boston. I talked it over with Harry Sinden, the Boston general manager. We decided that if he could sign McNab, and we would sign Savard, we'd do it. It wasn't a trade, as some people have called it. It was simply a mutual accommodation. Although the exchange seemed fairly equal at the time (or even favoured us, because Savard was a first-round draft choice and McNab a sixth-rounder) it did not turn out well for Buffalo. Savard is a strong hockey player but McNab is a fine natural goal-scorer, as he has proved since.

Every team in the NHL has horror stories about all the travelling that has to be done – the white-knuckle guys, the ones who like to anesthetize themselves with booze before stepping aboard a plane, and so on. I remember once in the early Buffalo years one four-games-in-five-nights stretch. To start with, landing in Chicago for the first game we were buffeted by high winds and then were delayed two hours waiting for a bus. We lost the game. Rushed to the airport after, to find that our chartered plane had just been declared unsafe. Waited hours for another, flew to Boston, arrived at 4 a.m. Lost that game. Next morning we left for Buffalo, circled for ninety minutes because of a snowstorm, had to land in Syracuse, then flew to Detroit. Lost. That night we went to the airport and found the wings on our plane iced up, got home late. Lost again. That's what players mean when they tell you that travel is the hardest part of being a pro athlete.

But nothing in my experience matched one weekend late in January, 1977. We played at home on a Thursday night, January 27, a 1-1 tie with Atlanta. I drove to Toronto after the game to do a few things on the Friday morning. Then I planned to take the train to Montreal in the afternoon to meet the team there that night. League rules change occasionally about the minimum amount of time before a game the visiting team should arrive, but most try to make it the night before.

On Friday it had started to snow in Toronto when I drove to the Guildwood station, the closest one to my home, and caught the Montreal train. It snowed the whole way and the train arrived in Montreal hours late. There were no taxis. I walked up Peel Street in the storm past the Mount Royal Hotel into the Ritz Carlton where the team was supposed to be staying. Bob Pickel, our comptroller, had flown in early to do some business at league headquarters. He met me and gave me the news – there was a blizzard raging in Buffalo. People were stuck downtown and couldn't get home. Some were staying the night in the Memorial Auditorium.

Pickel was really worried. "What are we going to do about the game?" I said, well, we couldn't do anything anyway until the next morning. We'd see then.

The next morning I guess was funny, if you have that kind of a sense of humour. I kept calling Buffalo and telling Smitty, "Get them on the bloody plane and get here!"

"But they can't even get to the airport, and no planes are flying anyway!"

I said, "They'll get to the airport somehow. Call them and tell them to get there by hook or by crook."

Some did. They walked, used four-wheel-drive vehicles, hitched rides on snowplows. Still, only the ones who lived fairly close to the airport made it.

The game was supposed to start at 8 p.m. At four they had managed to clear one runway in Buffalo during a letup. For a little while, anyway, our plane could take off. "How many you got there now?" I asked Smitty.

"Thirteen." Luckily enough, that included Desjardins. The twelve others meant we could play four on defence and leave enough for three forward lines.

"Get in the airplane and get going," I said.

I sat there thinking, well, I've often said it wouldn't be so bad if you only had four defencemen and nine forwards. Then the coach can't make any mistakes by putting the wrong people on the ice.

Another thing: Rick Jeanneret and Ted Darling, the broadcasters, were among those who didn't make it to the airport. Jeanneret lives on the Canadian side and couldn't get across the Peace Bridge. Darling didn't even make it out of his driveway. At such short notice they couldn't line up people in Montreal to do the game for them. Darling arranged a phone hookup to the radio station from his home and sat in his living room watching the game on television and broadcasting that way. And it was some game to broadcast. Our thirteen played like hell. We tied Montreal 3-3, Stanley Cup winners the spring before, and the team that was going to win it that year, too.

But the storm wasn't over. We couldn't get out of Montreal that night, and we had a game at home against Los Angeles the next night. Sunday morning I phoned to Seymour Knox. I told him not to cancel, that we should get the game in. Finally, he absolutely had to cancel. Orders from the city were that nobody was to go on the streets. The National Guard had been called out to help.

We did get out of Montreal on Sunday. Coming in to land I saw what had happened to Buffalo. There wasn't a road open.

I didn't know at the time that my wife had left Toronto that morning for Buffalo, took hours driving the last few miles to the Peace Bridge and finally got through only after an accident that bashed up her car a little. That night my wife and I went down to dinner in the hotel. A table nearby was filled with National Guardsmen. The girl that served us was also serving them.

She said to the Guardsmen, "Why aren't you out on the streets, cleaning up?"

Their officer waved at the storm outside the window. "You don't think I'm going to send my men out in that, do you?"

Everybody started laughing because, after all, what the hell were they there for?

Anyway, that was Sunday. And there was no game.

Dodo and I had planned to go to Florida for a few days. By Tuesday afternoon, when there were still no planes flying, I had to phone our Florida friend and tell him fate had intervened, or whatever, and we couldn't make it.

Here I have to bring in Al Smith. Even he used to use the word "flaky" about himself. But flakes come in several varieties, and he was one of the good kind. I've always liked him. I'd known him in Toronto. He'd played goal for me there, and he'd been around the league a bit and later came to us from the WHA. I saw him only as a backup goaltender. Desjardins played most of the time, but Al got in fourteen games in 1975-76, and part of one playoff game. This next season he was again strictly the backup. He played in seven games compared to forty-nine for Gerry, and I had him on a contract that gave him his outright release at the end of the season. Meaning, he had no place in our long-range plans at all.

Anyway, after the big snowstorm we had a goalie crisis. In a game with Boston, February 10, 1977, Gerry Desjardins was hit in the eye by a puck shot by Peter McNab. That was a Thursday night. Desjardins was taken to hospital. Al Smith replaced him in the rest of that game, but we didn't know how long Gerry would be out. With that kind of an injury some players never come back.

After my feeling that Gerry Desjardins hadn't played well enough in the 1975 Stanley Cup Final, I'd gone into the draft that summer looking for a goalkeeper. We drafted two – Bob Sauve our first-round choice (seventeenth overall) and Don Edwards our sixth-rounder (eighty-ninth overall). But a strange thing happened that hurt Sauve's development. He would not sign unless I guaranteed he would stay in Buffalo at least until New Year's. Edwards made no such conditions. We had the working agreement with Hershey in the American Hockey League then and Edwards had agreed to go to Hershey on a tryout. Normally Sauve would have gone there to get lots of playing time and a chance to develop. By the time I could move Sauve out at New Year's, Hershey loudly did not want him to replace Edwards, who was playing very well and was a great favourite of the fans. So Sauve had to settle for one stint in Providence, replacing an injured goalie, and another in Charlotte, North Carolina where, incidentally, people thought he was the best goalie they'd ever seen in the Eastern Hockey League.

The following year, again with Edwards well established at Hershey, Sauve played in a couple of games with Buffalo and then wound up in the minors again. So, when Desjardins was hurt and I had to decide on which of the two youngsters to call up, Edwards had been playing much more than Sauve, and had a better record. I got the word to Hershey on Friday, the day after Desjardins was hurt. Edwards played the next night for Hershey, and won. Then, very short on sleep (he had to catch a 7 a.m. plane for Buffalo) he arrived in our dressing room.

I was thinking about the goalie situation all day Sunday. Or actually, from the moment that Desjardins was hurt. I had not tried to con Al Smith at any time. He was our backup goaltender, but Smitty and I had agreed that he was not good enough to be our top man in that position. I knew we'd eventually have to go with Edwards or Sauve. First we had to decide which one of them was better. Edwards looked the better now, which is why I'd called him up.

About six o'clock on Sunday night, with the game against Minnesota only an hour or so away, I called Floyd Smith up to my office. "Who are you planning to start in goal?" I asked.

"Al Smith," he said.

I said, "Look, we've agreed that he is not good enough to be our number one, right? That means we have to find out whether Edwards is good enough. The only way to find out is to play him. Starting tonight."

He argued about how faithful Al Smith had been, working hard in practice, filling in when needed, and that he should get this chance. But he'd been in the league for more than ten years. He'd had lots of chances. "Play Edwards," I said.

"But I've already told Al he's going to start."

"Go and tell him he's not going to start," I said. "If it has to be, that's a direct order."

I know that I have often said that I don't interfere with how a coach uses the players I get for him. That's okay, but there are times when as manager, you've got to manage! You can't allow things to happen that are not in the best interests of the overall organization. I was the boss, and what I was stuck with was that our goalkeeper was in hospital, his backup was not a long-term proposition with us, and I had to find out right away whether Edwards was, or Sauve was, or whoever. If Edwards couldn't do it, or Sauve, it meant that I would have to give up a good player in a trade to get a good goalkeeper; or would have to go into the draft again looking for one. That's the way it is. I don't pussyfoot around when I have to do something. I think things work out better that way, even when it hurts. So Smitty either could have gone down and told Al Smith he had changed his mind, or he could call it a direct order from me, whichever he chose. He told Al Smith that it was an order from me.

Edwards had gone through the warmup thinking he'd have an excellent seat on the bench to watch the hockey game. Then Al Smith was called into the coach's office. When he came out he plunked himself down beside Edwards. "I might as well tell you," he said. "You're going to play."

Now, Al Smith was well-liked in the dressing room. Hockey players sometimes hang together on things that do not really have much to do with the long-term matters a manager has to consider. I don't blame them. Friendship is like that. They felt sorry for Al Smith, and that was all right. It could happen to any of them. They could understand how he felt. But what happened next was straight out of the old Al Smith so many hockey fans, managers, coaches, including me, had come to know and sometimes love. After he found he wasn't going to start, he just decided he would quit Buffalo. He felt we'd just been leading him on to think he was an integral part of the team, and now had yanked the rug. He did his quitting in his usual flamboyant way. He waited until the anthem was played, then skated over to Seymour Knox's box, gave a little wave and said something. He said later that he'd intended to say, casually, "Hey, Seymour, see you later," but that his voice squeaked and ruined the effect. After that he skated straight off the ice, walked into the dressing room, took off his equipment and left the Auditorium, which someone ran to tell me.

This left Don Edwards, twenty-one years old, never having played in the NHL, without even a backup. But the players, annoyed as they were with me, went to work to protect the kid, I'll say that for them. They checked and skated well. Rene Robert got a hat trick and we beat Minnesota 6-2. But in player interviews in the papers the next day, I got raked over the coals. When I look back, I think that was the start of the trouble I had with some players, directors, and parts of management. The fact that Al Smith was not a top-rank goalkeeper, and that all I was trying to do was start the process to find a first-rate goalkeeper to replace Desjardins, and put playoff money in the bloody players' pockets, didn't seem to occur to them. People asked me later why I didn't explain the whole thing to the players directly, so that they could understand what was going on. You can't do that. Suppose the kid doesn't work out and I have to use Smith again? At least doing it my way – and if Smitty had managed to soften the blow a little – we had a chance to keep him.

Of course, the dressing room that night became like a revival meeting. The team captain, Schoenfeld, instead of cooling it, said he thought Smith was justified. He did mention that Smith had lost both games he had started for us, "but that was because we played poorly in front of him." And, "When you work so hard and your chance comes and they take it away from you, you don't feel like waiting around to see if you ever get another chance." Jerry Korab, who usually roomed with Al Smith on the road, said that went for him, too. Brian Spencer chimed in about Smith being the hardest worker on the club.

Jeez, if teams were picked on who was the hardest worker, the league would be full of Al Smiths and Brian Spencers, while Rick Martin would be doing something else. Listen, I know how Al Smith felt. It had been a frustrating year for him, with only seven games and a rather poor goal average of 4.30. But to tell the absolute truth, there is no general manager with any sense who would not have done what I did. That did not save me from the long knives. Responsible sportswriters like Dick Johnston of the *Buffalo*

Evening News, and some of the television and radio people, reported what had happened and why. I've got no quarrel with that. I don't expect people to agree with me all the time. But the trained seals in places like the *Buffalo Courier-Express* had a field day, always ready anyway to harass me when they could.

Phil Ranallo, one of their columnists, recalled that when Floyd Smith was appointed to replace Joe Crozier, the only knock against Floyd was that he would be a yes-man to me; and said that had proved over the years to be wrong – "until Sunday night." He flayed me for embarrassing Floyd Smith and embarrassing Al Smith. Ranallo couldn't have done better if he'd been doing it on a street corner, playing a cornet. I guess they were disappointed as hell when Edwards beat Minnesota Sunday night, beat Toronto Monday night, was chosen one of the three stars each night, and went on even that late in the season to be a hot contender for rookie-of-the-year honours in the league. He also was Buffalo's number one goalkeeper from then until he was traded to Calgary in 1982. One of the league's best, still. And I stress again that none of this is intended to cast aspersions on Al Smith – only to say that if I'm running a hockey club I have the right to make decisions that have long-range effects. I made the decision and I was right.

However, the kind of news people who love big targets took up the cause from then on. They planted the seed that the coach was my puppet, on a string. I wish some of those bastards had been around, and listening, about four weeks later. We were in Cleveland around the middle of March. By that time we had played I think seventeen games with Edwards in goal and Bob Sauve as his backup, winning thirteen of them. We had just checked into the hotel when Schoenfeld came and said he wanted to talk to me.

"Okay," I said.

"I just want to apologize for saying what I said in the paper about the Al Smith thing. I was wrong."

That's well and good, eh? "Okay, Jim," I said, "I understand and appreciate you saying this. That's the way it is. Forget it." What the hell else am I going to do? It's like a story I heard about a drama critic who gave an actor a really vicious review and then met him in the toilet. They're standing side by side and the critic says, "I've decided I was wrong about you in that review I wrote. I regret it deeply." And the actor says, "Okay, but I'd appreciate it the next time if you criticize me in the can and apologize in the paper."

The damage was done by Schoenfeld's original quotes. My public reputation was injured and there was no way that it could be repaired. Schoenfeld was sorry. That's great, but he couldn't take back all the things that happened because of what he said. I wouldn't go to the newspapers and tell them he'd apologized. I could have said to him, "What the hell are you telling me for? Why don't you tell the newspapers you talked to in the first place?" But that would be opening the whole thing up again and I didn't really want to open it up. Let it die.

But it wouldn't and that was the start of the crap that hit the Buffalo team, and kept right on coming until the end, for me. With eight days to go that season, we were ahead of our main Adams Division rivals, Boston Bruins, 101 to 96. Even one loss by them would make it certain that we'd win our division and get that important extra home game in the playoffs. The Bruins were in Toronto that night. With six minutes to go, the Leafs led 5-3 and seemed to have it locked up, so Dodo and I left. By the time we got out on Church Street it was 5-5. When we got to the parking lot I heard somebody yell, "Boston's ahead!" Cars with keys in them were being warmed up. Boston had scored three goals in the last seventy-five seconds and won 7-5. I was so bloody upset at the Leafs folding that we climbed into the Lincoln Continental and slammed out of there. We were ten blocks away before Dodo noticed some cigarettes in the car. We don't even smoke! We'd driven away in someone else's car. Back we went. That's how calm my nerves were that week as Boston won five in a row and beat us out by two points.

But it was us folding as much as the Bruins going good that did it. Certain things stood out. We eliminated St. Louis in the preliminary round. In the quarter-final the Islanders took us four straight. The team wasn't playing for Smitty any more. You had to be there to see. Part of it had come as a result of Schoenfeld's stirring up trouble over the Al Smith affair, part was because he wasn't hitting any more. His every-man-for-himself attitude had spread and was hurting the whole club. The French Connection line also seemed to have fallen apart. I had to do something.

Quietly, without explaining anything, I relieved Schoenfeld of the captaincy and gave it to Danny Gare. Although Gare had had a bad 1976-77 season because of a back injury aggravated during the Canada Cup the previous September, he would give more of the kind of leadership I wanted. Also, I decided that Smitty had out-lived the time when his easygoing ways could motivate the club. I asked him to stay on as a scout, which he did, but then started to hunt for a new coach.

I offered the job first to John McLellan of the Leafs. We met in the Westbury Hotel in Toronto for lunch. After we'd talked a while about both the Buffalo and Toronto situations, Johnny said, "I don't think I'll take it, Punch. In a year or two you'll be back here – what's the use of me being over there, if you're back here?" I didn't know how right he was.

Then I talked to Al MacNeil, who was coaching Montreal's farm club in Nova Scotia but had been a Stanley Cup winner with Canadiens the only year he coached them; to Roger Neilson, who'd been coaching the Peterborough juniors; and to Marcel Pronovost, four times an NHL all-star defenceman and a good hockey man. MacNeil decided to stay with the Montreal organization, although when Sam Pollock retired a year later, maybe Al wished he'd come with me. Anyway, he went to Atlanta, not as good a hockey club as ours. Roger Neilson decided to take the job in Toronto. Marcel said he'd be interested in Buffalo, and on August 4 he signed.

CHAPTER TWELVE

Sixteen months to the end in Buffalo

To give you an idea of the job Marcel Pronovost faced in the next sixteen months before both of us were fired, I'll go back to a little before I relieved Smitty of the coaching. In his last few months as coach, I had brought in Allan Stanley as his assistant. Stanley was a good NHL player for twenty-one seasons with the Rangers, Chicago, Boston, Toronto, and Philadelphia. He'd been with me for four Stanley Cups in Toronto. Three times he'd made the league's second all-star team. He knew what it took to win.

At the end of every season I ask the people most concerned to evaluate the players and the team. So when we were bounced from the playoffs once again, I got reports from Stanley, Smitty, and John Andersen. Stanley's, which was hand-written, showed his frustration with what he found in Buffalo – and, as it turned out, the core of the problem Pronovost faced.

Stanley led off, "There are too many players here who think work, body contact, and aggressive play are dirty words and shouldn't be used. The players seem very complacent and talk tired all the time. Not from overwork, it would seem to me. To acquire a couple of hard-nosed hockey players who think it's worth fighting for, would make our big guns better hockey players."

I'm not going to run down his entire list of comments on individuals. A few will do. On most players, he used from thirty to fifty words. Only two rated his shortest report: "100%." They were Don Luce and Craig Ramsay. Gare probably would have been in that category, too, except that due to the back injury he had aggravated in the 1976 Canada Cup, he had played less than half the season, dropping from fifty goals to eleven. Even so, on Gare, Stanley wrote: "The only one who thinks it's worth fighting for."

On our big defence pair that at one time used to keep the opposition honest:

Korab: "Won't play it tough enough."

Schoenfeld: "Works hard, tries to do everyone's job, tires himself out. Has four or five basic bad moves in his defensive play which get him in trouble but could be corrected if he would listen to his coaching. Wants to be Mr. Good Guy to the opposition."

He thought Jim Lorentz, Fred Stanfield, Brian Spencer, and Lee Fogolin should be traded (although in my opinion Fogolin rated a plus as one of the few who would stand up for the others in the rough going). In the important matters, Smitty didn't disagree. He wrote that he found Korab: "Uncoachable." On Schoenfeld: "Has ceased to be a leader." John Andersen thought both Korab and Schoenfeld should be available for a trade, if they didn't rediscover what had made them good years before. All three reports said in various ways that the French Connection line was drifting down, not really trying, which showed in their goal production. Perreault's had held up the best, although even he sometimes played as if he was out to lunch. I'm giving these details because sometimes fans don't think club managements see what the fans have to put up with night after night. I thought an awful lot of it had to do with the every-man-for-himself attitude that had infected the team ever since Schoenfeld told me he wasn't going to fight for his team-mates.

Being able to put your finger on what is wrong, and being able to do something about it, are two different things. I had private conversations with each player after the season ended. I didn't let them get into their views on the coach. Mostly, what I heard was what you hear from everyone when things go bad on a hockey team. "I did my job, but the other guys didn't do theirs." The old refrain. It made me remember one time years earlier when I had a lot of bitching on a team and I went into the dressing room and told each of the players to look at the guy on his right and say, "You're a bleep-bleep lousy hockey player!" Then to do the same to the guy on his left. Then I told them that in case they were too stupid to realize it, every man in the room had someone who thought he was a bleep-bleep lousy hockey player. That was the Buffalo Sabres, by then, every one blaming everyone else.

Sometimes people have wondered why I didn't take Mike Bossy first in the amateur draft that summer. He went on to be a great goal-scorer with the Islanders. Some of the above will give you a clue. The last bloody thing we needed was another guy who could score goals! What we needed was to make the team more defensive-minded. That was why I chose Ric Seiling over Bossy. Seiling had checking ability, and a willingness to mix it. That summer also I almost had Charlie Simmer, who had become a free agent and was looking for a firm contract. I offered him one. I'd seen him play well against us for Oakland and Cleveland and always had in the back of mind, "That's a kid I'd like to have." We would have had him, I think, except that Los Angeles also offered him a contract. Looking at the two clubs, Simmer thought he had a better chance of making the team in L.A., which was probably right.

Late in the summer, I read the citation for Tim Horton being admitted to the Hockey Hall of Fame in Toronto. Johnny Esaw of CTV had put together a little film for me, showing Horton in action, which I showed along with the tribute I spoke. I was thinking while I was talking, "If Horton was still around, I wouldn't be having all this crap in our dressing room."

So we went into the season under Pronovost, and things went about as before. We had so much quality that we won our share of games, but I have here a note I wrote to myself about the French Connection one night: "French Connection – you're playing lousy, no drive, no fight, and the fans see it and I see it." There was a certain euphoria about them around the time of the league's all-star game, held in Buffalo for the first time, because Perreault scored the tying goal for our conference's all-stars, and Martin got the winner in overtime. (Alan Eagleson told the all-star dinner that I'd been the most important man in building that franchise, a tribute from where I least expected it! And at the game those great Buffalo fans played a gag on me. Five men in a row behind mine got dressed up in bald wigs and hats exactly like mine, and at one point all stood behind me and yelled, "Will the real Punch Imlach please stand up!" They had tipped off a photographer and the picture made the Buffalo front pages.)

But what I got out of that game, besides the few laughs, was the way Perreault and Martin played when you put a challenge to them, motivated them. It showed that they could still deliver if they felt like it. I decided to talk to them seriously about what was wrong. I went to each and to Robert separately. The answer was they didn't want to play together any more! You'd think that when they had established themselves as a line famous through all of hockey, the best line in the business, they'd want to keep on going. They didn't. It was purely mental, psychological. None of them had lost any ability. When I analyzed what they told me, I was sure that something had happened between Martin and the other two, especially Robert. I mean, Perreault, he just wants to go out and play. But he had given up on the line. "Ah-h-h-h," he told me, "it's time to break it up. We had a good thing, now we start something else."

Of course, you can never really get to the bottom of a thing like that because players won't tell you specific things that are wrong. But some things I knew myself. I zero in on Martin because he'd gotten a bit of a swelled head after his big scoring seasons, picked twice as first-team all-star, and twice on the second team. He didn't want to practise. I remember one time we had been playing badly, so had two-a-day practices going. He said he couldn't do it, he had to move his home.

"What's more important?" I asked. "You or the team?"

"Well, I'm not going to do it."

He missed the first day and I fined him $500. He was there the second day. I knew he had a home to move but when the team was on the rack of two-a-day workouts because they'd been playing lousy, we couldn't differentiate, couldn't say, "Hey, Martin, you're a fifty-goal scorer! You got it made!" But that insistence on doing things his own way wasn't only on the practice thing. And when he started pulling that "my way" thing on the other two, Robert having his say about how he wanted to play, and Martin insisting on his way, I noticed that sometimes when Martin, the shooter, should have been getting the puck, he wasn't getting it. As if the other two, and other players as well, just decided, we're not going to give him the puck. It ends up so stupidly, because they could have played a lot longer as the French Connection with nobody in hockey to challenge them, until Wayne Gretzky came along.

At the end of that season, when we finished a respectable fourth overall but were knocked out of the quarter-finals for the third season in a row, I took a real grilling from the reporters. They fired the questions: Why aren't we tougher? Why don't you trade for some players who will make us tougher? What the hell is going on? All I could say was that I knew these were questions our fans were asking, people who were frustrated from seeing the Sabres show no drive, desire, effort, and results in the playoffs. The fans were right. All I could do was assure them that I was twice as frustrated as they were.

So, finally, we come to my last six months with the Buffalo Sabres. I've done a lot of thinking about those six months and haven't come up with anything that I would have done any differently, if I'd been faced with the same circumstances. My summer life was pretty well the same as usual. I had to quit playing golf after my first heart attack in 1972, but went to the races from time to time, and did a lot of talking with other general managers about trades that never came off. I had said publicly after we'd been knocked out of the playoffs so quickly once again that I would trade anybody, even Gilbert Perreault. I would have been very reluctant to trade him, or Gare, or Don Edwards, but anybody was available if I could improve the team. Craig Ramsay said after I was fired that I had it coming to me, I should have made some trades. Well, maybe I should have traded him. Maybe then I wouldn't have got fired. But that gets down to what I said before. You don't trade a player just because you don't like him, if he can play hockey better than anybody you could get for him. And Ramsay was one of Buffalo's best hockey players, no doubt about that.

A team gets into a difficult position, making improvements, when it has our kind of record. Since 1975, when we tied for first place in the league overall with 113 points, we had always been fourth or fifth, well up there. That means that each year in the draft we didn't have a shot at the best young players, because we were always drafting late. There was also the point that only three or four teams in each of those years had better records than we did, before our flops in the playoffs. So I look at us and think, that's not good enough, but what can I do about it? Try, that's all.

Even with our bad position in the draft, we did well in 1978. We did a lot of kidding around the Buffalo table at draft meetings. That year the scouts were heavy on Larry Playfair, a six-foot-four 200-pounder from B.C. John Andersen was especially adamant about taking him. To kid John, I kept saying I was going to take Tim Higgins, a right wing from Ottawa, because I was pretty sure he'd be gone before our turn came. Everybody got upset. One of the scouts said, "Jeez, you'd better not take Higgins ahead of

Playfair, John will quit." I said, "So, he'll quit. But I've got to make the final decision." If Higgins hadn't gone (to Chicago) ahead of Playfair I don't know what I would have done. Anyway, we took Playfair.

While we were waiting for our next turn, we got lucky. Somebody dropped a word in John Andersen's ear that Tony McKegney, the young black player who'd been signed by Birmingham in the WHA, might be available, that he wasn't totally sewn up by Birmingham.

I said, "Are you sure?"

"Eagleson says so."

I found Eagleson in the crowd and went to speak to him. Of course, this stirred up a lot of talk at the other tables. Even the people at my table were saying, "What are you and Eagleson talking about?" I didn't want to say, because some people drafting ahead of us might hear about it. Finally I said to Eagleson, "Are you sure you can deliver?"

"I'm sure."

I said, "Jeez, if you don't deliver and I blow this choice for nothing, I'll be coming after you!"

He laughed and said, "I understand."

So I went back to my table and sat down. Then John Andersen thought he should warn me. He jerked his head toward the other end of the table where the Knox brothers and Bob Swados were sitting, and said, "I'm not too sure those guys would appreciate you drafting a black hockey player."

I said, "You've got to be kidding!"

"Well, I might not have read it right, but I think you'd better be sure."

"Okay," I said. When our turn came I went over to the Knoxes and Swados. "Look," I said, "this kid McKegney is by far the best hockey player available. It's a steal if we get him. If it's a hockey decision, we have to take him. That's the way I feel. If it's a political decision, I want you to tell me right now."

Everybody said, "It's a hockey decision." So we went ahead and took him, and it was one of the better drafts we'd had in recent years because of that. It turned out later that the Birmingham club owner Johnny Bassett, to his disappointment, had found that some of his supporters in Birmingham did not want to see a black hockey player on that club, so Bassett later in June turned him loose to us as Eagleson had said would be the case. To the kid's credit, all he said when he heard about the Birmingham opposition was, "All I want to do is be a good player in the NHL, and show those Birmingham people how wrong they were."

It was a few weeks after that when my contract came up with Buffalo. For the first time I was not offered a raise. Maybe that told me something. I did ask that my bonuses be doubled, which they agreed to. At the same time I was told by the Knoxes that they wanted me to be more active in a direct way with the hockey club, including going in the dressing room. Seymour Knox, questioned on this point when this book was being written in 1982, said his recollection was that no such order about going more to the dressing room was given. "We said changes had to be made, were in fact essential, but it was left to Punch what they would be. He rarely went into the dressing room, as I recall; only when he felt the situation demanded it." My recollection is different, that I was told directly to be more active with the hockey club, including the dressing room.

I said, "I don't want to go to the dressing room. If I go to the dressing room we're going to get into problems with the newspaper people. It always happens when somebody other than the coach makes a habit of giving orders to the players, or even opinions about game incidents. Like, maybe I'll say one thing, or tell a player one thing. The coach may say something else. Then the players and the newspaper people have two versions of the same story, and that causes trouble. I don't want to do it."

They said, "We want you to do it."

I said, "Okay, if that's the way you want it."

The trouble, as it turned out, was exactly what I had forecast. But when I did do it, and got the problem, the owners didn't back me up, ran away from me.

One other bit of trouble I had that fall was about playing the Soviets again in our building. I said at the time we were discussing contract that I was against it. Not much more was said then. Later I heard that a meeting had been held without me and the decision made to go ahead with a game against a Soviet team early in January. I heard this in two phone calls when I was in training camp at St. Catharines. The story I got was that the Buffalo club didn't care whether I liked it or not. One call was from NHL headquarters, where arrangements were being worked on.

"We're not playing the Russians!" I said.

"I think you'll find that you are."

What really riled me was that they had gone behind my back to do something that affected the hockey club. I thought about it from all angles. To myself I was saying, if they're going to force this issue, the hell with them. I'm losing my authority anyway, so I might as well get out. Meanwhile do I let them get away with knocking me down? Or do I stand up and be counted? If they were going to decide to play that game, they should have had a meeting with me present to give my reasons for being opposed. If they, as owners, want to overrule me in that room, in that meeting, that's okay, that's their prerogative. I'll walk out of the room and say we're going to play. I mean, I don't like it, but that's the way it is. I'm smart enough to know that's the way things should be done. Most times the Knoxes are very smart, they touch all the right bases. I don't know what happened that time.

Anyway, I sat on it for a couple of days. Then did something that maybe they should have fired me for, right there. I drove to Buffalo. The Auditorium is a municipal building, you know, with the Sabres only one of the tenants. I went in to see the man who handles bookings for the building.

"I want to rent the rink on January second and third, from 6 p.m. to 11.30 p.m. both days," I said.

Those were the only two days around that time when the Sabres would be free to play the Russians.

He was really surprised, and started to argue.

I insisted. "It's a public building. You have to rent it to me if it isn't being used that day."

Well, we worked it out. An agreement was drawn up, saying that I was going to present a concert on those two dates. I paid $100 down, and agreed to pay "12½ per cent of the gross receipts from all admissions sold, exclusive of tax, for each performance after deducting therefrom the minimum fee of $100 for each event, said payment to be made by certified cheque or in cash immediately following the event."

I got a receipt for my down payment, and a copy of the permit.

It was more than just me being stubborn. The Sabres had a five-day layoff in the schedule from December 31 to January 4. It's been my experience that such breaks often are essential to let injuries heal, and let healthy players rest. The next time I talked to Seymour was when he called me at St. Catharines. He mentioned the Russia game.

I said, "You can't play it, Seymour. I've got the building that day."

We had a fairly sizzling telephone conversation. He was insisting that the owners had the right to make the decision they had. I was saying that when any decision was made affecting the hockey team, I had to be consulted or my job was meaningless. After that conversation, I wrote him a letter dated September 28 in which I said, "I recognize the fact that you can, as owners, make a decision; but that decision" . . . I meant, when it affects hockey . . . "should be argued in my office or your office when we disagree. I find that my respect and integrity are at stake and I do not intend to jeopardize them. Therefore, if the Russian game is firmed up, you will have to find a new general manager."

Maybe they should have fired me then. A few days later – my diary says it was October 2 – Seymour and Norty came in to my office and we did talk about it. I told them my reasons. "After all," I said, "you've knocked hell out of the Russians already. Let them play everybody else. If they beat everybody else, let them come back and play us again. Then we'll be ready for them. Meanwhile, let's keep it that we're the only team that ever really clobbered them."

I also made the point that Gare had aggravated his bad back in another of those outside-the-league games, the Canada Cup of 1976. That had cost us a good player for half a year. "Suppose we got Perreault hurt, or somebody else, lose them for a few weeks – is that doing your fans any favour for what is anyway a no-win situation?"

That time, they accepted my view. It was a coincidence that on that very day, Gare had to go to hospital because his back was acting up again. Maybe I'm being selfish in my opposition to international games, television gimmicks like Showdown, or anything else that might, and quite often does, deprive home fans of a player they're counting on seeing when they lay out money for season tickets. From the personal standpoint, who can tell what the effect on me personally would have been if Gare had not been hurt in the Canada Cup of 1976? We might have got eight or ten more points a season, if he'd been a whole hockey player. Maybe his not being a whole hockey player helped cost me my job, eventually. Who can tell? But you can suspect.

To jump ahead a few years, try this one: In the Canada Cup of 1981 Gil Perreault broke his ankle and was out for about one-third of the season. As a result, Buffalo finished a few points behind Boston. That gave Boston the extra home game when those teams met in the playoffs of 1982. With that extra home game, Buffalo might have won the Stanley Cup – but didn't get that far at least partly because of Perreault's Canada Cup injury. One result was that Scotty Bowman's job as general manager and coach was put in jeopardy. So in the end it was Bowman who took the rap for the injury Perreault suffered. Eagleson, who arranges such series, has no one to answer to, of course.

But, back to the fall of 1978. When I look at the first twelve games that season and think that all I did was blow my top at one hockey player over one bad play, I am amazed at my self-control. In those twelve games we had three wins, five losses, four ties. And in the twelfth game, at home on November 9 against Pittsburgh, I blew up at Craig Ramsay.

Up until then, following the orders I had received when negotiating my contract, I had been going into the dressing room from time to time to make a point with individual players. Marcel knew what the situation was. I was trying not to tread on his toes and I think, in fact I'm sure, he did not resent it. He had gone out of his way to tell some reporters that our discussions helped him. He and I understood one another, and understood the problems each was facing.

Anyway, we're at home November 9 against Pittsburgh and it was a tight game. There was a face-off in our end, right in front of where I sat. I've always coached that when a team is on offense, has the puck, it's up to every player's skill and initiative, to use his brain to exploit situations as they come up (all while he's skating like hell, you hope). But when you're on defence there are certain things a player has to do, and he'd better do them. Ramsay was playing his left wing position right in front of me. His role, as soon as the puck was dropped, was to rush the point so that the guy there can't get a shot away. Ramsay didn't. The puck went back to the point where he should have been, the guy shoots, and it's in.

At the intermission I went to the dressing room and chewed out

Ramsay on that one play. He was furious. He didn't say a thing, but got up and slammed his stick against the wall.

I went in to Marcel and said to him, "Ramsay's the luckiest guy in the world that I'm not coaching this hockey club, because if I was he'd never see the ice again."

Of course, maybe I should have gone in and sat down beside him and said quietly, "Listen, Craig, old pal, about that play for the goal . . ." But that's not the kind of a guy I am. That's not the way hockey is. There's no time to treat everybody as if he's made of glass and might break. Anyway, I groused to Marcel but made it plain I was just letting him know; I was not telling him what he, as coach, should do. Besides, Ramsay knew as well as I did what he should have done – and that he hadn't done it.

But he isn't the kind of guy who lets a thing go by, either. We started the game again and I'll be a son of a bitch if a Pittsburgh guy doesn't take the puck away from Ramsay right in front of our net, and put it in. Then in the third period Ramsay scored a goal. As soon as it was in, he skated straight to the bench and sat down. No celebration, no nothing, just get off the ice and sit down.

I went in after the game, which we tied 4-4. I was still burning. Pronovost started to alibi for Ramsay. There were two or three other people around but I was mad, so I just said, "Marcel, I want to ask you one question – who scored the goal?"

"That defenceman."

"Who's check is he?"

"Ramsay's."

"That's it," I said. "No more to say."

I've mentioned before about the *Courier-Express* taking shots at me. Over the years a couple of their writers had broken down and told me that this was under orders from their editor, Doug Turner. The *Courier-Express* was the morning paper and not as strong as the *Buffalo Evening News*, so maybe that meant they had to try harder for sensationalism. The way it's done usually in sports is that a reporter starts using players, printing their beefs as if they're gospel, while neither the reporter nor the guy doing the beefing has the guts to name the source. As some of his colleagues wrote later, Warner Hessler of the *Courier-Express* was out to get me fired. He didn't do a bad job of it.

Three days after the incident with Ramsay in the Pittsburgh game, the Sunday *Courier-Express* carried a long Hessler story about what was wrong with the Sabres: me. A cartoon showed me and Marcel as a two-headed coach spanking a Sabre player. A lot of the quotes in the piece claimed that I had never stopped coaching (which is a bloody lie; I would have *liked* never to have stopped coaching, but had to) and that sometimes Pronovost told the players one thing and I told them another, then bawled them out for getting confused. Of course, none of the beefers were named. "A veteran player" said this and "another player" said that. No names, no pack drill, as they used to say in the army. But actually that was just the same old stuff. I had listened for years to the charge of interference, as if my forty years experience should be thrown out of the window just to please some newspaperman's stupid idea of what autonomy a coach was supposed to have. What really bugged me was right near the end of the piece where an unnamed player was quoted as saying, "The regular season is a drag. With eighty games you just try to survive until the playoffs. If you play hard every game, you'll be dead when playoffs come around." Hessler did remark that it didn't seem the players ever put that theory to the test, which was right because for the last three years the Sabres had been dead in the playoffs anyway. But the remark about the season being a drag made me see red. There we were, the owners and management, doing our best to sell the idea that hockey was the best, the fastest, the most of everything. For eighty games a season. Then some moron who is making his living off our selling job is saying that it is all a drag.

If I could have found that guy that day, he never would have put on a pair of skates in Buffalo again. We were playing Boston in Buffalo that night. We'd won in Washington the night before. I went into the dressing room and went around to all the players, one by one. I asked each if he had been talking to the *Courier-Express* and especially if he had made that statement about the regular season being a drag.

Did you say that, Ramsay? Did you say that, Gare? And so on. No one owned up.

"Well," I said, "if you can't show personal guts in a dressing room, how could anybody expect you to show it on the ice?"

However, I wasn't finished. To me, as bad as it was to have players saying things behind my back that they didn't have the guts to say to my face, or Marcel's face, the involvement of Warner Hessler and the *Courier-Express* was worse. He was making it possible for them to be cowards, the ones who needed any encouragement. Well, okay, his job is to report things as he sees them. I understand that, freedom of the press. But there was something a little different in this case.

Back in 1970, when the Sabres first came to Buffalo and Charley Barton was alive, we were coming up to our first road trip and I said, "Are you going to travel with us?"

"No," he said. "The office won't send me." I knew the paper was hard up, losing money, but in that opening year we really needed the coverage. We were competing with the Buffalo Bills in football and the Buffalo Braves in basketball. We were luckier than any expansion city I know in the United States in the quality of the two principal hockey writers in Buffalo, Dick Johnston of the *Evening News* and Charley Barton of the *Courier-Express*. I did not want to lose Charley's reporting on the road.

"If we pay your travel, hotel, and food, would they let you go?" I asked.

Well, he'd check. I don't even know whether all the higher-ups on the paper knew this was happening. If they didn't they were just turning a blind eye, because Charley was with us all the time and was never charging expenses to the paper.

After Charley died in 1972 and Jim Peters took over, and then Warner Hessler, the same system went on. I knew it wasn't really according to journalistic ethics. In fact, less than three months earlier there'd been a front-page story in the *Wall Street Journal* on the whole question of freebies for press people. Also, I'd found somewhere along the way some material from Sigma Delta Chi, the professional journalism fraternity, in which one line under ethics read: "Gifts, favors, free travel, special treatment, or privileges can compromise the integrity of journalists and their employers. Nothing of value should be accepted." The reason I'd been interested in such things was that some years before, during another phase of the *Courier-Express* anti-Imlach campaign, I'd written a letter to Doug Turner, the editor, withdrawing the freebies from his paper. But for some reason I changed my mind and didn't send it.

I simply decided now, however, that while Hessler had a perfect right and even an obligation to print what he thought was news, why should I pay for being dumped on when I could get it for nothing? Also, I was not going to hide behind any subtle sort of deep freeze, like saying nothing at all and starting to charge the paper for its writers' travel bills. Unlike some players I had with Buffalo at the time, I was willing to stand up and be counted.

I'm not a dumbbell. I knew what I was going to do was going to escalate things a bit. But also I thought maybe the *Courier-Express* would be so reluctant to admit in public about the handouts it had been taking all these years, that it would not make a big fuss. Anyway, why should it? I did not intend to bar Warner Hessler from anything, except that now he would have to make his own travel arrangements, instead of using my secretary to do so; and from now on the paper would have to pay his way.

I phoned him on the Monday morning, having taken the precaution of getting Paul Wieland and John Andersen in to listen to the phone call.

I told Hessler I was upset about what he had written and that the Sabres no longer would pay his travel and hotel bills. He said he had paid his hotel bill in Minnesota a week or so earlier. I didn't know that, but said it didn't matter much because his newspaper had been taking these expenses from the Sabres for eight years.

I told him that from now on he was not to ask my secretary to make his travel arrangements, as he had been doing. Also: "If you phone this office, I will not be available. If I run into you in the rink and you ask me a question pertaining to hockey, the answer will be, 'No comment.' " I said there was nothing personal about this, because I'd understood for years that *Courier-Express* writers had been encouraged to take shots at me, but I was no longer going to be the patsy by paying the bills.

You know, how a guy like this editor could justify the paper being on the take with one hand and firing dum dum bullets with the other is hard for me to understand. It must have occurred to him sometime that he'd be in a better position to criticize if his paper's own ethics were irreproachable.

Then came a major misunderstanding, one that caused more trouble than anything else. We had a game coming up in Toronto a couple of days later. When I was still steaming, I said something about not wanting Hessler on the player bus to Toronto. I did not tell Hessler this, but said it in front of Paul Wieland, the PR director. If the paper had called me to check, the misunderstanding might have been averted.

Instead, the paper called Dave Forman, our administrative vice-president, and said it wanted to clarify a couple of points. One, would Hessler be allowed on the team bus? Two, would he be allowed in the press box?

Because I had made the remark about the bus in front of Paul Wieland, the reply to the *Courier-Express* was that Hessler would not be allowed on the team bus. I might not have *wanted* him on the team bus, but that was not the same as barring him, even though some NHL clubs, including Toronto, do not let reporters travel with the team for the very reason that catching some players with their hair down can embarrass the team, and for what? So the writers who have some sense of proportion, respect for privacy and confidences, and honesty about putting names to quotes, have to suffer for what the other yo-yos do.

As to the other matter, the press box, of course there was no restriction there. I had only decided to stop paying the *Courier-Express's* way, not to bar it from normal news-gathering functions. I thought I had the right to refuse to talk to this one reporter, but that, plus the money side, was as far as it went.

Of course, this was a situation where they had me, to a certain extent. They pulled out all the stops. Some stories were ridiculous, like saying that poor Hessler now wouldn't be able to spend as much time with his wife and kiddies because he had to stop using team charters. But the funniest was Doug Turner, the paper's chief editorial officer, writing to Seymour Knox to say that my action was "just not major league." Them taking expense money for years was very major league of course.

I was amused by the *Courier-Express's* way of admitting it had been taking free travel and other favours from the hockey club for years. When it mentioned that *C-E* reporters had previously travelled with the team, it didn't add "at Sabres' expense" which would have been the direct way, but said "at no reimbursement to the Sabres," which seems to me considerably softer. A newspaper is fearless as hell when it's asking the questions, but when anybody dares to question it – look out! The crying towels are unequal to the crocodile tears.

I immediately got telephone calls and letters supporting my stand. Within a day or two several letters from paying customers started by saying, "Congratulations!" A note from John Andersen said that Max McNab, the Washington general manager, and Keith Allen, Philadelphia's general manager, called to say, "Good going." But they didn't have voting rights in Buffalo, of course.

I knew it wasn't going to blow over. Later in the week the players had a meeting. They asked the trainers to leave the room and although I can't verify this, I was told later that one of the events was a vote on whether somebody should go to the owners and have me disciplined, or fired. I was told that the vote was in my favour. Again, I can't verify that.

But on the Thursday of that week, I think it was, I came back to my office and found Marcel's office door closed and locked. I asked one of the office people, "Who?"

"Mr. Swados is in there with Marcel," he said.

Finally Swados came out. He said hello to me and then went on upstairs to the directors' room. Then Marcel came out, on his way down to the dressing room. He stopped in my doorway. Marcel – twenty years on defence in the NHL with Detroit and Toronto, Stanley Cups, all-star teams, a million stitches, and you can read it all on his face.

"I think I should let you know," he said to me, jerking his head at the departed Swados, "that guy is no friend of yours. Be careful of him."

Soon after, I was called into a directors' meeting. One club director was one of the *Courier-Express* owners, named Andrews. The idea was to put me on the grill. Andrews naturally took the side of his writer, telling me I had no business going into the dressing room, interfering with the hockey club, and that kind of thing.

I sat through it. I did not mention that I had been specifically requested to interfere more in the hockey club, including the dressing room if necessary. I was tempted to ask him what the hell he knew about the hockey business, and also to point out that maybe he should be spending more time interfering at his own paper and reducing the amount of money they were losing. But out of respect for the Knoxes, I didn't fire back. Once Dave Forman seemed about to say something, but I thought Norty Knox sort of nudged him, and he didn't. Finally, another director, Paul Schoellkopf, did give it to Andrews about the paper taking all that travel and expense money, and shut him up.

In the end, I agreed to have the club issue my statement that "the only thing I told the reporter was that in future he would have to make his own travel arrangements and pay his own way, and everything else stays the same." The statement was conciliatory to a certain extent. I agreed to it only on the understanding that the paper would admit it had been doing wrong to accept favours from us in the past. That admission was not made, so they really got my statement for nothing.

By the time these meetings had been held, and the statement issued, it was five days after Hessler's original Sunday story. For the next couple of weeks things went on as before, bringing us to a pair of weekend games against the Canadiens – Saturday in Montreal and Sunday in Buffalo. After the blowup over Hessler, we had tied Toronto, beaten St. Louis, Detroit and Minnesota, lost to Philadelphia and Boston, beaten Colorado, and lost to Boston – four wins, three losses, and a tie in eight games.

In Montreal on Saturday night, December 2, we were beaten badly, 8-1. During that game a strange thing happened. WGR-TV's cameras came and focused on me. I wondered why. It didn't take long to find out. Ed Kilgore, the station's sports director and intermission host, used the film of me during the game and said that my job was on the line. Unless we won tonight and tomorrow night I would be fired. My wife, watching the game on television, was badly upset as were other people – including me, when I heard about it before the game was over. In the airport I blew up at Kilgore.

"How come you are saying that I'm going to be fired?" I demanded. "If anyone is going to fire me it will be Seymour Knox, not you on television." I was really hot, yelling at him. Everyone around could hear. On the aircraft, Seymour came and sat with me for a while. I said, "Look, if you let the newspapers or television run this thing, or the players run this thing, you are making a big mistake. I've told you that a hundred times and I'm telling it to you again. It's up to you."

The next day my wife was still very upset. She hadn't been feeling well anyway. She decided she couldn't face going to the game. I went to the Aud. about four o'clock as usual. Montreal beat us 4-1. The next morning I told my wife that we'd drive to Toronto after the practice that morning, and to pick me up at the rink at 12.30. I kept a dentist appointment to have some root canal work finished, then went to the office in mid-morning.

When I walked in, one of the receptionists said, "Mr. Knox wants to see you upstairs in his office."

I said okay, did a couple of things, and then went up. He said hello and closed the door. After a minute or two he said, "You've lost control of the dressing room."

I said, "What's that got to do with it?"

He said that, well, things weren't going very well. I told him some of the problems – like, I'd had a battle with Jim Schoenfeld before we went to Montreal. He was out with an injury, but had been practising. After the practice he'd got to fooling around with another player, Ron Areshenkoff, and had separated Areshenkoff's shoulder. I'd told Schoenfeld if he was strong enough to wrestle with another guy and put his shoulder out, he was strong enough to be playing.

Knox was listening, but at the end he said, "But you've lost control of the dressing room."

And finally I got it. I stopped dead and looked at him. "Are you telling me that I'm fired?"

"Yes," he said. "How would you like to handle it? Would you like to resign?"

I said, "Are you kidding? You're going to have to fire me. If you've got the guts to fire me, okay, that's all there is to it."

"I've got the guts," he said.

I got up. "Okay, that takes care of it." I was walking out of the room when I turned around and said, "I wonder where that television announcer got the story about me being fired?"

"I don't know."

"There's only two damn people knew – you and him, apparently." And I kept going. I was very upset, of course. I went downstairs to see Marcel. He was still on the ice with the practice. I told Frank Christie, the trainer, that I'd been fired and wanted Marcel to know about it, because I'd be leaving right away and didn't want to leave without him knowing. I then went to my office for some things. When Marcel was told, he informed the players and then got a message that he was wanted in Knox's office, too. On his way up from the dressing room he found that I was still in my office.

"What do you want me to do?" he asked.

"What do you mean?"

"Do you want me to quit, or what?"

I said, "Are you crazy? Look, they've fired me. I expect you and everyone else to go on and do the job, that's all there is to it. I appreciate what you're saying, but you just do what you have to."

I heard later that Paul Wieland had been around a few minutes earlier when Marcel was talking about me being fired, and what a shame it was, and so on. Wieland was in a very bad position. He knew that Marcel was going to get the axe, too, but couldn't say anything about it. Marcel described his meeting with Knox as taking only about two minutes, with no rancour, no argument, just that he was fired. I have to give Marcel marks, offering to quit – before he knew he was being fired, too. If I'd been vindictive, I could have said, "Sure, quit." That at least would have taken a little away from them firing him.

Marcel told me later that after he was fired, he went down to the dressing room, let the team know and then walked a few feet into the medical room with a cup of coffee. Schoenfeld followed him in and said, "I didn't think it would go that far," I guess a reference to the players' indignation meetings. And someone told me that Perreault said, "Now you see what you guys have done." But it didn't change anything.

I'd been hoping to get out of the Aud. before I had to cope with reporters. I didn't make it. I had to talk to them. Dodo was waiting in the car. Finally I got in and we drove back to Toronto. I got her to drop me downtown. When she got home a young reporter was waiting, one with a heart – said he was sorry to bother her, he could see she was upset. Unusual.

In the press coverage immediately after, a lot of ink was given to the fact that I had built the team and had been treated badly in the way I was fired. I felt that way, too, but more than my own troubles, I regretted that I had been unable to bring Buffalo fans, and owners, too, the Stanley Cup that they maybe deserved – and would have got, I'll always be sure, if we'd had the best goalkeeping in that 1975 final.

I suppose there will remain a certain amount of mystery about what led up to my firing. I heard that a group of players had gone to see Seymour Knox and told him they wouldn't play for me anymore. I was told that this group included Craig Ramsay, the team's player representative, Danny Gare, and Jim Schoenfeld. I was also told that they wanted Gilbert Perreault to go with them, but he refused. When we were trying to get the exact details in the spring of 1982 to make this account entirely factual, Seymour Knox agreed to answer some questions. One was with regard to a statement that had been made by Alan Eagleson, executive director of the NHL Players Association, that the Sabres unanimously had gone to see Seymour Knox and demanded that I be replaced.

Knox: "That is absolutely untrue."

He wasn't anywhere near as definite in his response to questions about my so-called "losing control of the dressing room." To start with, he didn't recall specifically telling me to get more involved in the dressing room. That seems strange, to fire me for losing control in a place I would never have been, without his instructions at contract time. I was also curious about where his information came from that I had lost control of the dressing room. Had to come *from* the dressing room, right? When asked to verify my understanding that the final torpedo party had been Ramsay, Schoenfeld, and Gare, Knox said that was "partially but not entirely true." Later he did say that Schoenfeld was not part of the group. He wouldn't narrow it down farther than that. Knox also insisted that as far as he was concerned, Ed Kilgore had just been guessing when he put the TV cameras on me thirty-six hours before I was fired and said it was going to happen.

"Nobody knew but me," Knox said. "I didn't know it myself until hours after the Sunday game. The only other person who knew was my wife, because I was up until 3 or 4 a.m. agonizing over it."

One other thing we asked Seymour to comment on was the work of a group of sports psychologists called Team Management Consultants – Edmund J. Freeberg, U. Phillip Daniels, and Allan Turowitz – who had approached me in June of 1978 with a proposal that they interview some players and other team personnel during the season to see if they could improve the cohesiveness of the talents we had. Their tryout for the job, as it were, was a week of interviewing a few players as well as Marcel and me at training camp. Their preliminary findings (boiled down considerably) were that there was an absence of team cohesion; a high proportion of underassertive players; an absence of leadership skills in the players; "surprisingly strong evidence" of lack of self-confidence; a serious lack in inter-player communication; on both sides a desire for, but lack of, player-management communication; some "readily apparent" interpersonal difficulties; a serious motivation problem; and a few other things.

On the last day I worked for the Buffalo Sabres, Seymour told me to let the psychologists know that they could go ahead with their main program. So I phoned them.

The next day I was gone.

When I see those guys now I kid them, "Jeez, it didn't take you long to get me fired."

I also think it's worth mentioning that in the last four seasons I was with the Sabres we finished tied for first in 1975, with 113 points; were fourth in the league with 105 in 1976, fifth in 1977 with 104, tied for fourth in 1978 with 105. The year I was fired they dropped to seventh in the league with eighty-eight points and were knocked out in the preliminary round of the playoffs even faster than usual.

I got a lot of letters in the next few days. One was from Don Edwards, my goalie, "to thank you for everything you've added to my hockey knowledge," and to say that he would "truly miss" my "dedication and devotion to the game plus the inspirational leadership ability." He'd never forget that, he said, and "would be more than happy to have the opportunity to play under you again."

That, to me, is worth framing.

There were others from fans and one from Roger Crozier, by then with the Washington Capitals, saying he'd always been proud to have played for me and known me as a friend. Maybe I shouldn't quote some of the other nice things said, so I won't. I also had letters from Norty Knox, Dave Forman and Seymour Knox. Norty wrote, "You made the Buffalo Sabres' franchise . . . all of us here will be forever grateful to you." Seymour wrote me a longer letter talking about "thrills and excitement that will never be forgotten" and that "I hope you will think back upon your years here in Buffalo as being pleasant ones."

Which I will. Apart from the end, I was happy, often laughing at the crazy fights I got into, the crazy things that happened. Somehow I let the team slip away from its purpose in life, which was to win. One little record I kept was that over one stretch of 155 games from late in 1976 to late in 1978, the team never once had gone into a third period losing, and had come from behind to win. Never once. That tells you a lot.

I hope I'll be forgiven for quoting one more thing, a column written by *Buffalo Evening News* sports editor Milt Joffe, in which he said that in firing me and Marcel, Seymour Knox "had dismissed the guards and turned the asylum over to the inmates."

CHAPTER THIRTEEN

Back to the Leafs, with problems

As many a coach and general manager knows, being totally involved and fully in charge of a hockey club one day and barred from the premises the next takes some getting used to. Dodo and I drove home to Toronto through the early winter afternoon. She was badly upset in a different way than I was. We both go into things heart and soul, but let's say she has a more idealistic opinion of hockey players than I do. That some of her favourites had helped torpedo Marcel and me was hard for her to take. She wrote a letter to Danny Gare a day or two later pouring out her mixture of anger and disillusionment – "How could you?" But she showed it to me and I didn't think she should send it. That letter and others she wrote from time to time but didn't post, were her way of getting rid of frustration. But we've been through a lot together and by the time we got home to Scarborough, the home we'd bought when our kids Brent and Marlene were small, we could smile when Brent, born in another hockey town, Quebec, more than thirty years before, looked on the bright side. "Oh, well, we can all be together to take Mom out on her birthday" (only a few days away). Then he went out and as a Christmas surprise, put together on videotape big moments from the four Stanley Cups I'd won. Oddly enough, I've never played it. Maybe because of the emotion I would feel. But I know it's there. A reminder.

I hadn't signed the Buffalo contract we'd negotiated a few months earlier, but that didn't bother me in regard to the Knoxes. We had agreed verbally, which was good enough. A few weeks later I talked to the Buffalo people again to settle the details. They would continue paying my full salary for another year and a half unless I took another hockey job. If that happened, they'd still pay me half. In addition, hockey had been good to me and investments had helped make my financial situation solid enough.

Months went by before I stopped referring to the Buffalo Sabres, from long habit, as "we" or even "I." When the move from our Buffalo apartment had been tidied up we went to Florida for a while. Then I didn't want to be around during the playoffs, so we made a leisurely and relaxing spring trip to Paris and London and to find some relatives I'd never seen in Scotland. My Dad and Mother were both from Fraserborough in the north of Scotland but had been gone from there for nearly seventy years. Coming back to Toronto late in May 1979, I knew I was ready to start thinking about what I would do next, and the Leaf job came up.

To illustrate my feelings about the kind of team the Leafs had at that time, here's something that had happened a little more than a year earlier. I was still in Buffalo in March, 1978, when the Leafs made an unbelievable trade with Detroit. The best chance any club has to improve over the long-term is through the amateur draft (as I had proved in Buffalo, Bill Torrey had proved with the New York Islanders, and the Winnipeg Jets and Edmonton later proved). The Leafs traded not one but *two* first-round draft choices (1978 and 1980), plus a 1978 second-round choice, plus one of the team's few real skaters and scorers, Errol Thompson, to Detroit for Dan Maloney and a 1980 second-round choice.

I have nothing against Dan Maloney personally. I had appeared as a witness on his behalf when he was charged with assault after a fight in a Toronto game when he was with Detroit. But when the trade was made, I couldn't believe it. Next time I saw King Clancy I said, "What the hell are you trying to do over there?"

"What do you mean?"

"Who wins the Stanley Cup?"

"Montreal Canadiens."

"All right! If you want to beat the Montreal Canadiens for the Stanley Cup you have to have a team that can skate with them, not a bunch of plodders and grinders. Two first-round draft choices and a skater for Maloney! You know what that can mean for the Leafs in the future – missing good kids in the draft who might put them back on the rails again?"

Well, Clancy said they needed a tough guy, etc., etc. I just listened, wishing somebody would play Santa Claus to me in a deal like that. I heard later that the deal had been set up by Jim

Gregory, general manager at the time, because Harold Ballard, whose word is law around the Gardens, had said that the Leafs needed "someone like Dan Maloney." It's my understanding that the Leafs' captain, Darryl Sittler, had a hand in it, too. He and Maloney were friends from the time they played junior in London.

Let me indicate what the Leafs gave up to get Maloney. In 1978 they could have picked up any of these players – Larry Playfair, Al Secord (forty-four goals for Chicago in 1981-82), Keith Acton (thirty-six goals from Montreal 1981-82), Anton Stastny, or Tony McKegney. In 1980 those available to the Leafs would have included Brent Sutter who went to the Islanders, or Barry Pederson (forty-four goals for Boston in 1981-82). Any of those would have made the Leafs stronger today. Of course, at the time it was no skin off my nose. I didn't know that the loss of those draft choices was going to make my own life harder, before long.

I said in the first line of this book that the worst three years of my life in hockey began when Clancy phoned me on June 8, 1979, about returning to the Leafs. The time has come to document that statement.

At that time I had no quarrel with Darryl Sittler, Harold Ballard, Mike Palmateer, or anybody else. I was being asked to do a job I had done before: produce a good hockey team. I thought that at the end of my three-year contract I would hand over to my successor a contender for the Stanley Cup. They wouldn't necessarily win the Stanley Cup in three years but they would be competitive – and maybe they *would* win. One thing I knew for damn sure was that the team as it was in 1979 could not win the Stanley Cup, ever.

At the press conference on July 4 I spelled it out. I said that the reason the Leafs hadn't been getting anywhere in the last few seasons was lack of talent. I said the five or six good hockey players on the team were not enough to win the Stanley Cup. The only way to improve would be to buy players – it isn't easy to get good ones – or to make trades or get good young players in the draft. I said I didn't expect any interference from Ballard. "I run the hockey club," I said. "I take suggestions from anyone but that doesn't mean I go along with them. If I get into trouble, which I certainly expect to do, I expect Harold to back me."

Now, there were two ways the Leaf players could have taken that. They could have said, "We're going to show that s.o.b. that we are a good hockey team." Individuals could have said to themselves, "If I want to stay with the Leafs I'm going to have to dig deeper and make that s.o.b. want to keep me." I would have been happy if that had happened, but I knew that something else had to happen first – and it was something I didn't mention at the press conference, because I didn't want to spoil the chance that there might be a change.

In hockey, you hear things. Players talk to players and the word gets around. I knew that there was something like a country club atmosphere around the Leafs that had to be changed. They were a close-knit group with Sittler as leader. He hadn't led them anywhere, but nobody seemed to realize that. He was the focal point and the players practically ran their own show. If they'd been contenders, being close-knit would have been great. But they were a solid ninth-place team made up mainly of plodders and grinders, not skaters. A team like that will win a few, but not the big ones against teams that can outskate them. The Leafs had proved that. They were proud of having upset the New York Islanders in the quarter-finals of 1977, but instead of going up, by 1979 they had gone down. And were going farther down if they weren't improved. I always say, if you can't skate, you can't play successfully in the game today. Even the skaters they had weren't being played much, or given a chance.

Aside from that part about the country club atmosphere, I said what I thought at the press conference. There was no use saying everything was beautiful when it wasn't. Sittler later said in an interview that obviously I had made up my mind before I even talked to some of the players I was going to move out. He was right. I didn't have to talk to them. I had seen them play. Really good teams like Buffalo or the Canadiens or Islanders can afford to carry a couple of bad skaters, because they can do other things, but no good team can afford more. I didn't have one thing against players like Pat Boutette, a tough, hard-working kid, or Jimmy Jones, and others who would have to go, but I knew they had to be replaced with better players before the Leafs could challenge for the Stanley Cup.

My contract called for me to start work on August 1, but I really started the day after the press conference. Many people in the Gardens take holidays in July, so the place was quiet. I sat there for the whole month reading files, going over contracts and figuring out where my draft choices were. What I found shook me. I was jumping. I saw Sittler with a supposedly no-trade contract; Ron Ellis with a no-cut; and a lot of other things in which Harold and Jim Gregory simply had given up their right to manage. There was no depth. The farm system, in total, was a half-share of the Moncton franchise in the American Hockey League. The players we had there included only four who had any chance to make the big team, meaning that in training camp a few weeks away there would be no real jump for jobs. That's bad enough with a good team. It's murder for a mediocre one. I found also that Mike Palmateer, the goalie, was coming into his option year at a fairly low rate of pay. He deserved a lot more and would get an offer from me of about three times what he was making, but I had an inkling that this was going to mean trouble.

Ian Turnbull was the next problem. As a rushing defenceman, he was one of the best of the Leafs on sheer talent, no doubt about that. He was very friendly to me, those first couple of months. He had a restaurant down the street from the Gardens. After he'd cleaned out the lunchtime crowd he'd come up and talk. His contract had been more than half negotiated before I signed, which tied my hands. They had agreed to give him a five-year deal, which I never would have done. I tried to get that down, but couldn't. His pay had been agreed upon. So we were talking mainly about bonuses. He told me he'd been promised some kind of a signing bonus, or a retroactive payment which amounted to the same thing, of about $50,000 or close. There was nothing on paper about it. I went in to Harold and asked him. He wasn't really sure, either, but he said, "If we owe it to him, pay him." That was the way he was.

There is one thing about Turnbull I should mention because it bears on later events. During our meetings that summer, maybe ten or fifteen of them, he seemed to enjoy talking about hockey to me. Once he said something like, "You'll be seeing me. I'll be in to talk from time to time." But it never happened. Once that contract was signed – zilch.

I didn't realize for quite a while what was happening: that any player who was known to talk to me automatically became *persona non grata* in the dressing room. Carl Brewer laid that out clearly in a court case three years later when he was claiming that his pay cheques had been short about $8,000 in the first few weeks he spent with the Leafs. The judge asked him why he had not gone to me immediately to get it straightened out. Brewer replied, under oath, that to talk to me at all would have destroyed his chances of acceptance by the other players in the dressing room and on the ice. Sittler and others used to spout to the press about lack of communication. Now you know at least part of the reason.

Still, in the summer it didn't really bother me much. The players were off enjoying their last weeks before the start of training and I was busy enough. I signed Floyd Smith to rejoin me as coach and started putting other parts of my organization together. Dick Duff agreed to come in as Smitty's assistant coach. He'd won five Stanley Cups and knew what it took (a lot of good it did him, with this bunch). Johnny McLellan agreed to stay on as assistant general manager. The veteran chief scout and Leafs player from earlier days, Bob Davidson, had been retired – a bad move by Harold, I thought. For one thing, it meant our going into the amateur draft, which was in August that year, without the advice Bob's experience could have added to that of the other scouts, Johnny Bower and Gerry McNamara.

That was the year the four WHA teams joined the NHL. The draft was held late because details of who was entitled to what had to be worked out. Anyway, I was playing catch-up on the scouting and groaning over our lack of draft choices. We needed more depth everywhere but especially at centre. There we had Jimmy Jones who could check but couldn't score and wasn't fast enough; Paul Gardner who could score but wasn't fast enough; Walt McKechnie who could do a lot of things fairly well, except skate fast; and Sittler, who could score but wasn't quite as fast as he had been, and had some bad habits, like giving away the puck too often and frequently being caught out of the play when he went in too deep. If we had been doing player assessments, I'm pretty sure that most of them would have concerned improving a lot at centre.

When our first choice came, one player available was Laurie Boschman, who'd played junior with Brandon, centring a line with Brian Propp and Ray Allison on the wings.

Even though Boschman was a centre, I said, "Propp got all the goals. I think we should go with the goal scorers." But the scouts said Boschman did all the work and was the smart one on the line. I'd been in that situation in Buffalo once, picking a kid named Claude Deziel who had scored a lot in junior on a line centred by

Pierre Larouche. Later, Deziel never played in the NHL. Larouche did, and scored plenty. So when the Leaf scouts told me Boschman was the guy who made the line work, I had to think of Larouche. "Can he skate?" I asked.

"Good skater," they said.

So that's how Boschman was taken, and when you figure Propp got thirty-four goals that season for Philadelphia and Boschman sixteen for the Leafs, maybe we were wrong in that choice.

One other thing made a bad impression on me about the Toronto organization. Mark Messier was in that draft, then only eighteen years old. I was interested in Messier. The scouts told me he wasn't available. He'd played with Cincinnati in the WHA. I took their word for it. I didn't have a second-round draft choice that year anyway, didn't have another pick until fifty-first overall (when I took Normand Aubin), but on the forty-eighth pick Edmonton took Messier. It turned out he'd been available all the time! Now, with scouts I've always told them to live and die on their judgments; speak up loud and clear for what they believe, when choices are being made. Right or wrong, call it according to your judgment. But that word I got on Messier was not a judgment call. That was a mistake, and could have been a bad mistake. If I'd had a choice while Messier was still available, and hadn't taken him, then saw him go to Edmonton, I would have flipped. The kid scored fifty goals in the 1981-82 season, during which he turned twenty-one.

CHAPTER FOURTEEN

Life with Darryl when he wore the captain's C

No doubt about it, I would have preferred not to have to fight Darryl Sittler. He was a hard guy to fight. He had this great public image. Partly that was due to his reputation for leadership in a city where nobody said, "Yeah, but where has he led them?" Partly it was due to his appearance, his manner, the family-man sincerity of the guy. He was a good goal scorer, but the public and media did not understand the inside hockey part of it, that no team should be harnessed to one player the way the Leafs were harnessed to Sittler. The Canadiens were never harnessed to Jean Beliveau, Philly to Bobby Clarke, the Islanders to Bryan Trottier. And Sittler's image was also one of loyalty. I rather envied that. I wished he could have been loyal to me in my attempts to make the team better, or to Harold Ballard, or to the general good of the Leafs, rather than to the NHL Players Association, Alan Eagleson, and to those Leaf players who never, in a million years, were going to win the Stanley Cup.

Our differences eventually led Sittler to say that the trouble with the Leafs was Punch Imlach. I say that the trouble with the Leafs was that, with Sittler's leadership and Eagleson's backing, the Leafs did not want anyone to manage them. They liked things the way they were. My job was to change the team as quickly as possible into a Stanley Cup contender. This inevitably meant improving on what we had, which in turn meant breaking up their tight little group.

Maybe it would have helped people understand what was going on if I had shot back publicly at the players at the time they were shooting at me. But I hadn't done that in Buffalo and I wasn't going to do it in Toronto. If a player is on my hockey team I'm slitting my own throat if I cut him down in public. I might win the short-term argument but damage the man's usefulness to the team and, in the long run, his value as a hockey property I might trade for something better. So my method was to say nothing, to refuse to respond publicly to the things they said about me. I only mention that to explain why I will give background now that I didn't give at the time. And I challenge anyone to come up with a direct quote in which I spoke disparagingly about Sittler for publication as long as we were both with the Leafs.

I had only been in the job a few weeks when there was an opportunity to see exactly where Sittler's loyalty lay. In Buffalo I'd had trouble with the hockey television show called *Showdown*, because once a year, like clockwork, *Showdown* moved in on my right to manage. The producers did not call me and discuss which Buffalo players should appear on the show. Instead, there would be virtually an order from *Showdown* to the Buffalo trainer: "Send so-and-so's equipment to Toronto on such-and-such a date." Maybe I did not agree with the choice of player. Maybe sending one guy would upset another, which meant problems for the team. Once when *Showdown* wanted Perreault, Rick Martin was the guy who was doing all the scoring and might have felt slighted. Why should I help foster internal jealousy?

But that was not the main issue. There were many opportunities for injury in the *Showdown* taping. Rogie Vachon had been hurt once. In 1978's *Showdown*, Borje Salming of the Leafs had broken a finger. As Ballard pointed out (in a news report that Seymour Knox agreed with and circulated to the management group in Buffalo), "I've got a million dollars invested in a guy like Salming. He goes out and gets injured before training camp even opens. It could have been his leg." He said he'd never let another Leaf take part, a statement that was a definite factor the following season, when I had to handle the problem.

Even though the league had agreed to the deal with *Showdown* which brought money to the league and to the Players Association but not to the club, Ballard had voted against it. His argument was that the standard player contract gave the club the right to refuse to allow the club logo to be used, or a player to play hockey outside of the club. It was, quite simply, a property right and had to have Ballard's okay before it could become a league right. Anyway, in August of 1979 when *Showdown* asked for Darryl Sittler and Mike Palmateer, Ballard and I fought it.

In Buffalo, when I objected to a *Showdown* choice, I had simply called in the player and put it to him that the club was against it. These players included Gil Perreault and Danny Gare, at various times. In Gare's case, he still had not fully recovered from the back injury he'd suffered in another non-club competition, the Canada Cup of 1976. Anyway, both Gare and Perreault had seen the club's point of view, and complied. They might not have agreed but were loyal to the club first.

With the Leafs it was different. I called in Sittler. Of course, he had rather a conflict of interest. As vice-president of the Players Association, which supported *Showdown* because it brought in money, he had one loyalty. As the Leafs captain, he should have had another.

I told him my feelings, that the owners had certain rights and didn't want to get star players hurt playing a TV program. For instance, I told Sittler, I would have let Paul Gardner go. They're selling something, I said, while I'm trying to keep things as risk-free as possible at the club level. We were paying the bills and if any Leaf star was going to be injured it should be in a game played for our fans. *Showdown* doesn't give a damn what a fan pays to see a player who isn't there because he was injured in *Showdown*. That's my outlook and I put it to Sittler that way.

He said he couldn't accept that position. We had a fairly heated discussion and neither of us budged. Finally he said, "We're going to go."

"You're challenging management, that's all there is to it."

Then he said something a little strange. "The rest of the team is just waiting to see what I'm going to do. So I have to do it."

Lovely. He's saying he has to show other players that the wishes of the owner who pays their salaries don't really count. Palmateer came in later. He had the same party line.

I discussed it with Ballard. I mentioned that Sittler's insistence had something to do with not wanting to look as if he were backing down to us. But I didn't think he was totally happy with his position. If my impression was right, there was one way out worth considering. "We might be able to get a court injunction against them," I said. "If we win, he's off the hook. Nobody can say that he backed down to management if he's backing down to a court order. If we lose the case, the guy's off the hook, too, because then he's got the right to go."

So we went for the injunction, and lost. The media twisted the situation to make Ballard and me look bad because we took it to court for a ruling. The only reason for taking this action was to get Sittler off the hook.

The next order of battle was over club rules. In the NHL every club is supposed to post rules in its dressing room at the beginning of the season. These may cover dress regulations, fines for various infractions, and so on. The players are supposed to sign, to show they accept. I had a look at the rules we'd been using for years in Buffalo, always signed by a team that was a hell of a lot better than these Leafs. I had them typed up and told Floyd Smith, our coach, to post them on the first day of training camp before doing anything else.

The first mistake was that he didn't do it. It was the same old story. Smitty is easy-going. As a new coach coming in, he didn't want to risk starting a fight. Then when he did put the rules up, the players objected. Good enough for Buffalo, but not good enough for the Leafs.

One rule was the real stickler, Sittler said later in a radio interview. It was right at the bottom, intended to cover everything not specified in the previous ones. It read something like this: "Anyone who does anything that is contrary to good hockey discipline may be fined or suspended."

They felt that wording was much too loose and would allow fines or suspensions for anything we didn't like. Sure it was loose. On purpose. As I said when somebody brought it up, "Do you want me to put in there that if you get caught with some broad in your room, you're going to be fined or suspended? Or you get caught drunk driving, or whatever – is that what I have to spell out in the rules?" They wouldn't sign, but if it came to a fine point, they had a right to take anything to arbitration. I could only think that not signing was just part of the general down-with-Imlach attitude.

So we started the season and within three weeks I took a really terrible blow. Johnny McLellan, my longtime friend and one of the best people I've ever met, was the kind of assistant that every NHL general manager yearns for – good hockey man, honest, quiet sense of humour, a peacemaker wherever he went. On the Leafs' first trip to the west coast late in October we played in Colorado on a Friday night and flew to Los Angeles next day. That afternoon I got a message at our hotel. Johnny had been out cutting his lawn, on the kind of day he liked, home with his family, when he had been stricken and died from a heart attack. It was a tragedy not only for his family, but for the Leafs, to lose a man of his calibre. From then on the problems grew instead of diminishing. I know Johnny would have helped head many off. I flew back for his funeral. When I extended my condolences to John's wife she said, "You're going to miss your most important employee." And I agreed with her.

But the season, of course, went on – as it does no matter which of us dies. Hartford came in, one of the weaker teams taken in from the WHA, and beat us 4-2 with Dave Keon, thirty-nine, and Gordie Howe, fifty-one, getting goals. We went back to Hartford and lost again. The first time Buffalo came in, I went into the dressing room and used my knowledge of the Buffalo team to tell the Leafs of weaknesses they might take advantage of. Smitty was told later by a Buffalo friend that before the game, Sittler told Danny Gare right out on the ice that I had cut up Buffalo in our dressing room. Naturally that wouldn't hurt Buffalo's motivation at all, at all. They beat us 4-3. At the time, in our last six games we had lost five to teams that were no hell, except Buffalo, and tied one with Colorado. One point out of twelve, we'd got.

About that time I was asked to a private club in Toronto, the Albany Club, for dinner followed by a question-and-answer session.

"Would you trade Sittler for Bobby Clarke of Philadelphia?" one man asked.

I said sure. "Clarke has won two Stanley Cups. What has the other guy done? I would trade Sittler for any all-star."

The questions and anwers were supposed to be private, but that was going to come back to haunt me. Still, it was a plain fact. True.

With things going so badly, I asked Smitty to do something we had used to good advantage in Toronto when we were winning Stanley Cups and in Buffalo when we were coming close. We had scored only sixteen goals in our last six games, giving up thirty. Obviously, any possible improvement was worth trying. So we set up straight lines on the ice six feet from and parallel to the boards. These lines ran to six feet inside each blueline, and then diagonally to the far goal posts. Used intelligently, the lines indicated to the wingman what his position was in the up-and-down game, and also told him exactly how far he could penetrate and still get a shot away that could hit the goal. If he'd gone too deep, he could pass. It helped the goalies, too, by showing exactly where they had to stand to block a shot from that angle.

But this bunch of bastards knew everything. You couldn't tell them anything. They made jokes about the lines; and how if you went over one you'd get your wrist slapped, and so on. One point out of a possible twelve, and they wouldn't take coaching that *good* teams had found useful.

One day Smitty finally put his foot down in the dressing room, at least a little. He went in there a few minutes before a game and found some guys playing ping-pong! He ordered the ping-pong table taken out. Of course, the newspapers and the public had a lot of fun with that – but we didn't point out *why* it had been taken out. If we had, maybe even some of the yo-yos reporting on the Leafs might have gotten the point.

Then came one of the most misunderstood things of all. After that bad stretch, we went on a road trip. In St. Louis I was on the radio. The guy asked me if I thought Sittler had lost a step in his skating. I replied, "If he has lost a step . . ." but apparently I didn't say the "if" loud enough. It got to the papers that I had said Sittler had lost a step, was slowing down. We beat St. Louis. The fuss over what I was supposed to have said was raging when we got to Winnipeg. Everybody interviewed Sittler. Sittler said later that he just answered the questions calmly, but the net effect was the impression that I was hurting the team by knocking people. Team rapport had been good with Jim Gregory, Roger Neilson, and Red Kelly, but with Imlach – "I haven't had any communication with him." It got blown up in the papers. I said nothing but Ballard did. "If Sittler thinks he's going to run this hockey club he's got another think coming," he said in Winnipeg. "He wants us to hand him an all-day sucker every time he goes on the ice."

That night in Winnipeg the *Hockey Night in Canada* people

asked Sittler to appear on the intermission show. By league rules a club has the right to okay who goes on television. That had gone for me in Toronto and Buffalo, and for general managers everywhere else. Naturally if there's a controversy going on, the television people want to get in on it – might help to wake people up after watching *Showdown*.

I told Smitty to tell Sittler he was not going on television. He then was upset. No wonder. I'd found out that in the last few years, he'd been the one who okayed which Leafs went on TV! Actually, I can't blame Sittler for that. Leaf management had let him do it. As it was explained to me, sometimes players had been difficult about going on. The TV people would go to Jim Gregory and say they were having trouble getting players. And Gregory would say, "Well, go and discuss it with the captain." Soon Sittler was the gun on who went on TV.

But in Winnipeg, this time after I banned Sittler from TV, unfortunately Smitty was too easy-going. Instead of just telling Sittler he wasn't going on TV, he said something about letting him off the hook, letting the controversy cool a little.

Sittler said he didn't want to be let off the hook. Naturally. Might cool out the anti-Imlach publicity.

So then Sittler had to be told straight that I had told Ralph Mellanby, the executive producer of the intermission shows, "No Sittler."

More fun for the media, but I didn't let him on TV for months after that. Why should I, when he was going to go on and blast Leaf management? The other result was that that first time, in Winnipeg, my ban made the Leafs madder at me. Reporters told me that and asked me to comment. I just told them, "If the players are mad, let them prove me wrong by going out and winning a lot of hockey games." They did – went out and beat Winnipeg, on to Edmonton for another win, and back to Toronto for their fourth in a row. I think it was their best win streak of that year.

It was around then that a player's quote was printed which at first I misunderstood: "If we keep on trying, we'll win in the end." I thought, that's the spirit, that's pretty good, maybe I'm getting through to them.

But in the next month, no matter what the hell I tried to do, they challenged me. For a while I just bit my tongue. Then it finally got through to me that when they said, "If we keep on trying, we'll win in the end," they meant that *I* was the opposition, not the other teams. I was the one they were going to beat.

So I said to myself: I better start moving these guys and get it over with. This way I'm not going anywhere.

My philosophy in a bad hockey situation is simple. If you do something, there's a 50 per cent chance you'll be right, the same that you'll be wrong. If you do nothing, you're always wrong, because then nothing happens.

I believe in making things happen. If I make ten trades and six are good, the hockey club is improved. Of course, if seven are bad, you're out of a job. So I put the whole team on waivers. That meant every club in the league was informed by league head-quarters that any Leaf player might be available. But I made the waivers recallable. If I got a bite, I could withdraw that player from waivers and see what I could get from the club interested in him. It's an inside form of advertising. I did hear from a few general managers and got some talks going, but nothing immediate. At first I was just hacking around the fringes. The first deal that turned up didn't even involve a Leaf player. In the absorption of the WHA I'd got Reg Thomas from Edmonton on a complicated deal. If he played forty games in the NHL I had to give Edmonton a third-round draft choice. If he played less, I'd give them a sixth-round choice. This seemed pretty safe to me because we were plan-ning to send him to New Brunswick and not use him in the NHL. But he'd been a thirty-two goal scorer with Cincinnati in the WHA the previous season, and in a couple of months had scored twenty for New Brunswick, making the Quebec Nordiques take notice. On December 13 I traded him to Quebec for Dave Farrish and Terry Martin. Thomas only played thirty-nine games for Quebec that year (one more and we'd have owed Edmonton a third-round choice). A year or so later we picked him up again as a free agent and sent him to Cincinnati when we set up a farm club there. So for a sixth-round draft choice we got Terry Martin, who turned out very well for the Leafs; Dave Farrish who played useful hockey in the NHL and in the minors; and we still had Reg Thomas. Not a bad deal.

But I'd still been beating the bushes for anyone who might help at all. Which brings us to Carl Brewer. He'd been with me for seven years and three Stanley Cups in Toronto, an all-star defenceman. Now he was forty-one years old, but when I coached a team of Leafs' Old Timers in a charity game in the spring of 1979 I saw that he could still skate better than a lot of people in the league. He could manipulate the puck, make the plays. One day I got a call from columnist Paul Rimstead of the *Sun*. At the time I had just picked up Daryl Maggs as a free agent, out of hockey six years, on the off-chance he could still do it. He couldn't, but maybe that's what gave Brewer the idea. He had left the Leafs in 1965, blasting me. Maybe he didn't want to approach me directly. Anyway, Rimstead did it.

"How would you like to use Carl Brewer?" he asked. "He's dying to play for the Leafs again."

What could I lose? I called Brewer in. Dick Duff was with me when we talked. Carl said that he wanted to finish his career in a Leaf sweater. That was the whole theme. I told him to come and practise with the Leafs, and we'd see. We'd pay him something in expenses. Well, he said, first he wanted to go on a Florida holiday he'd arranged with his wife. I said okay, didn't make any difference to me, he wasn't on the payroll. He came back early in December and said he'd like to go to Moncton first and play a few games, see how it went. I thought that was a good idea. We announced that we were giving him a try and arranged to pay his expenses in Moncton. I went down there and watched him play. He wasn't that bad. I intended to bring him up to the Leafs in a couple of weeks, on December 26 against Washington. Everybody on the club was against it – Smitty, Ballard, and especially the players. Nobody seemed to realize that we were so thin in reserves that anybody who could help, even *might* help, should be made welcome.

About a week before Christmas I caught a bad case of the flu. And if I'd needed any jacking up about breaking up this outfit I got it when I was home in bed on a Wednesday, December 19. Harold had called a press conference for noon that day in the Hot Stove Club at the Gardens. He had mentioned to Sittler about a week earlier his plans for an exhibition game to raise money for Ronald McDonald House, a place that provides living accommodation for out-of-town relatives of children being treated for cancer at the

Sick Children's Hospital in Toronto. Harold's idea was that the Leafs would play the Canadian Olympic team early in February, just before the Winter Olympics at Lake Placid, when interest would be highest. He would donate the Gardens, sell television and radio rights, and all in all hope that close to $200,000 could be raised for this charity. Alan Eagleson was patron of Ronald McDonald House and Sittler was honorary chairman. Harold isn't basically what you'd call innocent, but I guess because of their connection with that charity he just couldn't imagine they were going to hose him.

Sittler actually heard about the thing twice, once from publicity director Stan Obodiac and once from Harold. He said later in a radio interview that he didn't comment on the project at the time, but did feel the players had a right to be consulted, and to say whether they wanted to play of not. When he did mention it to them he found mixed feelings, he said, really meaning it was up to him. With his clout, I always figured he could swing them one way or the other. Typically, he let Eagleson, but not Ballard, know about the doubts. Ballard had no inkling, none whatever. A lamb to the slaughter.

Ballard had set his press conference for noon. Sittler called a meeting of the players that morning in the dressing room. They asked Eagleson in. Even at that point, they could have called Harold in, too. Of course, that wasn't their idea. That would have spoiled the ambush. And never mind the money for a good cause that would be lost forever as a result.

When all the media people were assembled, by the dozens, including some from Los Angeles in for a game that night, and the announcement of the game was made, Eagleson got up and read his statement throwing egg into Ballard's face.

He said the Leafs would play Ballard's charity game only if certain conditions were met. For years Ballard had been refusing to let Eagleson book Soviet teams into the Gardens for exhibitions, Canada Cup games, or anything else. Now Eagleson was saying that the Leafs' conditions were that they would play a game with a touring Russian team and give the proceeds to the NHL Players Association; their favourite charity obviously being themselves, because such a game would draw. Then they would play the Olympic team for Ronald McDonald House only if it was a fun affair, the teams trading goalies and defencemen. Like a glorified practice. It would not draw flies.

When I heard all this on radio and television, I was sickened, especially by the fact that with Ballard in the building, they'd kept him totally in the dark. But it figures. No way they wanted to spoil the egg-in-the-face by letting him know what was going on. Eagleson must have come prepared with a sheaf of press releases announcing the players' decision, because he and Sittler came to the noon press conference straight from the team meeting. What they had done, it seemed to me, was set out deliberately to humiliate Harold Ballard, which ain't easy. But for once Ballard was absolutely caught off guard. This under the leadership of the same guy, Sittler, who had insisted on his and Palmateer's right to play for *Showdown* and make some money for themselves.

I don't think I've ever seen Ballard so hurt. You could tell by how subdued his reactions were.

"They're an ungrateful bunch," he said the next day. "You wonder how this could happen over such a worthwhile cause. All I wanted to do was help because I lost my wife, my parents, and a lot of my friends to cancer. It means a lot to fight this thing. Instead, the players on my team acted like a bunch of idiots."

He also said that if the game was cancelled (which it was) Ronald McDonald House would get a large donation out of his own pocket; but it's hardly likely that he planned to match what the game would have brought from his donating the rink free of charge, selling TV rights for $30,000, and filling the rink. The next day I was still sick but went down to the office anyway, sore enough at Eagleson to take the shot at him that I thought he deserved.

For months he had been telling the media about his troubles in trying to get a new contract for Mike Palmateer. I was willing to give him the money he wanted, about $1,000,000 over five years. But I would not give him the five-year guaranteed contract Eagleson demanded. A standard NHL contract, agreed to by both players and owners, has what is called a buy-out clause. If a player's performance deteriorates to the point that he is put on waivers and there are no takers, meaning nobody in the NHL wants him, his club can buy him out at one-third of what's left on the contract. It's fair both ways. For instance, if Palmateer signed on my terms he'd get around $200,000 a year, about triple his pay at the time. If he was traded, his contract would go with him as is. But if the time came when he couldn't play and there was, say, three years left on his contract, he could be bought out for one-third, or $200,000.

It was Eagleson's opposition to the buy-out clause in Palmateer's case that made me think he was guilty of a double-standard. That clause apparently was okay for rank-and-file players but not for Palmateer. I tried to point this out in a statement. I said I wouldn't negotiate through the media, and neither Eagleson nor Palmateer had been near me for months; but, about the buy-out clause, it seemed funny to me that he was saying the clause is okay for the ordinary members of the association – but for players who retained him personally as an agent, it was not a good deal and they should not sign. I asked: "Would you say this is a conflict of interest or would you not?"

Meanwhile, I felt the one guy who was suffering was Palmateer. If he had signed, his pay would have tripled immediately. I called him over to the boards one day at practice and tried to explain that even if he signed a guaranteed contract with some other club after this year, he'd have to get quite a bit more than he was asking from me, just to get the total up to what I was willing to give him, if he played five years for me. But he paid no attention. The thing that wasn't mentioned publicly was that one of his knees swelled up so badly after some games that he couldn't play if we had a game the next night, which didn't make a five-year guaranteed contract a very good proposition for any club, including ours.

On the Wednesday of the hullaballoo over the Ronald McDonald game, we tied Los Angeles 4-4. We flew to Boston and on the Thursday night it was Boston 10, Leafs 0. Palmateer told reporters that he had played well. Big joke all around. Finally I could see there was nothing else for it. I had to start moving people. I dealt Pat Boutette, a regular for us (thirty-two games, no goals, four assists) to Hartford for Bob Stephenson, who was with Springfield in the minors. Bad deal but the best I could do at the time. I had to start somewhere.

Right after the 10-0 Boston game Ray Miron in Colorado called me. He had a hunch that I'd be jumping. I was. He knew I wasn't going to turn the club around just by trading Pat Boutette. For nearly a week Ray and I bandied names. Meanwhile we squeezed out a Saturday night win against Detroit, 2-1. We got bombed Sunday 8-4 in Montreal. Played bad hockey. Ray and I were getting down to cases. I knew who I wanted the most, Wilf Paiement, and that I wouldn't get him for nothing. Ray wanted Lanny McDonald.

"Lanny McDonald for Wilf Paiement and Pat Hickey," I said, at one point. In trading, you always ask for more than you think you'll get.

Ray: "Maybe you got a deal, but I need somebody besides McDonald."

Things were at that stage when Washington came in the day after Christmas and hammered us 8-2. That was the first game for Brewer. He was far from being the worst defenceman on the ice. In fact, he was the only Leaf player who wasn't on the ice when any Washington goals were scored, which made a total of thirty-one goals against us in five games.

Meanwhile, I was getting close with Colorado. When Ray said, "Throw in Joel Quenneville," I said, "I'll call you back." He was a big young defenceman, but in my opinion at that time showed bad judgment in critical situations and would commit himself in a way that caused three-on-one or two-on-one breaks. Eventually, those cost goals and games.

I knew there would be an uproar about trading McDonald, a crowd favourite and Sittler's buddy. I talked it over with Smitty and spent Thursday thinking how lousy we'd looked against Washington. On Friday morning I called Ray Miron and said, "You've got a deal." He had to go to his owner, Arthur Imperatore, for a final okay. I didn't. But I went in to Ballard and said, "Look, I'm trading McDonald and Quenneville for Paiement and Hickey. It's a good deal. Sure, McDonald can score but Paiement can do more things for you than McDonald. Hickey has one forty-goal season behind him. Quenneville, I feel we can let him go."

Soon Ray called me back and said the deal was on. We arranged that we'd release the news at four o'clock Eastern time, two o'clock in Denver, to give us time to tell the players. I went to the dressing room to tell Smitty, but he wasn't there. So I called McDonald and Quenneville into the coach's room.

I had just started by saying, "This is the toughest part of my job . . ." when McDonald got it. Right away.

"To where?" he asked. "Who for?"

I told him he was going to Colorado, but didn't tell him the players we were getting back, because it was still before the release time Ray and I had agreed on. He rushed out. When Smitty was told a few minutes later, he was described as being shocked. He might have been shocked, but he'd known what I was working on.

Of course, there was an uproar. Some people in the media claimed that I was making the trade to get at Sittler by trading his close friend and linemate. As usual I said nothing, but Ballard replied that if the Leafs had been able to trade Sittler, he'd have gone, not McDonald. But dealing Sittler was never discussed at that time. Ray Miron and others knew about his so-called no-trade contract, so they hadn't even mentioned him. I made the trade simply because I thought it would improve the hockey club. When McDonald sounded off later about the Leafs being a nuthouse, it was even plainer that the trade was a good idea because he was certainly part of the nuthouse.

First he went to Eagleson's office, found he wasn't in, and went home. When Eagleson did get into it he fuelled the fire by pointing out that both Mrs. McDonald and Mrs. Paiement were about to give birth, and couldn't I have waited a couple of weeks? He'll use anything. Pictures in one paper showed Darryl Sittler in tears. The deal was front-page in all the papers, bulletins on radio and TV, no holds barred.

Naturally, this got the fans all riled up. They showed up for our Saturday game at the Gardens carrying signs and placards blasting me and praising McDonald. But nobody who knew anything criticized the deal, as a deal. Both Quenneville and Hickey were happy with the move and said so. So did Paiement, after the initial shock. One writer for the *Globe and Mail*, Jim Christie, made rather a point about my trading away an Eagleson client, McDonald, for Paiement, apparently not being aware that Paiement was an Eagleson client, too. Eagleson, I thought, was being disruptive – telling one reporter, "I'm not sure Paiement will ever report."

The next twenty-four hours or so after the trade included another interesting move by Sittler and Eagleson. When I came into the Gardens Saturday night one of the first people I saw in the press box was Louis Cauz. He's an old friend from hockey trips when he worked for the *Globe and Mail* years earlier. By then he was with the *Star*, writing racing. I hadn't seen him for a long time.

After we shook hands I said, "What the hell are you doing here?"

"Covering the game."

"Yeah, but you're a racing writer!"

He said that at 11.30 that morning he had been called by his sports editor, Ken McKee, and told to come down.

Then he said, sort of deadpan, "What have you got to say about Sittler taking his C off?"

I said, "What are you trying to tell me?"

"Well," he said, "that's what they sent me down for, to get a feature on it."

I said, "You're kidding me! You mean to tell me that they phoned and told you to come down and cover this game because Sittler was taking the C off? And the papers have known since noon but we don't know anything about it?"

"Gospel truth," Louis said.

When I looked around I could see that all the papers had extra people there, photographers all ready to record the big event. Of course, what happened next had been planned well in advance, another Eagleson-Sittler production for maximum publicity, another ambush.

As sports editors had known for all that time what was going to happen, Sittler could have told Smitty and the players that morning at their regular game-day meeting. He didn't. They got there around 6.00 or 6.30 and dressed and went out for the warmup and still nobody had been told. Then just before the team was to come back on the ice, with the maximum audience on hand and the television cameras ready outside, Sittler took a pair of scissors in the dressing room and cut the captain's big C from the left shoulder of his jersey. I can't imagine a player with his team's best interests at heart doing it just in that way. Sure, resign if you wanted to. But to stage and time it carefully so that the team would go on the ice still shocked, concentration broken to hell, seemed to me wrong. It had to destroy team morale. This was the great team leader I'd read so much about.

Luckily that night the Zamboni ice-flooding machine broke down. The teams had to stay in the dressing room fifteen or twenty minutes longer than usual. At least that gave the Leafs a chance to regain enough composure to beat the weak Winnipeg team. Some of the stories later gave the impression that cutting off the C had been a sudden impulse, despite the fact that after the game Sittler distributed a hand-printed statement on his own stationery. Now when in hell did he write that statement? Did he make it up between shifts when they were out on the ice? It had been photocopied so that everybody could get one. He'd been in the rink since six o'clock or so, and I was assured that no Gardens copier had been used to make the copies, so they must have been done somewhere else, earlier.

When I was going to my car after the game that night, suddenly I was hit very heavily from behind. I staggered. When I turned around ready to slug whoever it was, I found that a woman had hit me with her purse, which must have been loaded with bricks. She was screaming at me for trading Lanny.

I just turned away from her and got into the car.

Somebody asked me once if the public outcry over trading Lanny McDonald was anything like the one when I traded Frank Mahovlich from Toronto to Detroit back in 1968. Hell, there was twice as much fuss about McDonald. And he wasn't half the hockey player Frank was.

CHAPTER FIFTEEN

Life with Darryl, without the C

So there we were going into the second half of the season with the newspapers and other media now well aware that anything I thought would improve this hockey team was going to be done, if I could do it. Reporters with sources in other clubs picked up rumours of deals I talked about, and some I never talked about, but when nothing more happened immediately they had another story: Carl Brewer. It would only have made me laugh, if it wasn't so stupid, but the players thought I'd planted Brewer among them as a spy!

What happened to him had to be seen to be believed. Dave Hutchison sat out the first four games Brewer played, and resented it. Brewer was no spring chicken, but he played competently, including not looking out of place in a 3-1 game we lost to the Islanders. But Hutchison was fuming. There was all this talk, from the other players, about Brewer being too old. In workouts, Hutchison didn't take runs at anybody except Brewer. I couldn't help wondering what would have happened if Tim Horton, at forty-three, had been the older guy out there, or Allan Stanley, or Gordie Howe. All three played in the NHL, a lot older than Brewer. Against them, Hutchison never would have lived to tell the tale.

The other players were in on it too. They wouldn't pass Brewer the puck even when he'd made a good play to get open. It was such chicken stuff it was unbelievable. Of course, Smitty could have controlled it if he'd been stronger in the dressing room, but he was being Mr. Nice Guy. Anyway, Brewer never did get a proper chance to show if he could still play anywhere near the pro-rated $125,000 salary I had given him, a ridiculous one, but one I'd based rather sentimentally on our old Stanley Cups. Smitty didn't play him enough, because of the dressing room opposition. When you're that age, you have to play or you deteriorate fast. I've told older players, like Horton and Stanley, the older you get the *more* you have to practise, not less. You've got to work harder to stay where you were. At best Brewer wouldn't have been better than the fifth defenceman, but if he was better than the other fifth defenceman, that was all I would ask. I won't even try to describe the kind of things the players – rarely, if ever, identified, of course – were unloading to the reporters around that time. The whole outfit was more a talk show than a hockey team.

And still, I'm looking for trades. I thought Hutchison was hurting us and when Bob Pulford of Chicago offered me Pat Ribble, another defenceman, I traded him. It was on the day of the Hutchison move that the famous, or infamous, incident happened in Delaney's bar in downtown Toronto. A bunch of players had gone to drink there after practice and wound up putting my picture on a dart board and throwing at it. This prompted another prime round of gutless criticism, made possible by a *Star* reporter who printed everything they said cutting me up, celebrating, as they said, Hutchison's escape, but never giving their names. I knew who they were anyway, so the *Star* reporter could have done his job properly for his newspaper and its readers instead of for this bunch of players.

I was trying to find Hutchison that day to tell him he'd been traded, but couldn't find him. This he translated later into a story saying that he had to hear it on the radio, not from me. I just hadn't thought of phoning bars, until I was talking to Eagleson about the deal and said I couldn't find Hutchison to tell him.

"I know just where he is," Eagleson said. "Delaney's."

So we phoned him there. Anyway, I don't think Hutchison would disagree – it was a good deal for him. I didn't see him as good enough, but Pulford did, because Hutchison had played very well for Pulford in L.A. a few years earlier.

I used to get mad at the TV people. Every time a new guy would come in, I'd talk to him and say, "Look, you've heard a lot about what I'm trying to do here, but I just want you to play the best game you can. Go out there and do what you have to do. I consider you're a good hockey player. I got you, that should tell you I want you." But the TV people would want him right away, and that's okay, fans like to see what a new guy is like personally, but the questions were always the same: "What do you think of the situation here?" What the hell is the kid going to say? He's right over a barrel, having to declare himself.

I told Paiement something a little different, when he came in. I said that the club was changing, and that he had a chance to become its leader. He was tougher, stronger, a better skater and a better checker than McDonald. True, Lanny has a hell of a shot. That's his game. But finding a centreman who could bring out the best in Paiement was another thing. He wound up playing most of the time with Sittler, who wasn't the best kind of centre to play with him. In fact, I had an idea early on that if we were smart, we'd play Paiement at centre, let him do the checking and the heavy work, as we had done with Pulford when we moved him off left wing to centre for the Leafs in the 1960s. But it was a few months before we tried that.

Now the players had a new excuse for losing. They were shooting at Smitty, saying that he didn't have any system. It wasn't their fault that they couldn't get the puck out of their own end, they said. Nobody was telling them how. Around the middle of January we had a game in Montreal. Going down on the train once again I read this line in the papers from the usual unidentified players about Smitty having no system. I was burning. In Montreal I said to Smitty, "Look! I want you to have a meeting with every damn hockey player and tell them what your system is." Duff was there, too. "Duffy," I said, "you're going to be in those meetings. After Smitty has explained the system to them you're going to ask, 'Do you understand the system?' They say, 'Yes,' and you say, 'Okay, I'm a witness.' And both of you tell them that if we ever see in the papers again that they don't understand our system, they're going to practise twice a day until they do know the system."

I've used the twice-a-day-practice before. You know, these guys usually come to the rink after the morning rush hour and go home before the afternoon one. But at twice-a-day practices they have to come in during the rush hour, like working people do, and go home during the rush hour, like everybody else. Usually after about two or three days of that, they begin to get the message.

A few weeks later I'd finally had enough of Sittler. After he'd cut off his C, I had offered him a week or so off, a paid trip to

Florida, in case the pressure was getting to him. I just thought that time away to think things over might do him some good. He turned it down. When he persisted in his public criticism, I got mad. I studied Sittler's contract again, and found that although the original had been on a no-trade basis, in 1978 the contract had been revised by Jim Gregory and Harold Ballard to increase his pay from about $170,000 a year plus bonuses, through the 1983-84 season, to a rising scale giving him $190,000 plus bonuses by the end of the contract. But the amendment really constituted a new contract and did not mention the no-trade clause. I thought there was a loophole there and I intended to use it.

I went into the dressing room with him alone on Friday, February 15. He'd been quoted a couple of times as saying that maybe he should get out of Toronto. I told him I was prepared to take him up on that.

He said, "Eagleson says I can't be traded without my consent."

I said, "Well, I'm telling you now that Eagleson did his work very sloppily when you changed the contract, and I think we can get away with a trade."

"I don't think you can."

"I think I can and that's all that matters. I'm going to try."

Then we got around to other things.

He said, "Smitty can't coach."

"Is that right?"

"Yeah, he's no good."

Dick Duff, with all his Stanley Cups behind him, much more than Sittler's accomplishments in hockey, was Smitty's assistant. "What about Duffy?" I said.

He called Duff a name that I won't even repeat, and added, "He's worse than nothing."

I blew up. "Will you get the hell out of this room? I don't want to talk to you again!"

If Sittler would say that kind of thing to me about the coaches, he'd say it to other players. If I could have traded him that day I would have. After that I started actively trying to trade him. We weren't thinking of just anybody. Talking to Philadelphia, it was Sittler for Paul Holmgren and somebody, Bill Barber and somebody, Brian Propp and Behn Wilson, Propp and a goaltender, some kind of a deal like that.

When they brought up the stuff about his no-trade clause, I'd say, "The way we'll make the deal is that he'll be dealt for future considerations, which we'll agree on, and keep secret. If we make the deal and he doesn't go to you, you suspend him and that's it. It doesn't cost you a nickel or a player. But if you can make the deal with him and he'll report to you, we get the future considerations, the players we've agreed on."

That was a legitimate way of doing it. If we did it he could go home, maybe, and sit there or maybe he'd go where he'd been traded. At least we'd get it going. Eagleson heard about it and sent a telex to all clubs, warning them of the no-trade clause, making some people back off, but in the next few months I did have at least two good chances to make a deal. We'll get to them.

A funny thing about that club – they could be going nowhere for weeks and then I'd do something that woke them up and they'd win a few. Sometimes, anyway. In the two weeks before my dustup with Sittler we had lost to Chicago twice, then to Boston and Los Angeles, beat Detroit, and lost to Pittsburgh. Two points out of twelve. Enough to put anybody on edge. We went out the next night and beat Hartford on Saturday and the New York Rangers on Sunday.

That was the night when Jake Milford of Vancouver and I made our final phone calls on a deal for Bill Derlago and Rick Vaive. They weren't going well out there. There were stories about coming in overweight, drinking, all that kind of stuff. Hell, the only time you're going to get anybody good is when a club is having trouble with him. You don't get a hockey player when he's going great. You always hope that you can straighten him out, or he'll get smart and realize he's going no place if he doesn't change his ways. This does happen, especially with kids. You're talking about a twenty-one-year-old kid who doesn't know which way is up. All of a sudden he's got everything. Half the people in the world, if they got the same opportunities, the same money and fame, would go crazy. So you've got to take that into consideration when you're making the deal and know that the kid is having problems.

These two were both first-draft choices, good skaters and good scorers. I would have traded Sittler for Derlago and Vaive, if I could have. Of course, all hell would have broken loose on that one, too, but today it would look like a hell of a deal. As it was, I wound up giving Tiger Williams and Jerry Butler. I liked Williams, no doubt about that. He is the kind of guy I like to have in a hockey club. Okay, he's a bad skater. If I had everybody else flying, I could live with Williams. But when everybody else is a damn plodder, there's no way. Somebody had to go, somebody had to take the brunt. I was sorry it had to be Williams.

That deal, Williams and Jerry Butler for Vaive and Derlago, came on February 17. We'd beaten the Rangers and were staying over to play the Islanders. I got to Tiger after the game and we sat up over a few beers. I could always communicate with him. He'll talk frankly to anybody. Like one time somebody asked him what was the greatest problem facing the Leafs, and he said Harold Ballard. That night I told him I'd been fired a couple of times, which he knew, and that I felt the way to take a move was to look forward to what you were going to be doing next, rather than back at what went wrong. He took it pretty well that way. I got a bad press because I didn't tell Butler at the same time as Williams. Well, I tried, but that night I was up fairly late, and couldn't find him. If he'd been in his room, I would have told him when I told Williams.

A footnote to that move, not known at the time, was that I got Curt Ridley, the goalkeeper, in the same deal by the back door. Vancouver had put him up in a draft, for $7,500. I'd taken him because with our goalie problems I wasn't letting anybody go by without a look. I still owed Vancouver that $7,500 when I made the Williams deal. I said, "Look, you're going to get Williams, he's going to put a lot of people in your rink. I owe you $7,500 for Ridley. Let's wipe it out." And that's what was done.

When the deal was announced, Sittler was front and centre again. He told a television reporter that he was very unhappy, it wasn't a good trade, getting rid of two good team mates and all that. Don't break up that old gang of mine – what's that got to do with running a hockey club?

People have wondered why I didn't sign Palmateer somehow. There were two reasons. One was the bad knee. It was swelling up after nearly every tough game. No one could tell how long it was going to last. I told Ballard, "I'm not going to put you on the hook for a million dollars for a goalie with a bad knee." The other reason was something I couldn't mention, but that was even more important to me. I was trying to put together a team that could win the Stanley Cup. To me, Palmateer is not the type of goaltender who ever wins a Stanley Cup. He's a gambler. When things are okay he can stop anything. He's a fine competitor, a colourful guy, and he can put a lot of people into a rink and make them like him. He does a lot of good things. But when you're playing for the big money you don't need a gambler. The goalies that always win the Cup are the Terry Sawchuks, the Johnny Bowers, the Bernie Parents, the Drydens, the Billy Smiths, people that stand up in the net and don't go running all over the place. So what the hell, if you're looking for a championship team you'd better start trying to find a goalie who's steady, and get it over with. If Palmateer had signed on our terms I would have been quite happy to have him, but I still would have been looking for the kind of guy who, in my opinion, wins championships.

That is where Jiri Crha came in, even before that season began. We didn't have any goalie in the minors at that time, just Vince Tremblay straight out of junior. But before training camp opened I had a tip from a good friend about Jiri, who'd played international hockey with the Czechs, had defected, and was in West Germany. Here was a goalkeeper I didn't have to give up a player for, or a draft choice, if I could get him.

While we were arranging to get him out, we sent him goal equipment in Germany so he'd be ready to play when he got here. But when he showed up at training camp we ran into trouble; the NHL had an agreement with the Czechs that said we had to pay the Czech hockey federation $50,000 for him. I wouldn't put $50,000 up front sight unseen, so I was told I couldn't play him. We were also having trouble getting him papers to cross the border to play in the States. We got him in shape and sent him to Moncton, where the NHL ban didn't reach. I'd hired Joe Crozier to coach there and Joe told me, "We've got a hell of a goaltender here."

Things moved slowly on Crha until late December. Then we got permission for him to play in the U.S. About that time also, the Russians went into Afghanistan and there was a public outcry about it. I took the advantage to tell John Ziegler, the NHL president, that considering Afghanistan, I thought the NHL had a hell of a nerve ruling that a kid who had defected from that sort of society could not make a living playing hockey in North America because of some technicality.

Soon after, it was agreed that if I put up $25,000 on an irrevocable letter of credit, good for one year, they'd give the okay. I did that, telling Crha that if the Czechs didn't pick up the money I'd give it to him. There was the second $25,000 to pay if he made the Leafs. For some reason the Czechs never picked up the money so Crha got most of it.

When we did get Crha playing with the Leafs, he was vying with Palmateer as to who was the best goalkeeper. To my mind, Crha won out. Anyway, with Palmateer still unsigned we were going to have to find out what Crha could do, and it was pretty good. Although he only played fifteen games to Palmateer's thirty-eight that year, Crha had a slightly better goal average.

But then, in this seemingly endless season, we had one more disaster.

On Friday, March 14, after practice, Smitty was going to go home to Buffalo. At lunch I was in the Hot Stove Lounge with Clancy and Smitty so I know he didn't have a drink. He stopped in at Archie Katzman's Parkway Hotel in St. Catharines and had a couple of beers. When he got out on the highway again something happened and he lost control of the car. It went across the median and hit another car. Two people in the other car died. Smitty was taken to hospital. I got a call saying that he had broken a leg. Actually, the leg was badly battered and X-rays showed bone chips lying around, and a crack, but it was an old hockey injury. We didn't know that for a while, though. I was told he'd be in a cast for some weeks at least, and certainly wouldn't be fit to go behind the bench for the rest of the season.

I had some ideas percolating but there was only one thing to do right away. Duff was assistant coach, he'd take the Saturday night game against the Rangers. But the Leafs wouldn't play for him. No wonder, the lousy things Sittler had said about him, which meant everybody in the dressing room probably was saying the same. The Rangers clobbered us 8-4. I went over to see Smitty on Sunday in the hospital and we talked about all the alternatives. Judging from the night before, the team wouldn't play for Duff. I mentioned Joe in Moncton. And I also tried out another idea I was toying with. "Maybe I'll take over as coach myself," I said. I think he thought I was kidding, and he kidded back. "If I thought you'd do that," he said, "I'd get right out of this bed and *walk* to Toronto."

I went back to Toronto thinking I'd see what happened the next night against Atlanta, and then decide. Leafs lost 5-1 to Atlanta. It was then I made up my mind. They'd been giving themselves all those outs about part of their trouble being lack of communication with me. They couldn't say that if I was a coach, right there in the dressing room every day. On the Tuesday, I phoned Joe and told him that I was going to be the coach and he would be the assistant coach. He would be behind the bench, but for all other purposes of communication and so on, I'd be front and centre.

I made the statement at four that afternoon that I would be coach of the hockey club. I planned to let that sink in and then at 7 p.m. announce that Joe was going to be my assistant, and run the club behind the bench. The only trouble was that my second announcement got torpedoed. Joe couldn't resist phoning a TV friend of his in Buffalo, Rick Azar, to tell him so that he'd have it at the same time as the Toronto media. Azar was a good friend of Dave Hodge of CFRB, and phoned to tell him. When Bill Stephenson from CFRB came in to do a tape with me about the coaching change, I told him Joe was coming to help me. Immediately he phoned the radio station with what he thought was hot news, but Dave Hodge already knew. There's quite a grapevine in hockey. Hard to keep a secret.

Joe's a good coach, a very aggressive s.o.b. Just the opposite from Smitty. Between the two of us, I thought we might get somewhere. There were points I would have told the team before if I hadn't wanted to avoid interfering with Smitty, but I did get a few things off my chest right then. For one, I talked to Salming privately. He had a bad habit of winding up flat on his ass after a play on our goal. You could see it time after time in the video tapes. After a goal went in, there'd be Salming down on the ice. I told him, "Look, do me a favour. Stay on your feet. If they score anyway, at least stay on your feet."

I told Joe other things that needed correcting. Sittler and Salming led the team at giving the puck away. Sittler was getting caught out of the play a lot because he went in deep all the time looking for goals and didn't have the speed to get back into the play when it went to our end. Joe's toughness after Smitty's easiness made the usual impression. The first night he was behind the bench, we massacred Winnipeg 9-1. We went to Philadelphia and the next night played one of our best all-round games of the season, a 3-0 shutout for Palmateer. That was sort of the honeymoon, and then we went back to the more usual winning-a-few-and-losing-more. "This is a very funny team," Joe said once. But he was trying to get the operation running smoothly and at the end of the season we were at least in the playoffs, eleventh overall in the league.

Our preliminary playoff round was against Minnesota, and this brought the final example of what a strange bunch of people I was dealing with.

There are players and sportswriters who are fond of talking about how the game has changed, and how coaches and managers must change with it. In some ways I agree. Some of the old methods don't work any more. And any group of players on any pro team – hockey, basketball, whatever – can get together and undermine the coach or manager to the point that he's fired. But it is mainly teams that are going nowhere anyway who have the time and inclination to do that. The winners work at their game, their profession, instead of at shafting management. Anyway, there is one thing that does not change and never will, and that is honesty, and that's what my final letdown of the season involved, a lack of honesty. I might be tough on some people, but I don't lie.

We hadn't done badly against Minnesota that year, won two in Toronto and lost two in Bloomington. They'd finished thirteen points ahead of us, which gave them the advantage of opening our best-of-five round with two games on their home ice. On the last Saturday night of the season we'd beaten them 2-1 in a pretty good game. That day, for some reason, nobody on the team had skated before or after the morning meeting. Normally that would be a disadvantage, but I'm superstitious. If a thing works once it might work again so I did two things. On Monday a couple of hours before leaving for Minnesota, I called down to the dressing room and asked Joe Crozier if anybody wanted to see the film of the 2-1 game. Sometimes it helps to remember what you were doing right, when you win.

Nobody wanted to see it. Not interested.

I also told Joe, "I don't want anybody to skate in Minnesota when they have the game-day meeting tomorrow. Just like Saturday."

We flew to Minnesota, spent Monday night, and the next morning I went over to the Metropolitan Centre. Who do I find coming off the ice but Sittler, as well as some others. I suppose when the captain disobeyed an order, the other guys figured they'd do it too.

I said to Sittler, "What the hell are you doing on the ice when I said nobody was to skate?"

He looked at me with that honest look, like in the TV commercials. "I've got new blades on my skates," he said.

What could I say? That was a legitimate reason. New blades need a little breaking-in. I didn't say anything more to him. But I called the trainer out and gave him hell.

"Why weren't Sittler's new blades put on so that he could have used them in practice Monday in Toronto?" I demanded.

He just stared at me. "Those blades went on ten days ago," he said.

I told him, "Go back in that dressing room and tell that so and so that you just got hell about his blades. Don't let him get away with it." I don't know whether the trainer did that or not, because I didn't intend to carry the incident any farther.

I suppose the game that night had more to do with the Minnesota team's character than with Sittler leading the way to show the s.o.b. (me) that I couldn't tell *them* anything. Anyway, with Crha in goal, we lost 6-3. Second game, the next night, Wednesday, we used Palmateer and lost even worse, 7-2.

We had a charter back to Toronto after that game, and arrived about three on Thursday morning, not leaving much time for sleep. Our third game – last one if we lost it – was Friday. To give the players a chance to get a good sleep Thursday night before the game and a good rest Friday, too, I put them in the Westbury Hotel on Thursday night. Meanwhile, Ballard had blasted them for playing as if they wanted to get their golf clubs out, and saying that he expected Sittler to ask to be traded, at the end of the season. When I pick up the *Globe and Mail* the next morning I see on the front page that Sittler is blasting back at Ballard for "demeaning" the team. So what else is new, they'd been blasting each other in public all season, while anything I said to Sittler was in private. But the story went on with the usual quotes from unidentified players, saying the Leafs had no system. They said Crozier had been out-coached in Minnesota and went on to say that "privately" several Leaf players said they expected to lose the game that night. Now, I don't know if any player actually said that, but the last paragraph had one unnamed player giving his version of why I had ordered all the players into the hotel for the night before the game.

"They want to keep us off the booze," this guy is supposed to have chuckled. "But have they ever heard of room service?"

Yeah, I'd heard of room service – I paid the bills and knew which rooms were getting it, and what. But I kept quiet. I didn't call the papers and say that we had caught one player with a girl in his room, and another bringing in a case of beer. I could have said, "It really looks like they want to win, eh?"

If I'd done that I would have been using the same tactics as that reporter, blackening the whole team because of a few bad apples, the ones who didn't know how to be winners.

That night, with Crha back in goal, the Leafs did make it close. I did something I'd been thinking about for weeks, put Wilf Paiement at centre against Minnesota's best, Bobby Smith. He just about smothered him. Smith didn't get a point all night, and Paiement set up our first goal. Regular time ended in a 3-3 draw. In the overtime we went down and I think it was Terry Martin who hit the post and the puck was loose in there, just needed to be knocked in. But nobody could get to it. Paiement was hanging back to try to prevent a break. But they got it anyway, went straight back to the other end, and Al MacAdam got the winning goal thirty-two seconds into overtime. Season over.

All I could think was, now maybe in trades or the draft or somehow, I can do something about next year.

CHAPTER SIXTEEN

When not to have a heart attack

There is no doubt that during that season, my first year back with the Leafs, Ballard supported me like there was no tomorrow. As I wasn't talking for publication, reporters went to him – and he said a lot of things that I didn't think he could ever take back. Over the course of the season he had called Sittler just about everything, including a cancer. "There is no place for him in the Leafs any more," he said. After the last game, pictures in the papers showed Sittler carrying some of his equipment out of the rink. One caption read "Sittler leaving Gardens . . . for the last time?"

A spread in the *Toronto Sun* was headed, NO ROOM FOR SITTLER, SAYS BALLARD.

I thought Paiement at centre might be the wave of the future. Against Bobby Smith in that one playoff game he had shown he could do it. I would have loved to have seen him against some of the other good centres in the league, like Bryan Trottier. Trottier is a tough little son of a gun, too, but I was sure Paiement could take the game away from any good centre man. He might yet, if somebody is smart enough to play him there. He hadn't wanted to play centre in that last playoff game, but when I put it to him that it was for the good of the team, he went along and played one hell of a game.

After Minnesota knocked us out, I started thinking about what I had to do between then and the draft meetings in June. Some players, hired for a short time and knowing it, like Brewer and Larry Carriere, wouldn't be back. Brewer, in fact, made an announcement of it, to the effect that nothing could make him come back. I wasn't sorry I'd given him a chance, but he hadn't done much. We would pick young defencemen in the amateur draft and

I was looking for defencemen in trades as well. Since Mike Palmateer wasn't going to sign with us, I wanted to make a deal for him before he became a free agent – and did, giving Palmateer and a third-round draft choice to Washington for Robert Picard, Tim Coulis and a second-round draft choice. Then it became Washington's job to sign Palmateer to the no-cut, no-buyout contract he was demanding. Max McNab, the Washington general manager, signed him for three years plus an option year on that basis. That year we had no first-round choice. It had gone earlier in the Maloney deal. But we had our own second, Washington's second, and Colorado's third. With them we took three defencemen – Bob McGill, Craig Muni, and Fred Boimistruck, all eighteen years old. If we got enough good young ones, some at least would develop.

But much of my time before the draft meetings was spent trying to deal Sittler, again. Bob Pulford in Chicago was very interested in trading for Sittler. He was prepared to accept my idea to trade him first and worry about his reporting, second. Pulford and Alan Eagleson are good friends and I thought maybe they had come to an agreement that Sittler would take that trade. I would have been prepared to take the first-round draft choice Chicago had got somewhere, third choice overall. That's the one Pulford used to pick Denis Savard, a really good kid, although I probably would have used it to take Larry Murphy, who was taken next, fourth overall, by Los Angeles. But Pulford wouldn't give me that one for Sittler. I wasn't giving him away for anything less. I didn't think the Leafs could be winners with Sittler running things, but in a different atmosphere he'd be still a good hockey player, too good to just give away. I couldn't believe that Sittler didn't know about those conversations with Pulford. When they didn't work out, he knew that, too, and also heard just about every day that Harold was adamant he would not play with the Leafs again.

A few weeks after the draft, while I was working at signing players, Sittler phoned and said that he'd like to come in and talk to me.

"Well, okay," I said. "Why don't we come down on Saturday when there's nobody around?" Then we wouldn't have to cope with another round of bloody headlines just because we'd had a talk. We set a date and he came in.

One of the first things he said when he came in was, "I just want to let you know that Eagleson is no longer my agent for dealing with the Leafs. I'm going to deal for myself and the only thing he's going to handle is a few commercials." Another thing he said was, "I don't want to talk about last year at all." In other words he'd written last year off. I thought it's not so easy for me as manager to write it off, but it's easy for him. He'd been quoted as saying, "As long as I think I played as hard as I could, well, I don't have to worry about it." I used to read that and I'd say well who the hell *is* supposed to worry about this thing, just me? But this was his attitude: forget last season.

I said, "Well, if that's the way it is, that's the way it is."

We talked on. I've got nothing against him. When we get away from the personalities, it is business. He said he still wanted to play for the Leafs. I said, "Well, I'll call you sometime and let you know what's doing. Go have a good summer. Forget about hockey if you can. I'll call you later on in August."

Not long after that I flew to Sweden to talk to Salming. His option year was coming up, and neither one of us wanted to go through the kind of year Palmateer and I had had, a public argument every second day. I wanted to sign him, but he wanted a guaranteed contract for something like $400,000 a year. My working figure was about $250,000 a year, but I started with $200,000 and wound up offering him $250,000.

Our meetings were in the Sheraton Hotel in Stockholm. His agent did most of the negotiating, but Salming did get into it. He's a good hockey player, but not as good as he thinks he is. In fact, the year before he'd played lousy hockey. He and Sittler were giving away the puck more than anybody. I had nightmares thinking of some of the power plays we'd had against us in the Minnesota series. Salming would stand there in our end and whenever he got the puck he'd shoot it around the boards and it would be stopped at the point and bang, there'd be another shot on our net.

In fact, Sittler and Salming between them stood for a lot of what was wrong with the hockey club. Sittler controlled the play, harnessed it to him, in the other team's end. Salming controlled it in our end. Sittler kept getting caught, not able to get back. Salming slowed the forwards down by the way he circled and diddled around, instead of head-manning. The forwards couldn't get steam up because they were always waiting for him at the redline or the blueline. When he did catch up, they'd be stopped, not skating. If they skated, they'd be offside. It's quite evident to me that Salming does slow the forwards down. The other thing is that defensively he is by no means great. He's not strong in the corners. In front of the net he's on his ass too much of the time.

I told Salming in Stockholm I frankly didn't think he was worth the money he was asking, when I took into account that he was on the ice for more goals than anybody else on the defence.

"Well, I play forty minutes a game!" he said.

I said, "Yeah, you play forty minutes a game. That's a hell of an argument but it's the wrong argument with me. If you're so damn good and you play forty minutes a game, why aren't I in first place?" That settled that argument. Then I said there was another statistic that maybe he didn't know about.

"What's that?"

I said, "You and Sittler give the puck away more than anybody else on the team."

"Oh, I don't know anything about that."

"Well, I do. That's my business."

So I didn't sign him at the time.

When I did get back a few days later, Clancy said, "You know, Harold was very mad because you didn't call him."

I guess I swore a little. "I got nothing to call him about! I'm not going to give Salming what he's asking! He isn't worth it."

Maybe I should have twigged right then that Harold wasn't backing me quite as much as he had before. I understand Harold, you know. The hockey club and his Hamilton football club are his life. He gets his kicks by talking to the press, having his name in the paper. He'd been doing things his own way so long that he missed it. He'd told me, "You run it," but he just couldn't keep out of it. And the next few weeks showed how damaging his way of doing things could be, for me.

In mid-August I was getting ready for training camp. Naturally all the players and their records, and so on, had to be printed up in the training camp guide for the media. I had put Sittler in. These things go across Ballard's desk. This day he came into my office waving the camp guide page proofs. "What's Sittler doing on the roster?" he demanded, and called Sittler a few names that I won't put in here. "I don't want that so-and-so in a Leaf sweater ever again."

I explained my way of thinking. He was still owned by us. "If his name's on the roster and he comes to camp, there's no flap. If he doesn't come to camp, that'll be obvious but either way we're covered. It's crazy to leave his name off and then have him show up and you have to explain why he's there when his name isn't in the guide."

He ranted and raved a little but I thought I had made my point, except there was no doubt about where he stood on Sittler.

So I phoned Sittler, as I had promised I'd do at our July meeting. I said, "Look, Darryl, he's adamant you're not going to play for the hockey club this year. I can't fight that situation."

I was letting him know that I didn't intend to go in and fight a battle for him after what had been going on. I wanted him off the hockey club. He knew that. But I could see his dilemma. I've been in dilemmas myself.

So he said, "Well, could I talk to Mr. Ballard?"

"Why not?" I said. "If I were in your position, hell, I think I would want to go to the owner and discuss it face to face."

"Would you set up a meeting for me?"

I said, "Sure, I'll set it up."

As long as a thing like that comes through me it's okay as far as I'm concerned. If it doesn't come through me, then it isn't okay. I'm with the old army idea – if you want to see the officer go through the sergeant. So Sittler knew where he stood, and that the meeting was okay by me. When I told Harold about the conversation, he said he'd see him. I said, when? He said, "After Labour Day. Set it up."

All this time I was still working away at trying to find someone who would make a deal for Sittler the way I thought it might work – meaning, to make it and see what happened. Some people might remember in that summer of 1980, there were a lot of rumours that Sittler was going to Calgary. That was the summer the Atlanta Flames moved to Calgary, and Cliff Fletcher, the general manager, was looking for a way to start off with a bang. After I got back from Sweden, he and I talked quite a few times. Eventually I had a chance for the best deal I'd ever had for Sittler.

Fletcher said, "You can have anybody off my team." He meant any one player. I told him I wanted Kent Nilsson and Bob Mac-Millan. He argued but I said, "Look, he's better than anybody you've got, right? Otherwise you wouldn't be telling me I can take anybody on your team. So I want MacMillan as well." I might have had to throw in somebody else, too, but maybe not. Nilsson and Sittler, both centres, had been forty-goal scorers that year. MacMillan was down a little but was a good skater and scorer. Fletcher then told me that because of the rules governing the expansion draft the year before (they'd got Nilsson from Winnipeg when the four WHA teams joined the NHL) Nilsson could not be traded for another year.

Remember, none of these names were going to be mentioned at first. The deal was going to be announced as "future considerations." The names we had agreed on would not be released until Sittler reported. If he didn't take the trade, those names would never be released. You can see the reason for secrecy. If somehow word leaked out who Fletcher was thinking of trading for Sittler, and the trade didn't come off, he would have a couple of disgruntled hockey players on his hands. Being an expert in that field, I wouldn't wish it on anybody.

When he said Nilsson could not be included in the trade, I thought, "Okay, give me Guy Chouinard and Bob MacMillan." Chouinard had scored fifty for Atlanta a year earlier. I thought further: "If at the end of the season I want to keep Chouinard, I keep him. If I don't, I send him back to you and take Nilsson." Around August 23 or so, that's the way it might have worked out.

The trouble was, I made the mistake of telling Harold my thoughts.

I got up on the morning of August 25, a Monday, and there it was in the paper, quoting Ballard that Sittler was going to Calgary, and who for. Of course, this was the one thing that Fletcher and I both had insisted on: that no names be mentioned until Sittler reported, and the trade was certain. When Ballard let it out I knew that Fletcher would have to deny until he was blue in the face. Yet, once it was out in the open like that, he would have looked like a fool denying it and then a couple of weeks later saying, "Yeah, it was true all the time." That season Chouinard scored thirty-one goals, MacMillan twenty-eight, Sittler forty-three. We'd have been getting a fifty-nine-goal potential, two young skaters, and the chance to pick up Nilsson (forty-nine goals that season) for Chouinard a year later. It gives you a bit of perspective on the deal the Leafs eventually did make for Sittler after I was gone.

That morning when I read in the papers and heard on the radio what Ballard had done, it was a blow to me. A terrible blow. It wiped out something that might have changed the Leafs entirely. I left the house between 9.30 and 10.00. I was somewhere on Eglinton Avenue, driving west, when suddenly I got this pain in my arms. Then it started to go through my chest. I realized it was the same kind of pain I'd had when my first heart attack came, in Buffalo more than eight years before. The traffic was just crawling along. I know now I should have pulled over and called an ambulance. Instead, I was wondering where the nearest hospital was. I was past Scarborough Hospital. I decided to go to Wellesley Hospital. As I was travelling down the Don Valley Parkway the pain was hitting me hard. Traffic was bumper to bumper. Finally, when I got to Wellesley the pain had gone away. So I thought maybe there was nothing wrong, and went right by.

I went into the Gardens and I saw Clancy. I guess Ballard wasn't in the building, because the first thing I said to Clancy was, "I read in the paper that Harold said that we're going to trade Sittler to Calgary for Nilsson and MacMillan. Will you tell that guy please to shut up? I tell him what the hell's going on, and he goes and blabs it to the newspapers. What in hell do you think Fletcher's going to do? If the deal doesn't go through, if Sittler won't report, he's got two guys on his team that are hostile towards him. He's going to have to say right now that there's no deal! And once he says there's no deal he makes himself look like an ass if he comes up and *makes* a deal later. Lord Almighty, this is getting to be ridiculous!"

When I blasted like that at Clancy I realized how upset I was, that it might have triggered the pains earlier. I thought, ah, hell, I'd better call the doctor. So I called Dr. W. F. Greenwood, my heart specialist, and told him what happened. He said I'd better come to the hospital right away. "I'll meet you at Emergency."

I said I had a couple of things to do, first.

"Be there!" he said.

"I'll be there in half an hour, don't worry."

I made a phone call or two. I think one was to Sittler telling him to see Ballard the following week, the meeting I had set up. But I don't remember that day too well.

Joe Crozier was in the office. Just as I was saying that I didn't want to go to the hospital, the pain came back. After it subsided, I said, "I guess I'm going in."

"I guess *so*," Joe said.

He drove me to Emergency at Toronto General. Dr. Greenwood met me and looked me over a little and said, "We'd better book you."

"I don't want to go in," I said. "I've got some things to do. I'll come back in two days and you can check me over." While we were arguing about it, the pain came back. It was bad. When it was over I said, "I guess I'm going in."

They wheeled me upstairs into Intensive Care and got me all set up. I knew I had to phone my wife and that she'd be upset. Actually, she kept a sort of diary of the next few days and a lot of this is her recollection, because for a few days I was so sick that I didn't really know what was going on in detail.

When I phoned her, it rang a long time. Turned out she was up a tree, trimming branches. As soon as I said, "I thought I should let you know I won't be home tonight," she knew something was wrong.

"Are you in the hospital?"

"Yes."

She left everything right where it was, tree branches all over the place, and drove to the hospital. Of course, I looked fine. Those pains had just been warnings, I guess, not a real attack. But they were getting me hooked up in Intensive Care, putting me on blood thinner, and so on. She wanted to stay overnight but I told her to go home. She says I even phoned at ten o'clock to make sure she was there, and she told me that she had let Brent and Marlene know.

It was about four the next morning that I had the real attack. Lucky I was in Intensive Care. At noon Dr. Greenwood told Dodo that my condition was so serious that she should get someone to lean on, as if I wasn't going to make it. She said the doctor had tears in his eyes. She called Brent, who left work right away, got his sister, and came over. All three of them were there.

I can remember saying to Dodo, "Why isn't Brent at work?"

I insisted that they go home that night but in Dodo's diary she said they stayed up all night and that it was a "nightmare of fear." But she didn't sit there wringing her hands. She did some cooking and washed and ironed. Wednesday morning she was standing by the bed when the doctor said to me, "You're a lucky man, Punch. We just about lost you last night." By that time I'd been on oxygen

I don't know how long, and it seemed I'd turned the corner. But then I got worse again. Fluid gathered in my lungs. Dodo told me that she was next to me watching the gauge on my blood pressure going way down. They couldn't get it back up. I think the technical term is vital signs. Mine were no hell, no hell at all. They gave me a transfusion. I was on intravenous. The crisis seemed to go on all Wednesday and Thursday into Friday before things levelled off and my blood pressure began to come back up again.

Dodo did not want anything to bother me, anything that might give me worry. She blasted a couple of people from the Gardens who did get in, on the first day. I had no radio or television for days, but even when I started to get brighter again, move around a little, she was giving me papers with the sports pages torn out. But she couldn't keep things from me very long, like the big reconciliation between Ballard and Sittler.

That was a surprise, after all Ballard had said about him. However, I'd set up their meeting and Ballard at least had made a logical decision. Sittler was better than the kids we had in the minors. Until we could move him, we might as well use him.

Sittler said in the interviews, I finally heard, that the only thing he was sorry about was that I wasn't there. He mentioned the secret meeting we'd had a couple of months before and said that from it I'd laid the groundwork for his meeting with Ballard. He and his family sent me a get-well card. Both Sittler on his card and Danny Gare on his said "we had our differences in the past, but . . ." There was a card from Tiny Tim in New York, and a lot of others from hockey people as well as fans. Laurie Boschman and family. Sam Pollock. Tommy Ivan of Chicago phoned Dodo every day. But from Ballard no calls, no cards, nothing. He said in the papers a few times that he didn't want me involved in anything that would cause me worry – and then he said a guy who's had two heart attacks, "you've got to wonder what he can do for your organization." Very soothing for the nerves.

Also, he didn't level where it counted. Training camp started and Sittler's name was not on the roster! Ballard had taken it off without telling me. Yet he managed to let Milt Dunnell of the *Star* think that I, dirty old Imlach, had wiped Sittler's name from the training camp list. This column of Milt's was published September 4. The pertinent line read: "The fact that Sittler wasn't even listed on the training camp roster is evidence that Punch had not changed direction." Ballard certainly should have corrected that, but didn't. It wasn't up to me to call Milt.

I was in the hospital three weeks before I was allowed my first visitor. A few days later I went home to convalesce. I was getting stronger rapidly. I had to! With me away, Ballard signed Salming to a long-term contract averaging around $325,000 a year, a lot longer term and more money than I would have given. And then there was this strong rumour going around – that Ballard was going to give Sittler back the captaincy. I couldn't believe it. How could Harold have his face rubbed in the dirt by this guy over that charity game, call Sittler a cancer, call it "treason" that Sittler had cut the C off his sweater after the McDonald trade, and then give him back the C?

I was home on September 24. Montreal was in for an exhibition game and that day Clancy came out to the house. Training camp had been going very well, with Picard one of the stars. We talked about this and that player. Somebody had phoned me to say that Ballard had asked him, "What would you think if I gave Sittler back the captaincy?" So I knew for sure he was thinking about it.

I said to Clancy, "Look, tell Harold under no circumstances give Sittler back the C. What the hell was the fight for all year long, to try to get back the authority for management to run the club, if you're going to turn around and give it all back to him." At the same time, however, I was aware that Ballard might already have made up his mind. I tried to cover that, too. I said to Clancy, "Tell Ballard under no circumstances should Sittler be both captain of the team and vice-president of the players' association! He's either got to decline one, or resign from the other!" Sittler seemed to want to be all things to all people, which just doesn't work.

I don't even know if Clancy got to Ballard before the deed was done. Sittler and Ballard had a meeting after the workout that day. A little later I got a phone call, from Joe Crozier. He hummed and hawed first and then said, "Sittler's got the C back. I've got to tell you because you're going to see it on television tonight. Didn't want it to be too much of a shock."

Of course, I understand if I'm sick and can't make a decision, someone has to make it. You can't stop the hockey season because I'm sick. But that time I was plenty well enough to make a decision, and Sittler would never have got his captaincy back from me. Over my dead body. That was when I started to lose. Harold was doing things, like the Sittler C and the Salming contract, that he knew I would not have done. He was enjoying being in full control again. Doing things right or wrong and getting them all done fast, before I got back.

Well, in a month I was back. I went in to see Harold and said, "Here I am. The doctor says I'm okay. I'm back to work." So we chatted awhile and then he said, "Okay. Go to work."

CHAPTER SEVENTEEN

Goodbye Joe, goodbye Ronnie, hello Nykoluk

I guess this chapter could also be called How To Get The Coach Fired. But you wouldn't have known it from the first month of the season. We lost our opening game to the New York Rangers and then won six in a row. The media euphoria, as usual, was something to see. Some of the columnists, forgetting their anguished outcries over deals I'd made less than a year before, spent their time singing praises. A line with Bill Derlago, Rick Vaive, and Pat Hickey went well for a while. Ballard called it the Punch Line because I'd traded for them all. Sittler with Wilf Paiement and Terry Martin was another effective line. So was the Kid Line, Laurie Boschman, Rocky Saganiuk, and John Anderson.

But the columnists were just as wrong to over-praise as they had been to over-criticize. We were skating and scoring, but the defence was erratic and I knew I had to get a good goalie backup for Jiri Crha somewhere. Ridley and Tremblay weren't it. In those first seven games when we picked up twelve points out of a possible fourteen, the only disciplined defensive games we played were 4-2 and 6-2 over Philadelphia and 4-2 over Buffalo. In the seven games we had allowed twenty-seven goals, too many.

Robert Picard, who'd been one of the best hockey players in training camp, one of the three stars of exhibition games a couple of times, was punched out badly by Tom Laidlaw in our first home game and rarely played well after that. It wasn't more than a couple of months later that I mentally put him on my trade list, although I didn't take kindly to Sittler telling Johnny Bower, "What's wrong with that boss of yours? Can't he see Picard's no good?" If Picard, a first-round choice, third overall, was going to recover his form, it wasn't going to help to have Sittler – which meant others on the team, his old guard – talking like that. A guy knows when that's going on. When he's struggling already, it gets worse.

After that streak of six wins, we gave up twenty-two goals in four games and got only one tie out of them. I was trying to make deals, but the first one was really borderline, Dave Burrows and Paul Gardner to Pittsburgh for Paul Marshall and Kim Davis. I still think Paul Marshall will play in the NHL, but not many agree with me. I like Gardner, he's a scorer, but he wasn't fast enough. He was in the minors at the time, on a major-league salary. Burrows wasn't doing much for us. Maybe I wouldn't have made the deal except that Baz Bastien, general manager in Pittsburgh, was in job trouble there; so two guys we didn't want might help him. Also, it would help Gardner to be back in the NHL again. As soon as I got off the phone I said to my wife, "That wasn't a good deal." But it saved the club $250,000 in salaries for two men who weren't going to play for us anyway.

I picked up defenceman Barry Melrose on waivers from Winnipeg, sold Richard Mulhern to Winnipeg, and traded a pretty good youngster, Mark Kirton, to Detroit for goalie Jim Rutherford. The simple case was, we needed a goalie and I hoped Rutherford would fill the bill, which as it turned out he didn't.

And the trouble on the team was getting worse. Soon I had a distinct feeling that the team was trying to get Joe fired as coach. They were just going through the motions.

By early December they were well on the way down, or back to normal, however you want to put it. Frank Orr of the *Star* put his finger on it when he did a major piece on how other teams viewed the players who were supposed to be the core of the Leafs. "Salming is Leafs' greatest talent, but if harassed in his own zone he tends to bang the puck off the boards, to no one in particular." Usually winding up in a giveaway, he might have added. "Sittler is back in command of the dressing room, but off to a slow start on the ice." "Turnbull forgets he has teammates, carrying the puck as though no one else is on the ice."

Early in January the Leafs were in Edmonton. Since the middle of December we'd lost 5-3 to Detroit, 5-2 to Chicago, 7-2 to Hartford (!), 6-3 to Boston, and 5-3 to St. Louis, while only beating Chicago 6-3. Lost five games out of six, allowed thirty-one goals.

Joe phoned me from Edmonton.

I wished him Happy New Year and asked, "How's it going?" –
hoping that they were showing signs of snapping out of it.

"Had trouble with Turnbull," he said. This was the guy Joe had
been praising to the skies earlier, trying to get him playing the way
he should have been able to play.

"What happened?" I asked.

"He showed up late for practice. When he came on the ice I said
to him, 'I'm going to fine you,' and he says, 'Fine me!' And skated
away. He's making so damn much money, what's five hundred to
him?"

In the circumstances I knew it was pretty tough for Joe. Joe must
have known that the way the team was playing, his job was in
danger. That's the way the papers had it, anyway – that Joe, I, or
maybe both of us, were soon to get fired.

I went in and talked to Harold about it.

"The team is not playing for Joe," he said.

"They're not playing, in my opinion, because they want a
coaching change," I said. "Unfortunately you can't get rid of
everybody on the bloody team. So the question is, would they
play better for somebody else? If you think that's the case then we
better be prepared to do something about it."

Harold said, "Okay, then. Let's move right away."

"No, you can't do that," I said. I mean, he'd done that once suddenly with Roger Neilson and then when he couldn't get anybody
else, had to take Neilson back. I said, "You make a list of people
you think you'd like to have coach. I'll do the same. Clancy the
same. Go from there. Then if the team doesn't get straightened out
we'll be ready."

So we made out our lists, put them together and shortened that
list until the only two left were Mike Nykoluk and Doug Carpenter. After eight years as assistant to Fred Shero in Philly and New
York, Nykoluk hadn't been able to get a coaching job and was
doing colour commentary on the Toronto radio broadcasts, so at
least he would know the team. Carpenter was doing well in New
Brunswick, coaching the team we shared there with Chicago.

When we got down to two, I made arrangements to interview
them. All this was done with Harold's agreement, on the assump-
tion that Joe's days probably were numbered. In other words, the
players who felt he was too tough on them had won. You might
think that is a harsh way to put it, but the next summer when I was

180

trying to sign a goalie, and telling him he hadn't played very well for us, he said, "It wasn't my fault, the team wasn't trying to win. They were trying to get rid of the coach."

I heard the same later indirectly from another goalie.

That was the situation when the team got back from the road trip (lost 4-1 in Edmonton with Turnbull caught up the ice five times in the first few shifts, and lost 8-5 in Calgary and 6-3 to the Islanders). Their next game was a Wednesday night in Toronto, against Winnipeg, the worst team in the league then. You'd think coming home from that trip, they'd try to show something, because by that time they'd lost eight games out of nine, and had forty-nine goals scored against them in nine games. Well, that day Borje Salming went skiing. He was supposed to be having sinus trouble, be weak from overwork, etc., and instead of resting on the day when his coach's job was on the line, he's skiing.

Carrying out the arrangement I had with Harold, I had set it up to interview Nykoluk the next day, Thursday, in a room at the Westbury. Carpenter was flying in from Moncton to meet me at an airport hotel after I'd seen Nykoluk. If the team turned around, we wouldn't move Joe, but we had to be ready.

Winnipeg stoned us 8-2. At the end of the second period I was upstairs. The game was on TV. At that time, because of my heart condition, I was usually leaving with ten minutes to go. I was just going to leave the office when Dick Duff, who was up there too, yelled, "The television has just said that Harold says Joe's job is safe until the end of the year."

A few minutes later, the same thing was repeated.

I was thinking, 'I've got interviews with these two people – what am I doing, if Harold says Joe's safe until the end of the season?' That would be okay with me. But I was puzzled. I put my hat and coat on and went down to the box Harold watches games from at the end of the rink, shut the door behind me, and said, "What the hell is going on?"

Harold's statement had come when he'd gone out of the box in the intermission. With us getting beaten so badly, he'd been met by a swarm of reporters asking if Joe was going to be fired. And he'd said no.

"I've got to know what's going on," I said to him.

"Oh," he said, "you know me. I had to say something to them so I told them the exact opposite of what we're doing."

I couldn't help it. I started to laugh. Here he's saying that Joe's got the job, and it's going out on television and will be in the newspapers, and he means the exact opposite. How can he do that kind of thing?

"Okay," I said, "I'll go through with the interviews. I'll talk to you on Friday."

Talking to Dodo on the way home, I said, "How about the people, you know?" I said. "Joe's people are listening to the game. they hear that, they're going to be all hepped up. And it's not the truth. That's playing with people's lives. I just can't go for that. I don't think it's right."

Nevertheless, it was done, so what am I going to do? Next morning I went in and talked with Joe. I laid it all out for him, exactly what had happened.

He said, "Why don't you fire me now?"

I said, "Joe, no way – what are we, crazy? You don't know what's going to happen and neither do I. Maybe these people are not going to be good enough or I won't recommend them to take the bloody job. If so, and you're not fired, everything's all right. What the hell, I'm not going to fire you if I haven't got somebody I think is ready to take the job or good enough to take it. I just want you to know the truth."

He said, "Okay."

Later that day I met with Nykoluk. I asked the questions and let him do the talking. I told him what I thought was wrong, and did he think he could handle it? I listened and that was that.

I was just going to leave to meet Carpenter when I had a telephone call from someone in the news media. He said there was a kid in his office from United Press Canada who had been talking to Harold just a little while before, and Harold had said Joe was fired.

The reporter said, "It was supposed to be off the record, so the kid might not write it, but is it true?"

I said, "I don't know what Ballard said, but as long as it isn't printed it can't do any harm."

He said all right, but then phoned back to say the kid had changed his mind, to hell with the off-the-record, and it would be in the paper in the morning. I can't blame the UPC kid. Probably the biggest story he'd got up to that time. An older writer might respect the off-the-record, but most of the young ones don't.

I was very upset. It's all right if Ballard wants to play games with people, but I can't do that. I wasn't going to let it go and have Joe read it in the morning. So I phoned him. I said, "Look, this is in the paper. Harold should not have said it, but I can't muzzle him. I don't want to put you and your family through any more of this. Come in in the morning and I'll fire you and it'll be over."

"Fire me now," he said.

"No," I said. "You've got to do it right. You come in and see me in the morning and I'll tell you that you're fired. I got no alternative, now."

It was a disgraceful performance by Harold. Joe is a good hockey man, coach of the year in the NHL when he was with Buffalo, knows his stuff. He didn't deserve this.

Then I had to go and see Carpenter. Because I was upset, I felt I didn't interview him properly, but still he really impressed me.

At the Gardens in the morning, with the papers full of Joe's being fired, Joe and I met and made the announcement official. We all have to go to the guillotine, it seems. I was mad and sad. Joe went down and told the reporters they'd been a great help, meaning what a bunch of jerks they were. I was in my office when Clancy came in. I was talking to him, madder than hell at Harold, when Harold walked in.

He sat down and I looked at him. I said, "Harold, what in hell did you think you were doing when you talked to that UPC kid?"

"I thought he would hold it," he said.

"You should know better than that. I'm going to tell you something. You've got the biggest case of foot-in-mouth disease I ever saw in my bloody life."

He looked at me, never said a word, got up and walked out of the office. But I had to say it. Then I had to go right after him because now we had no coach. "I talked to Nykoluk and Carpenter," I said. "As far as I'm concerned, I think Carpenter would do a better job for you as coach of the hockey club, than Nykoluk. But I don't like the idea of throwing a kid who has a future into an outfit like this that wanted to get rid of the coach and was prepared to lose to do it. I don't think the kid could handle Sittler. So I guess I have to go with Nykoluk."

Harold made a definitely derogatory remark about Nykoluk.

I said, "Well, you know him better than I do." He'd played

junior hockey for Harold years earlier. "I think the other kid is a better coach but I hesitate to ruin somebody until we get this other thing cleaned up." Meaning, getting Sittler out of there.

He said, "Okay, we'll go that way. Nykoluk."

That was Friday. I talked to Nykoluk further. We agreed on pay but there were still some terms I had in mind that had to be negotiated so we arranged to meet again the next day.

I was busy because Philadelphia was in to play on the Saturday night and I was trying to make a deal with them. I wanted one of the Philly goaltenders, specifically Rick St. Croix. Keith Allen and I talked off and on most of Saturday. I have my notes from that day. As usual in a trade, we were both throwing out names. The two I was throwing out were Sittler and Turnbull. In return for both I wanted, basically, a first-round draft choice, one of Philadelphia's goalkeepers – preferably Rick St. Croix – and two other players. Names bandied around included a big winger from Brandon, Don Gillen; another big defenceman, Blake Wesley; and Mike Busniuk, Mel Bridgman, Brian Propp, goalie Phil Myre, Rick MacLeish. As you can see, I wasn't thinking small. For Sittler alone, one of my offers was to deal him for a first-round choice, plus Brian Propp and my choice of Mel Bridgman or Rick Mac-Leish. For Turnbull alone, I might have taken a second-round draft choice. I would have Keith Allen in my office, then Nykoluk, then Keith again. One of the times with Keith, I thought of something. "Nykoluk – you had him as an assistant coach to Freddie Shero. Why did you let him go?"

Keith was very evasive. Said he couldn't remember. When he left I called Nykoluk. "Why did they let you go in Philadelphia?"

"Oh," he said, "they were trying to reprimand Freddie." Within an hour he was in my office repeating that he'd been fired for that reason, which I thought was nuts. When you want to reprimand a coach, you don't fire the assistant coach.

By then it was Saturday afternoon. "Okay," I said, "I'm going to hire you. Come back about six o'clock and we'll sign the contract." He did, and after he'd signed for one year with an automatic second year if he achieved certain things, I said, "You've seen Keith Allen around here all day. We're trying to make a deal for Turnbull. Just thought I'd let you know." I took him down to the dressing room and introduced him around and told the team he had my backing, and let's get cracking and accomplish something.

I couldn't make a deal with Keith. The various combinations kept us talking all day. We weren't that far apart, but I wanted more than he wanted to give. That happens. If we hadn't been in such a turmoil over the coaching situation I might just have got rid of Turnbull for whatever Allen would give me, but I didn't. I said, "Okay, we'll try again sometime."

That night after Keith and I called it off, we tied Philadelphia 4-4. Soon after that, I sure wished that Nykoluk had told me some of his great ideas before I signed him. I had told him I was trying to unload Turnbull. Also he knew that Ron Ellis had been put on waivers and passed through the league. So he made them both alternate captains! Along with Laurie Boschman and Borje Salming. He made Dan Maloney assistant coach. The word got out that this was sort of prime minister Nykoluk and his cabinet. Nykoluk said he had decided on the alternates after talking it over with Sittler. The first decision of all that brain power showed up a few days later when Nykoluk came to my office and said, "We don't think we want you to trade Turnbull."

I said, "Look, it's in the book, he's going, that's all there is to it. If somebody comes up with a deal, he's going."

The next thing was Ronnie Ellis. I like Ellis. He did a hell of a job for me when I was with the Leafs before. Anything I asked of Ronnie, I got. He is a good man, you never had any trouble with him. But I felt we had to improve on him, make room for some of the younger players to get in. So the previous summer, before my heart attack, I had made an offer to buy out the last two years of his contract. He was making $140,000 a year, no-cut, no trade, whatever. I thought the best thing for him to do was retire, take a lump sum settlement and call it a day. The agreement with the Players Association calls for such a settlement to be one-third of the balance on the contract. In Ron's case, the balance was $280,000. So I think my buyout offer was a little over $90,000. That could have been negotiated upward a little, because Ron had been a good player for the Leafs. However, the answer I got from his agent, Alan Eagleson, at the time (the summer of 1980) was that we owed Ron Ellis the full $280,000, but he would knock off $100,000 and settle for $180,000. I thought that was too much. Then I'd had my heart attack and we'd gone into the season with Ellis. In twenty-seven games into early January, about the time Joe was fired, Ellis had two goals.

Obviously if I was going to change the team I had to keep going at it. I don't know how much Eagleson had to do with Ronnie's stonewalling at the time but there was something – who was using whom as a pawn? Eagleson knew there were moves I could make to get Ellis out of there. He knew that they would be pounced on by the media as being cruel and unusual punishment. The reaction of most media people in these situations is totally predictable. They take what is on the surface and run with it. I knew that too. But I needed another hockey player playing better than Ellis was.

His contract was no-cut, no trade, sure. But there was nothing in there saying he couldn't go to the minors. For me to send him, I had to get him waived through the league. I didn't like any of that, for his sake, but I was damn sure that he would be waived by every other team. In this era of eighteen-year-old NHL players there is no great demand for a thirty-six-year-old with two goals in twenty-seven games.

When I'm forced, I'm not bloody afraid to take the next step.

That's why I put him on waivers. He cleared waivers just a day or two before Joe was fired and Nykoluk hired. I was then contractually free to send him to Moncton at, of course, the full Leaf salary. Okay by me, but it would still be his decision.

I hope that newspapers are generally more accurate than they've been in reporting items I happen to know about. Even guys who normally have some sense get swept away with the pack. John Iaboni of the *Sun* I count as one of the better hockey writers, but even he made a lot of mistakes in his final story on the Ellis affair. First, he and every other reporter said I had been opposed to hiring Nykoluk. Maybe Ballard had told them this, but I had recommended him, hired him, negotiated his contract. Second, Iaboni wrote that the whole Ellis thing was an attempt by me to show that, even though Nykoluk had been hired over my objections and was buddy-buddy with Sittler, I was still the boss. For gosh sake I started the Ellis negotiation six months earlier when Joe Crozier was the coach! It had nothing to do with Nykoluk! Or rather, it shouldn't have.

In the middle of it all, he came to my office. He brought Gerry McNamara with him as support. Nykoluk doesn't like to go in alone, anywhere.

Nykoluk said, "I've talked to the people in the dressing room, and they don't want you to move Ellis."

I said, "Look, this hockey club is trying to get along, trying to get better."

"Well, we don't think we want to be disturbed at this particular time by losing Ronnie."

He talked and I listened, but finally I said, "Who runs the damn hockey club, the dressing room? If you walk downstairs and ask the gang that he's part of what they feel, do you think they're going to say, 'Sure, get rid of him?' You've got a goddamn nerve to come up here and tell me you want me to change my mind. You got a job to do, and so have I. Stay the hell out of my end. I'll handle it and that's that."

What the hell, I don't like letting good people go because they haven't got it any more. But I've done it. That's the nature of the business. You have to keep bringing kids in and getting rid of the older guys whether you like it or not.

The only thing is, you do it as well as you can. If we'd been able to settle it all when I made the original offer the previous summer, that would have been it and Ron Ellis would have retired with the kind of general good feeling that he certainly deserved. But this was the crunch. I told him he could call the shot: either retire with a lump-sum payment or go to the minors. He wanted a few days to think. I called him back two weeks later, Friday, January 23, and asked if he'd made a decision. He told me he had – he wouldn't go to the minors. Then he said he'd appreciate it if I'd meet with him and Eagleson the following Monday. On Monday at two, Ellis came alone. Eagleson had told him if it was over, to come in and tell me he was retiring and settle the financial end. That night about seven, Eagleson came along and brought with him an agreement in his own handwriting, calling for a $100,000 settlement. I had to get Ballard to approve it.

The next day when they came in I had the cheque ready. Ronnie was satisfied and so was I. I think he understood all along that I had a job to do, and that I liked him, but had to do the job. I made sure that my admiration for him, and his contribution to the team over the years, got into the statement about his retirement. When I handed him the cheque I asked him to sign the club's copy of the settlement. He signed it: "Punch. We started together and I'm happy we were able to end it all on a good note. Ron Ellis."

Something I didn't know at the time was that the next seven months were going to be the last time in my life I would call the

shots for the Toronto Maple Leafs. It wouldn't have made any difference if I had known. We had two months to go until the playoffs and about five or six weeks to the trading deadline. I knew we
needed improvement on Crha in goal. I sounded out Buffalo for
Don Edwards, having heard that he and Scotty Bowman were not
getting along. No dice. Our three eighteen-year-old defence picks
in the 1980 amateur draft all were back in junior where they
belonged, but we had them. On January 30, I got Rene Robert
from Colorado and on February 18, Ron Sedlbauer from Chicago.
I tried for Blaine Stoughton from Hartford. At one point I offered
Turnbull, Rocky Saganiuk, and a second round 1981 draft choice
to Edmonton for Kevin Lowe and Blair MacDonald. I talked to
Quebec.

We plugged along through February with the team falling back a
little after getting in one good opening burst for Nykoluk. He'd
been sucked in, too, like Smitty and Joe. And he didn't grab opportunities when they presented themselves. When Robert came in
to report, he was really excited, practically ran up the stairs to my
office. In that frame of mind, if he had been put on the ice right
away he would have been capable of playing a hell of a game.
When he's in the mood, there aren't many people better. But I
guess that was another case of Nykoluk and the dressing room not
liking something I had done, because Nykoluk said something
like, "He's got to practise with us first, show he belongs on our
team." So the chance to get him going all jacked up, was lost.

I talked to a lot of general managers in the first week in March,
dangling Sittler, Turnbull, Picard, Dave Farrish, Barry Melrose,
and others. Goal was top priority. By the last day I was mainly
concerned with trying to get Chico Resch from the New York
Islanders. I was offering Turnbull from our end. The trading
deadline was noon in each time zone, meaning that in the East, for
instance, it was noon but in Minnesota, one o'clock our time,
Colorado, two o'clock, three on the coast.

I'd talked to Bill Torrey of the Islanders the day before the deadline, trying to get Resch and another player – six or seven were
named, but I would have taken Steve Tambellini – for Turnbull. I
found out later that while Torrey was willing to give up Resch for
a defenceman (with throw-ins on both sides), he also was talking
to Colorado about Mike McEwen. That's why I wasn't getting

either a yes or a no from him. But time was running short. I'd heard that another goalie, Bunny Larocque, wanted out of Montreal. With only hours to go I phoned Irving Grundman, the general manager there, and said, "Look, Picard is a natural to go to Montreal. We'd be interested in Larocque for Picard."

"I'll call you back," he said. When he did he said, "All right, but you have to give me a draft choice with Picard for Larocque."

I said I would have to think about that. Then he added, "Away up, for the draft choice, eighth or ninth." I said, "Okay, I think we've got a deal, but I've got another goaltender deal in the works and I've got to call the guy and say, 'Look, do you want it or don't you?' " I wanted to get rid of Turnbull more than I wanted to get rid of Picard.

Grundman said, "Well, I'm talking on a deal for Larocque with another team, too, so we got to get cracking."

I called Bill Torrey and said, "Dammit, Bill, it's fifteen minutes to twelve. I got a chance to make a deal for a goaltender. I want to make it with you. Yes or no."

After a pause he said, "No, I don't think so."

I called back Grundman and said, "I'll take the deal, Picard and the eighth-round draft choice for Larocque." So I made that deal and I was no sooner off the phone than Craig Patrick of the New York Rangers called. He'd heard already. "What about Larocque?" he said. "I've been trying to make a deal for him. Now you've got him, I'm still interested."

I said, "Well, hell, I've got to go with him now. Maybe later on, who knows, but right now, no."

Now I'd like to explain something else. By this time it was past twelve o'clock, but there were still trading chances with the teams in other time zones. I was on the phone or didn't want to leave the phone, so I didn't have a chance to call or send down to the dressing room and let Nykoluk know that we had got Larocque for Picard. And it turns out that when noon passed, he said to the players something like, "Well, the deadline has passed. I guess we stay as we are."

About that time, the phone rang from Minnesota. Lou Nanne. "Are you interested in Ron Zanussi?"

I said, "Maybe."

He wanted a second-round draft choice.

I said, "No way, but I'll tell you what I'll do, you give me Zanussi and your third-round, and I'll give you our second." So I'm losing something in the exchange, but I already had a second-rounder from some other deal, so I was covered if somebody came up in that round that I wanted. And Zanussi I knew might help us.

Meanwhile, all the trades made up to the deadline in the East had been released, so naturally the newspapermen got to Nykoluk and the players before I did, because I was still on the phone into other time zones. As soon as I got Larocque, I could trade Jim Rutherford. I got on to Los Angeles and moved him for a fifth-round draft choice.

But all this, Picard and Rutherford out and Larocque and Zanussi in, got to the dressing room from the press while I was still on the phone. Of course, this caused the usual fuss in the media about lack of communication, keeping the coach in the dark, and so on. He could have been up there listening, if he'd ever wanted to listen to me at all, which he didn't. Still, that's always a worry I have, that deals get to the newspapers before I have a chance to tell the players involved. It makes you look like a yo-yo, you know. People don't understand how much is going on in such a short time.

Harold wasn't around the office at that time. I was still on the phone when Clancy came in. I called, "Tell Harold I made a deal for Larocque."

He came back in a little later and told me, "Harold doesn't like Larocque. Says it's a bad deal." I had to laugh later, because that explained why Harold made it clear to everyone who would listen that he didn't want Larocque, get rid of him, he's no good. Harold didn't seem to understand what kind of position that put Larocque in. Nobody in authority in a hockey club can run down a player. The player somehow senses what's going on. In Harold's case, of course, eventually Larocque was hearing it and reading it in the papers, getting the idea, "I'm not wanted, they don't like me." And when that happens you don't play well.

Anyway, when Joe Crozier was fired, the Leafs were in sixteenth place overall, clinging to the league's last playoff spot. They won four, tied three and lost only one of their next eight, the usual honeymoon with a new coach, and then the basic troubles of the club asserted themselves again. By March 26, the Leafs were seventeenth. We came down to the last game of the season, a Sunday night game in Quebec. We had to win or tie it to get back into sixteenth place and a playoff spot, exactly where we had been when Nykoluk stepped in.

Something happened before that game that really annoyed me. John Ferguson phoned in the afternoon and said he wanted to take something like five players from the Leafs to play for Canada in the world championships. He wanted permission to talk to them. I wasn't around when the call came or I would have given him hell. Here we are life and death to make the playoffs. I knew he had a team to put together from players not in the playoffs, but to talk to ours with a game like that left to play! There are always some who will let it bother them. They're thinking, we can go over there and make as much money as we could if we lose in the first playoff round to the Islanders, and don't play with full intensity that night in a vital league game. That's wrong.

Anyway, we won 4-2. I liked the heading on Milt Dunnell's *Star* column the next day: IT TOOK LEAFS 79 GAMES TO GET GOING.

But it didn't last long. The Islanders won the first game 9-2 and the second 5-1 on their home ice. After the second beating in New York I saw a kid carrying two cases of beer into the Leaf dressing room, plenty considering that some of the players didn't drink, which meant more for those who did. There was also beer on the plane. They couldn't have done better in the beer department if they'd been two games up instead of two games down. In Toronto Saturday night it was all over: Islanders 6, Leafs 1.

There were the usual post-mortems and some unusual ones. A day or so later Harold called me in and said, "What's this in the paper about Nykoluk hiring Dan Maloney as assistant coach? Who gave him permission to do that?"

"I don't know. I was just going to find out."

I went to Nykoluk and said, "Did you make Maloney this offer?" He had. I asked, "Where'd you get the authority?"

"One night on the plane Harold said, 'I'd like to see Maloney as assistant coach for a whole year.' "

I went back and told Harold that as far as hiring Maloney was concerned, Nykoluk thought he was doing what Ballard wanted. He looked at me with a little smile on his face. I don't know why.

For various reasons I wasn't in any hurry to sign Nykoluk again. Harold had said right away that Nykoluk would be back, but I made a mental note there. When he was hired, he was assured of a second year on the same contract – if the club did certain things. It didn't. I was against hiring him for a second year, but when Harold insisted, I at least put into the next contract a job description to spell out his areas of responsibility so that he wouldn't feel he had to give me so much advice.

I had another year on my own contract. Ballard told the press, "If Punch chooses to resign, that will be his decision, not mine. The thought of him resigning is one I don't relish because if he leaves I don't know where to start looking for a replacement with his hockey knowledge. Maybe he won't want to carry on. I don't know. I'm not the easiest guy in the world to work for, you know."

After the things I'd called him a couple of times, that was a fairly generous statement. But that, too, is Harold.

In the last few weeks of that season, I did make peace in one direction. The previous year I had been named to the Buffalo Sabres Hall of Fame but hadn't felt ready to go back there, face that crowd, even to be honoured. This year was different. Seymour asked Dodo and me to be his guests at dinner before the game and ceremonies April 1, 1981. We didn't do that, but we did go up and say hello around the office and then walked out on the ice so that Seymour could present me with a sword and a lot of warm words. I said a few true things about Buffalo hockey fans being the greatest in the world. There was cheering and applause. As I recall, Dodo and I didn't talk much on the way home. Too many memories.

CHAPTER EIGHTEEN

The roof falls in

On September 7, 1981, the day the Leafs' rookie camp opened in St. Catharines, I went down to the Gardens while the medical examinations of the players were being done. I went around and saw everything was okay, then drove to St. Catharines. I couldn't find a parking place except a fair way from the door of the Holiday Inn. I carried the bags in myself. I had brought a lot of clothes because I'd be there for the best part of a month (I thought).

The months since the playoffs had been okay. At the amateur draft in Montreal I'd done better than I had a right to. After Dale Hawerchuk, the kid who was automatic first pick overall by the Winnipeg Jets, the one I wanted was Jim Benning, an eighteen-year-old defenceman who'd played with the Portland Winter Hawks. As we were drafting sixth, I didn't think he'd still be available when our turn came, but he was and I grabbed him. He's a very smart offensive hockey player and frankly, if he develops as he should, he might be the best defenceman Toronto has ever come up with. That's saying a hell of a lot. He has to work on his skating and manoeuvrability but when he's in full flight he has the capability of penetrating the other team's defence. I said at the time he could be a superstar, and I mean it. We picked up some other good prospects as well, maybe not as talented as Benning, but with excellent futures. However, I struck out on one thing at those meetings. I'd invited Doug Carpenter to come up from the farm club and see how the meetings were run. I made sure Carpenter was introduced to Nykoluk, and that they spent some time together. I hoped that Nykoluk, seeing Carpenter's quality, might be impressed enough to suggest that Carpenter come in as his assistant. It didn't work.

Also, I'd talked with Don Luce in Burlington because I was considering making a deal for him with Los Angeles, who'd got him from Buffalo. I thought highly of him, but didn't want any misunderstanding. I spelled it out that I probably only wanted him for a year, with the option of buying out his contract in the second year. He would be fourth centreman and penalty-killer, do those jobs, and, as a veteran, help the kids we were going to have to use. Luce agreed all the way. I made the deal. It was similar in intent to one I'd made in the previous season for Rene Robert from Colorado. The escape clause in the Robert deal was that he could be returned to Colorado at the end of the 1982 season. Both were hired, short-term only, to do specific jobs and also help develop our kids.

In retrospect, I guess as the summer wore on there was no doubt I was ready for another heart attack and should have been more careful. Since then I've had plenty of time to think. The work was extra heavy in July and August. Besides all the usual contract negotiations, we were putting our own wholly owned farm team into Cincinnati in the Central Hockey League. If you're counting, you might notice that in two years I'd built the Leafs' minor league system up from the four players in New Brunswick to a team and a half; about twenty-six more players to pick from. I moved Doug Carpenter to coach Cincinnati because I knew he could do a first-rate job of developing the young talent we would send him. All this was going while I tried to get everybody signed and things in order before training camp.

But I wasn't feeling so hot. Sometimes just walking a block or two after lunch would tire me out. A couple of times I'd had slight pains. Sometimes I would be pale and sweating at my desk. I talked to Dr. Greenwood in June or maybe July. He examined me, and said I should check into hospital and have an angiogram. That's a way of checking how the main blood vessels around the heart are working. He thought if some were plugged, or partially plugged, that would be causing my tiredness. I said, "Look, I can't do it now." I was thinking of it as a checkup, you know. I just wasn't paying enough attention.

"You shouldn't leave it too long," he said. "There's quite a waiting list for this procedure."

I said, "Okay, book a time for me around November. By that time I'll have training camp over, Cincinnati going, and the first few weeks of the NHL season behind me."

When I got into the room in St. Catharines on the Monday night I lay on the bed and read for a while and then about 2 a.m. I had chest and arm pains. I phoned Smitty. His new job with the club was as advance scout. I said, "Look, get out of bed, I want you to take me to the hospital."

He'd been with me when I had my first attack in Buffalo nine years before. He didn't waste any time getting to me. At the hospital, the doctor on duty said, "We'd better put you in for observation."

I told her okay, and was put to bed. The next morning another doctor came to see me. I hadn't had any more pains. But he said, "We'll keep you in for another day. Let you out tomorrow morning if everything's all right."

I told them I didn't want to let anybody know. Especially not to call home and alarm my wife. I didn't want to upset her if everything was going to be okay, anyway. But the next night, again about two, I had another pain. A real one. They started giving me nitroglycerin, and the pain – I thought my fingers were going to fall off. Then they gave me an injection of something, morphine or another drug. When I started to feel better I still knew I was in trouble. "You'd better call my wife," I said.

My daughter Marlene answered the phone. Dodo told me later that Marlene came into her room and just said, "He's had another one." They were all out of bed and dressed and on the road within ten minutes. They got to St. Catharines about dawn, I think. Later that morning the doctors decided to move me to Toronto. Somebody in St. Catharines had let the Gardens know and the news got out. When I was wheeled into Toronto General on a stretcher reporters and photographers were there. Pictures in the papers the next day showed me strapped onto the stretcher with the intravenous bottles hanging above me and tubes running down. I did not look good. I could have done without that publicity. And it didn't get any better. A day or so later a nurse came into my room looking upset.

"Is it true that you're losing your job?" she said.

"What are you talking about?"

"It's in the paper that you're out as general manager. How could he . . .?"

"Ah," I said, "that's just paper talk. The main job is for me to get better, not worry about that." But afterward I lay there thinking about how Ballard is always firing people in the papers. Not only with the Leafs but with his football team, too. Anybody wanting to know where he stands should read all the papers every day, never miss a word Ballard says.

I started to feel better in a few days and wanted to get out of there, but Dr. Greenwood thought we should go ahead with the angiogram. He said there was a little danger in it, because the procedure of pumping dye in, or whatever they use, involves a rush on the heart. That's when they take the X-rays and see what is going on. I was lying there day after day thinking about how they had wanted to do this earlier in the summer. I should have had it done then and said to hell with hockey. Instead, I had been working for the Leafs, taking a shot at my life.

Anyway, they did the angiogram and found that I had two complete blockages and one other 75 percent blocked. The doctors told me I was very high-risk now, and should have a by-pass operation. They would take a vein from my leg, right from the groin down to the ankle, and replace the blocked veins. They said that if I didn't have the operation, I wouldn't be able to count on anything. The alternative was that every time I'd walk down the street I'd be open to another attack. In other words, no alternative at all.

I said, "Okay, there's no way around it. I take my shot, take my chances." Then I said, "I want the best man to do it, too!"

The doctor said, "They're all good."

"Listen!" I said. "I got a lot of good hockey players on my club, but some are better than others. There's got to be somebody here who's better than the others. That's the guy I want."

He looked at me and started to laugh. I ended up with the head man. He came in, drew a diagram to show me where the blockages were, and explained the risks. That was a Thursday about three weeks after my first attack. They were going to do the operation on the following Tuesday. "Could I go home until then?" I asked. I felt good. One doctor said no, but the guy who was going to do the operation said, "Yes, go on home and take it easy for a couple of days. Around here all you'll be doing is going crazy. Come back on Sunday."

All this time, Dodo had been guarding the door. She wouldn't let Clancy in, or anybody else. Again, Dodo received a call every day from Tommy Ivan, which helped her. I never heard from

Ballard. He said later that Dodo had prevented him from coming, but he never tried, or called her, or sent a card. All he did was talk to the papers.

When I got home I called the Gardens and on Friday and Saturday had some people out to see me – Doug Carpenter, Gerry McNamara, and Smitty. I had them on different days, Carpenter just to wish him good luck in Cincinnati. A month or so earlier Ballard had made McNamara chief scout the same way he'd eliminated Sittler from the training camp roster a year before – without telling me. For one thing, I would have liked to talk to Gerry and give him a raise. Anyway, I wanted to tell him and Smitty a few things to do with the club. The matter of Bunny Larocque had to be settled, I said, by playing him for the Leafs' first twenty games. That would give him a chance. If he was good enough, we could relax on the goalkeeping end. If he wasn't, we'd have to start looking elsewhere. Jiri Crha had developed a bad back. Tremblay had missed the playoff games the previous spring because of an appendix operation, so my idea was he should play in Cincinnati and be ready if needed. Give Normand Aubin, who'd scored forty goals in the minors the year before, a good chance to make the Leafs. Along with Paul Marshall. Another thing I said was that we should start the season with three kids on defence. Any that showed they were ready we'd keep. But if some needed further development we should send them back to junior. If Benning could play, get rid of Turnbull. Those were my instructions.

I went back in on the Sunday afternoon. The next day they prepared me. The anesthetist came in to explain his end, and the doctor from the intensive care unit, and the ones who were going to do the operation. They did a tremendous job of answering every question before I even asked it. I'm not a medical person but I know a good deal about doctors and hospitals because that's part of the hockey business. Dr. H. Aldridge was the angiogram expert, Dr. J. R. Baird the surgeon, and Dr. W. F. Greenwood my own heart specialist. The way they explained that operation to me, I never felt nervous or anxious. Actually, I was surprised that I was taking it so well. I was even feeling upbeat about it, and I was right. When it was done, I was up in a matter of days. Ten days after the operation I was walking a mile. In a month I could walk three miles in an hour with no trouble at all, ride an exercise bicycle, do whatever I wanted. The blood was getting to my heart.

That was the difference. I would drive myself out to the Oshawa shopping centre, which is about half a mile long, and walk back and forth three times, about three miles. Army pace. I felt better than I had in years.

The only problem bothering me was Ballard. After the operation I'd found that when Ballard heard about the guys coming to visit me at home, he apparently gave orders that no Gardens person was to visit me, or call on the phone, or anything else. He said he didn't want me disturbed. But all that really disturbed me was his attitude, the way he was freezing me out.

I had been told to see the doctors for a checkup six full weeks after the operation, and learn when I could go back to work. But after only a month I felt well enough, myself, to get involved again for at least a couple of hours a day. I was eager. Heck, if I could walk three miles without stopping I could do some work, so I got Clancy to line up a date for me to see Ballard. That was late October. When I got there, Ballard didn't show. He'd gone on the road with the team, with no call to cancel the appointment, and no message. I decided the next time I went in would be when the doctors told me I was fit and ready to go back to work.

That time came on November 17, a Tuesday. I saw the doctor first thing. We talked about what Ballard was saying. He checked me over and told me, "Ballard doesn't know what he's talking about. You can go back to work fulltime." I got into the Gardens about 11, checked around the office, talked to Clancy a bit, and then went in to Harold's office.

To get there you go through the open area of the hockey department just outside my office, walk through a door into a sort of vestibule with a washroom off it, and then open his door. His office is about the same size as mine, and crowded with pictures – a couple of Sittler, some of Harold with other people, and stuffed tigers and things connected with his football team, the Hamilton Tiger-Cats.

He was sitting behind his desk, which is never really cluttered but always has some business going across it. There's hardly a thing done around the Gardens that doesn't go by him at one time or another.

That's his working place. His living quarters are right behind that.

I walked across to his desk and shook his hand. He waved me into a chair and asked me how I was.

"Great."

"Have you got any pain?"

"None at all."

I got the impression that he was looking right away for something to substantiate what he'd told one reporter when discussing me – that he was running a business, not a hospital. I sometimes wonder if Harold is so afraid of death or illness himself that he just doesn't want to be reminded that it exists.

I said, "Actually, I feel better than I have for the last couple of years. I saw the doctor today and he told me I'm ready to go back to work fulltime."

He asked me something about the scars. "You wanta see a scar?" I said, and showed him the one on my left leg where they took the vein out for the bypass. It runs like a sort of angry crooked line right from my ankle to the groin.

He just looked at it.

I was well, and it seemed to surprise him.

I thought I'd better get to the point. "All I've seen in the paper is that you don't want me as general manager any more," I said.

"Ah-h-h, don't believe half of what you read in the paper."

"Okay, I won't believe half. What about the other half?"

Then he was direct. "Well, I think it would be better . . . I'd like to keep you here as an advisor."

"That's not acceptable," I said.

He tried to persuade me.

I said, "It just wouldn't work."

"There are lots of jobs around here you could do."

"That's not the way it is," I said. "If I'm going to be your advisor, the first thing I advise you to do is put me back as general manager."

He didn't seem to know what the hell to say to that one.

I went on. "Before I got sick, I told you what we had to do. I told you that Turnbull you'd have to get rid of, Maloney you'd have to get rid of, Melrose you'd have to get rid of because none of those guys can play on the hockey team we're trying to build."

"You also said to get rid of Salming."

I didn't remind him that he had told me, the year before when

Salming wasn't playing well, "Look, try and trade him."

"Yeah, I said to get rid of Salming," I said, "because I don't think you can win with him. Now's the time to make a deal for him, when he's playing well. You might be able to get something really good for him."

"Well, everybody's available," he conceded.

We talked about Salming for a while, Sittler, Turnbull, the others who are supposed to be the guns but I didn't think the Leafs could win with. Then I said, "Look, I'm your general manager, that's what you hired me for, that's what the contract says."

He thought that over. "Well, I'm not going to fire you."

I said, "That's your prerogative. You can do what the hell you like. There isn't anything I can do about that."

"I won't accept your resignation," he said.

"I never offered my resignation!"

At that, he kind of smiled. That's Harold. He isn't unaware. I didn't have any farther to go, I guess. I was not going to plead. I was just telling him the facts as I saw them. "Look, Harold, put it this way. I'm your general manager. I'm under contract to you. When you think I can help you as general manager, call me or send somebody for me. I'm available, as per my contract. That's all there is to it."

And I walked out.

As I've said before, in a lot of ways I like Harold. All I'm saying here is exactly what happened. I understand him, too. It wouldn't mean anything to him that the manager of the Milwaukee Brewers had had a quintuple bypass operation, and had gone back to his job a few weeks later; that Rock Hudson had one and was checking out a place to make a movie a few weeks later; that Arthur Hailey had one and went back to work on another multi-million dollar book. I know exactly what happened with Harold. He wants to be general manager. He likes to travel with the team, give the interviews, be front and centre, the unchallenged boss, calling all shots. With some general managers he can do that, but not with me. That's why each time I was sick he dove in and did things that I wouldn't do, and that he had agreed with me we shouldn't do: sign Salming to a long contract that makes it much harder to trade him, give Sittler back his C.

When he hired me, he'd been taking a lot of flak and thought he'd like to have me in there to take the load off him. But when I took the load, as he knew I would, that void in his life began to bother him. His life, getting close to eighty years of age, is that hockey team and his football team. His life is talking to the papers and knowing that he can make the front page of any paper in town any day he wants to. I understand all that. He's an active man, used to the limelight, and missing it when anybody takes some of it away. He's even found that he can say one thing one day and the exact opposite the next, and both will be front page, while he's laughing.

But his life also is expressed in something he said once when a reporter asked when he would retire. "What would I do?" Harold said. "Sit around and watch the sky stay up?"

In a hockey club you can't fight the owner, just like you can't fight city hall. It's just that Harold has no accurate sense of what the things he says do to other people. He could have waited out my operation, and my getting back into shape, saying something like, "Well, Punch and I will discuss his future when he's okay again. Then we'll see." That way, I could have gone in to him that day and he could have told me substantially the same things, and I could have argued, but it would have been between us, and then announced, instead of being in the papers from day one that because I'd had another heart attack I was through.

Even after we had that meeting, he didn't let up. It was like rewriting history. He said two or three times that I had quit, not that he'd fired me. On Bill Stephenson's radio show on CFRB a few weeks later he used the phrase, ". . . when Punch made up his mind not to come back as general manager. . . ."

Stephenson: "It's been my understanding that Punch wanted to come back and you said, no, he could not come back."

Ballard: "Oh, that is true in one sense . . . but he's had three heart attacks, new plumbing put in his heart. How can a guy come back and be general manager? A general manager should be in Flin Flon tonight, probably Chicoutimi tomorrow night, and back in Winnipeg the following night to see what his scouts have raked up for him. I don't think a man sixty-two, sixty-three years of age is able to do that." Stephenson didn't mention to Harold that there is no Junior A team in Flin Flon anymore, or ask him just what general managers did that sort of thing; certainly not Bill Torrey of the Islanders, or almost any good g.m. you can name. That's what scouts are for. A general manager's main job is to know what is

201

going on in his own hockey team and farm system, direct and lead them, and once or twice a year go out to see young players that he might want to draft.

This radio program was on, I think in December, after Darryl Sittler had finally said that he would accept a trade if it was one he wanted. It's a phone-in show. One caller said, "I know for a fact that a lot of people have had bypass operations and come back working harder and stronger. Why can't Punch come back into the picture again?"

Ballard: "Because I don't want to have somebody that's a cripple, here. I'm not going to put him in the pine box. . . ."

He calls me a cripple when I'm not. He says he doesn't want to put me in a pine box, doesn't want to be responsible for my being sick. Well, that's my responsibility, not his. It's my life, right? I'd made the decision the previous summer not to have the angiogram when, if I'd had it, I might not have got a lot of his players signed, or got the farm club going in Cincinnati.

Somebody once asked me if I'd ever thought about what had happened to me with the Leafs, in comparison to what would have happened if I'd had a similar job with another big company. All I can say is that if I'd been with another big company and had had a heart bypass operation, it wouldn't have been front page in the papers. Not ten people would have known about it – only family and friends. And the guy who was my boss would have said, "Look, get better, don't worry about a damn thing. We'll look after your job until you get out and then we'll sit down and talk about it."

That's exactly what would happen not only in industry, but in a lot of hockey clubs, as it had when I was in Buffalo. I still knew my business. After Harold had put me out, and I was sitting at home, I would get calls from other top men in hockey. Like one that went, "How are you? What are you doing? How do you stand with that s.o.b.?" And then, "Can I ask you a few questions?"

I said, "Look, I'm still being paid by the Leafs and I'm not going to answer any questions that might be at odds with that, but anything else I'll try to answer." And I did. I went away from the phone and said to my wife, "Isn't this ridiculous? Some other hockey club phones me to ask my opinion on certain things, and the club that is paying me has given orders that nobody is to consult me on anything."

It seems to me that the reasons I got fired three times were the stupidest reasons anyone can imagine. First, by Stafford, because I was too old. Next, by Seymour Knox, because I couldn't control the dressing room. And then by Harold, because I'm a cripple. All very strange. I guess that's the word. But neither Stafford Smythe nor Seymour Knox played games with me the way Harold did.

Yet I can understand all he did, because what he really enjoys most in life is being out there making news, good or bad.

And maybe this is the place to add a small footnote on the Palmateer deal. He played much of his first year with Washington, but was not able to play at all in the 1981-82 season. I certainly hope he can make a comeback but even if he doesn't Washington is on the hook for that big contract in full, for two more seasons. That's why I had been trying to save Ballard a million bucks. Taking that into account, plus the fact that Picard didn't work out for us and was traded, one Washington newspaperman dubbed the trade "a lemon for a lemon." That was harsh, but not far into the 1981-82 season when Palmateer was not playing, Max McNab was fired and the Palmateer contract was at least a contributing factor. Anyway, Max wrote me a card that Christmas with a note on it: "That Palmateer-Picard trade didn't do us very much good. You got a heart attack and I lost my job."

CHAPTER NINETEEN

Goodbye Leafs

When I walked out of Ballard's office and the Gardens that day in November, I didn't really know whether it was all over or not. I know better than most people the impossibility of predicting what Harold will do. In some ways, it was hard to take, psychologically. You come off a heart attack, out of an operation, you look at yourself in the morning and see the scars have faded a little, you feel good, you feel ready to work – but the rug has been pulled. You've made a great comeback from the surgery – for what? To be told you're obsolete, have lost your touch. Like hell! I recognize that I am a stubborn, tough bastard to deal with, but that's why I've been successful, so why change it? If that makes me unacceptable to the chronic losers, so be it. But it is a little bit different from losing my touch.

One day I went down to the Gardens and my parking space had been taken away. I had to laugh at how ridiculous the situation was becoming.

Then, oddly enough, early in 1982 they needed me. Carl Brewer was suing for money he claimed he should have been paid for the two weeks he spent in Moncton before joining the Leafs on December 26, 1979. As I was the man who had hired him, the Gardens treasurer, Don Crump, asked me to help contest the case. Of course, Brewer didn't have five cents coming to him. He had come to me and told me he'd play for nothing if I'd just let him end his career as a Maple Leaf. I wouldn't do that just on the grounds of what he'd been doing in old-timers hockey; I had to see him in practice or in games. So when he said he thought Moncton was a good idea, I went along with it, gave him air fare and expenses. When he came back I signed him to a five-game tryout contract, the kind that free agents and amateurs get. The NHL wouldn't approve it, said he was a pro. So for sentimental reasons I gave him a $125,000 contract, pro-rated from December 26. Can you imagine a guy who said he would play for nothing, then going to court and trying to collect $8,287.32 for two weeks in Moncton? That's what he was paid when he did join the Leafs, about $4,000 a week.

But I wouldn't have missed that court appearance for the world. Although I got angry a couple of times, in other ways it was revealing. There is Brewer not denying that he'd said he would play for nothing to die a Maple Leaf, but at the same time taking a case to court to collect money that he didn't have coming to him. And there is also Brewer confirming under oath the matter of what the Sittler-led dressing room would do to any Leaf who dared to talk to me.

Judge Keith Gibson said to him, "When you noticed what you felt was a discrepancy in pay, why didn't you mention it right away?"

Brewer said he failed to act immediately because, "One of the things that concerned the players was that I was a lackey, or spy, for management. I avoided any contact with management because, invariably, it would get back to them."

And they're the bunch of bastards who used to whine to the newspapers about lack of communication.

I got mad a couple of times during the hearings. Once Judge Gibson reminded me that I was in a court of law and not in a dressing room. This was because I had said a few things like hell, bloody, and bugger-all. But he was very fair. When it was over, he said, "I saw you play with the Goodyears and I saw Carl playing with Toronto Maple Leafs . . . I'm glad to see that you haven't lost any of your fire."

I said, "Goodyears! You're sure dating yourself!"

What the hell, that was more than forty years ago when I played senior hockey, starting in the fall of 1938.

When I was going out of the courtroom, there were a lot of photographers around. In the papers the next day I looked as good as I've looked in ten years. I wouldn't normally mention such a thing, but some of my friends had been telling me I should get out more, go to hockey games, show the flag. I still had my tickets for the Gardens but I hadn't felt like going before. Now I did feel like it. The Edmonton Oilers were in town on January 16. Dodo and I went to the game. As the guy who used to tell the *Hockey Night in*

Canada people who they could have on, and who they couldn't, maybe I was more amused than somebody else would have been that no camera came around to show Dodo and me in our usual seats; the cameras had shown us there hundreds of times before. Talk about the Iron Curtain. Leafs played a hell of a game that night. They beat Edmonton 7-1 and from Bunny Larocque on down, the Leafs looked like the team I'd thought they could be. Because of all the Gretzky publicity, for once they had motivated themselves. It's a wonder that didn't tell Nykoluk something about what he should be doing about motivating them for other games.

But to go back a bit, from November on I was sitting at home watching the club that I tried to build up going downhill. There was an assortment of reasons. Ballard had moved Gerry McNamara up from being head scout to being acting general manager, but the word "acting" tells you that he was not being allowed to do much on his own. And Harold is far from the best hockey man around, as he has proved time and time again, from his trade of first-round draft choices for Dan Maloney – a blow that the Leafs still haven't recovered from – to his negative attitude toward Bunny Larocque before even seeing what the guy could do for the team.

But in my opinion one reason for the decline was the coaching. As I've said, Mike Nykoluk's idea that he didn't have to bother motivating players is wrong, terribly wrong. Once, late in the season, he was quoted widely as saying, "I just hate that word, motivation. It's just another poor excuse for the players. I don't get my wife to give me a pep talk to get me to come to the rink every morning. These guys are paid well to do a job and I don't think any athlete, after they've won something, remembers what the coach said. Can you imagine me trying to motivate Borje Salming?"

Well, I could certainly imagine *someone* trying to motivate Borje Salming! Why not? Very few people ever do anything so well that they couldn't do better. I say 10 per cent of players can motivate themselves. Let's take the other 90 per cent. You drive the hell out of them and most of those people will thank you later. Many times people have said to me after it's all over, "Jeez, I didn't know what you were doing, but I understand it now. I appreciate what you did." It's like the kid who gets himself in trouble and says, "Nobody cares. If somebody cared about me I might not have got in trouble." Well, when you're driving them, you're caring about them. The most important job of any coach is to motivate his players. If I'd been general manager when the above Nykoluk quote was published I would have called Nykoluk in and asked if he had said what he was quoted as saying.

If he answered yes, I would ask, "Do you believe that? Or were you just talking for some guy to write a story about?"

If he said he believed it, I would fire him.

Back to my impression of the Leafs. The goalkeeping was okay. Larocque and Vince Tremblay showed that. When the guys up front felt like playing, they could do it, too. But the defence was simply not good enough. Among the experienced players, I'd picked up Bob Manno from Vancouver and he played well in spots; as for the others, the tough ones weren't fast enough and the fast ones weren't tough enough. Greg Hotham was okay but couldn't handle the rough stuff in front of the net or in the corners. That means the Leafs had a hell of a time handling the corners, because, as I've said, Salming couldn't handle the corners either, and he was the best the Leafs had. They sure as hell needed help. Okay, the only way to go is to develop it. You usually can't go out and trade for it. They had a group of young defencemen around twenty years old, some less. Out of Benning, Boimistruck, McGill, and Craig Muni, some are going to develop into top-notch players. So that's not bad odds. After all, you can play the game with four defencemen. It's like anything else, if you've got seven defencemen, as the Leafs had most of the year, some of them have to be fifth, sixth, or seventh best. So when you put your fifth or sixth out, you're making the team weaker.

But kids that age are better if they play a lot more, play steadily. What's the matter with sending some to what was supposed to be the development team in Cincinnati, for gosh sake? How long does it take to get somebody up from Cincinnati, if a player gets hurt? Why treat the Leafs themselves as the development team? I've always said that if you're going to lose, you should lose with your best, not with some kid you're just putting out there for the sake of putting him out there.

I'd told them about Benning, that unless he was good enough to play regularly it would be better if he went back to junior hockey for a year. A lot of other clubs did that with their young ones, called them up from time to time and they did well. But the Leafs kept Benning, and after he'd played the ten games allowed a junior, they couldn't send him back. One time he missed a game because of food poisoning. That was a Thursday. Friday there was no game. Saturday he didn't play. Sunday they don't even practise. Kids like that should be getting all kinds of ice time whether it's with the Leafs, Cincinnati, or back in junior. None of the young ones got it. Those kids don't want to sit around doing nothing and go home and moan because they're not playing, not doing the job they're supposed to do.

The same thing goes with the forwards. You get your nine best forwards and you play them. And furthermore, if it got down to a tight game you play your six best, and short-shift the guys that aren't good enough. So that you've got your best out there more of the time. It's only common sense. Especially if you've got a team like the Maple Leafs. If the game is gone, one way or another, okay, give those guys on the bench a chance to play, get them in as much as you can. But when you're stuck and you've got to win, you better be playing your best.

So generally speaking I think the Leafs are in good shape. They have a bunch of young players who have the potential to become big leaguers. My concern is with the word potential. If they try to force-feed these kids into the lineup just to say they're a young team, it's not going to work. These kids have to have the atmosphere and the competition to develop their skills naturally. If they're in over their heads they won't get that opportunity because all they'll be doing is trying to hang on.

One time Nykoluk was quoted as saying that he wished he had guys like Williams and Boutette back. Grinders, is the hockey term. Maybe by the end of the season when Vaive had fifty-four goals and Derlago thirty-four, he wouldn't have said it, but that's the way he was thinking.

When Sittler let it be known at the end of November, 1981, that he wanted to be traded, the club should have said to him, "Okay, go home. We'll let you know when we've got a trade for you. Sit there." Then you could bring a kid in who wanted to play, go for the future. Sittler wasn't going to be there in the future, so why should he be playing and delaying the development of some kid who was going to be there, if he was good enough?

I would have sent Sittler home or even sat him out, but that takes guts. However, if somebody had told Harold that he was going to be on the front page for two weeks if he sent Sittler home to wait for a trade, Harold probably would have had his chauffeur drive him there.

The trade eventually made for Sittler with Philadelphia was laughable, if you compare two kids, Rich Costello and Ken Strong, plus Peter Ihnacak in the 1982 draft's second round to one I could have got from Calgary in 1980 – Guy Chouinard and Bobby MacMillan – or even any of the ones I could have got from Philadelphia the time I was trying to move both Sittler and Turnbull in one deal. What the Leafs got for Sittler might turn out okay in the long run, but the Leafs needed help right then, the day Sittler quit playing.

Partly that was Ballard's fault. He missed a big chance. Sittler went in to see Ballard early in the season, and wanted a new contract. You can understand Sittler's motives: the contract Ballard had given Salming was more than $100,000 a year higher than Sittler was getting. Ballard turned Sittler down. I would have said to Sittler, "Sure, I'll give you the new contract. You had a better year than Salming and he shouldn't be making more money than you. But you understand that I'll be trading you." My way, he would have got the money, would have been traded faster, and the Leafs would have got someone for him who could play right away with the team, not years from now, if ever.

That would have avoided what eventually did happen. Sittler asked to be traded and five weeks later when there was no trade he quit the team, pleading mental fatigue or whatever. In that situation another team can say, "Well, hell, if he isn't in a frame of mind to play hockey, why should we give up a lot to get him? We're taking a chance giving up anything."

Money had a lot to do with the Sittler decision to get out. Alan Eagleson's reading of the 1981 Canadian budget was that it would hurt Sittler financially. When Team Canada is front and centre, Eagleson claims he is a true patriot. But he said publicly that because of some tax changes in the budget he would recommend to his clients that they sign with U.S. clubs. This is not for patriotism, but for money. He and Sittler forced the issue on the deal the Leafs eventually made. They were frustrated for weeks waiting for the Leafs to make a deal when Sittler was playing. When Sittler quit the team early in January it was to force some action. He said he was sick. Of course, he was well enough to make automobile commercials along the line – "I've made my best trade, what about you?" Through all this, incidentally, Eagleson was doing much of the talking for Sittler, making me recall Sittler's assurance the previous summer that Eagleson wasn't his agent for dealing with the Leafs any more. That apparently had just been lip-service to try to smooth that one particular situation, a ploy by the same partnership that had master-minded taking off the C, the Ronald McDonald fiasco, and other sources of friction between Sittler and the Leafs.

Eagleson's advice to his clients to sign with U.S. clubs, obviously is creating a serious problem for Canadian teams in the NHL. I'm concerned that the best hockey players in Canada will want to go to the U.S. when they become free agents. In the long run this would weaken all Canadian teams, practically make them a minor-league feeding system for the U.S. teams. The league should be aware that this might happen and take steps to ensure that it doesn't. I can't really blame the players – it's a business decision. But the league rule requiring adequate compensation for players lost through free agency is one that in my view must be retained. It simply means that if a Canadian player is lost, someone of equal merit must be awarded to the Canadian team.

As you know, I would have been glad to see Turnbull and Sittler go, anytime. But I always hoped they could find themselves again, play out their careers with some kind of satisfaction. I found Turnbull an enigma, lots of talent but unable to use it fully. Sittler I thought had been spoiled by being allowed to run the team and setting himself up for a fight that sooner or later he was going to lose. He would have been a lot better to take a trade a couple of years earlier and get a new lease on life that did not include all the tired, worn-out, monotonous Toronto battles.

But the trade I never would have made was dealing Wilf Paiement, one of the few genuine hockey talents on the team, to Quebec. I had lots of people trying to get Paiement into deals, but my answer was always no. The player the Leafs did get for him, Miroslav Frycer, might be all right, but nobody in his wildest dreams would say he was the equal of Wilf Paiement. I would have liked to see a tough coach get on Paiement's back and motivate him, bring out the great talent that he later showed with Quebec in the playoffs. You don't trade a player of that calibre just because he's having a so-so season (everybody has one of those), when down the road, under different conditions, a different coach, he might well have been the team's main star. Nykoluk's self-motivation theory failed most miserably with Paiement, by letting him go his own way, not challenging him, not giving him something to strive for.

When the season ended with the Leafs drifting down into being the third worst team in the league, I thought it was sad. I thought of Winnipeg the year before, and Edmonton a couple of years earlier, persevering with kids but working the hell out of them, giving them pride, convincing them that up ahead were going to be some good years, which now have come. I still think that the Leafs have the basic foundation to get there, if the management doesn't keep on screwing them up.

Once in Toronto I took a last-place team into the Stanley Cup finals, and then won four Cups – the whole cycle taking nearly ten years. In Buffalo I took a team not nearly as promising as today's Leafs and in five years was in the Stanley Cup final. We were beaten only by fantastic goalkeeping. But I still left a nucleus that today makes Buffalo one of the best in the league. In Toronto this last time I tried it again and do not doubt for an instant that I would have made it three good building jobs in a row, if I'd had the time.

But I'm lucky in many ways. I have a lot of good days to remember, right back to the morning I carried my skates into the Gardens for the very first time, and the big clock in the lobby showed that it was 5.25 a.m., and I went out to try to be a good hockey player, never even guessing where it was going to lead – sometimes to heaven and sometimes to hell, but with a lot of just plain good times in between. To see great players like Gil Perreault and Tim Horton night after night, to win with the good teams that my old Leafs were and my best Buffalo Sabres were, to take men to heights in hockey that they would remember forever, and to be there with them and share it all with my family, that has been my life.

Index

215